The Marketing of Rebellion

How do a few political movements challenging Third World states become global causes célèbres, whereas most remain isolated and obscure? *The Marketing of Rebellion* rejects the common view that needy groups readily gain help from selfless nongovernmental organizations (NGOs). Even in the Internet age, insurgents face a Darwinian struggle for scarce international resources – and, to succeed, they must aggressively market themselves. To make this argument, Clifford Bob systematically compares two recent movements that attracted major NGO support, Mexico's Zapatista rebels and Nigeria's Ogoni ethnic group, against similar movements that failed to do so. Based on primary document analysis and more than 45 interviews with local activists and NGO leaders, the author shows that support goes to the savviest, not the neediest. *The Marketing of Rebellion* develops a realistic, organizational perspective on social movements, NGOs, and "global civil society." It will change how the weak solicit help, the powerful pick clients, and all of us think about contemporary world politics.

Clifford Bob is Assistant Professor in the Department of Political Science and the Graduate School of Social and Public Policy at Duquesne University in Pittsburgh. He specializes in transnational politics, social movements, human rights, and ethnic conflict. His published work includes articles in *Foreign Policy*, *Social Problems*, *International Politics*, *American Journal of International Law*, *Journal of Human Rights*, and *PS: Political Science & Politics*.

Cambridge Studies in Contentious Politics

Editors

Jack A. Goldstone   *George Mason University*
Doug McAdam   *Stanford University and Center for Advanced Study in the Behavioral Sciences*
Sidney Tarrow   *Cornell University*
Charles Tilly   *Columbia University*
Elisabeth J. Wood   *Yale University*

Ronald Aminzade et al., *Silence and Voice in the Study of Contentious Politics*
Charles D. Brockett, *Political Movements and Violence in Central America*
Gerald F. Davis et al., *Social Movements and Organization Theory*
Jack A. Goldstone, ed., *States, Parties, and Social Movements*
Doug McAdam, Sidney Tarrow, and Charles Tilly, *Dynamics of Contention*
Charles Tilly, *Contention and Democracy in Europe, 1650–2000*
Charles Tilly, *The Politics of Collective Violence*
Deborah J. Yashar, *Contesting Citizenship in Latin America*

The Marketing of Rebellion

INSURGENTS, MEDIA, AND INTERNATIONAL ACTIVISM

CLIFFORD BOB

Duquesne University

CAMBRIDGE
UNIVERSITY PRESS

2005

CAMBRIDGE UNIVERSITY PRESS
Cambridge, New York, Melbourne, Madrid, Cape Town, Singapore, São Paulo

Cambridge University Press
40 West 20th Street, New York, NY 10011-4211, USA

www.cambridge.org
Information on this title: www.cambridge.org/9780521845700

First published 2005

Printed in the United States of America

A catalog record for this publication is available from the British Library.

Library of Congress Cataloging in Publication Data

Bob, Clifford, 1958–
The marketing of rebellion : insurgents, media, and international activism / Clifford Bob.
   p. cm. – (Cambridge studies in contentious politics)
Includes bibliographical references and index.
ISBN 0-521-84570-X (hardback) – ISBN 0-521-60786-8 (pbk.)
1. Insurgency. 2. Government, Resistance to. 3. Human rights – Cross-cultural
studies. 4. International relief. 5. Non-governmental organizations. 6. Public
relations. 7. Mass media. 8. Ejército Zapatista de Liberación Nacional (Mexico)
9. Ogoni (African people) – Government relations. I. Title. II. Series.
JC328.5.B63 2005
322.4 – dc22   2004024987

ISBN-13   978-0-521-84570-0 hardback
ISBN-10   0-521-84570-X hardback

ISBN-13   978-0-521-60786-5 paperback
ISBN-10   0-521-60786-8 paperback

To Joan

Contents

Maps and Tables

Maps

Tables

Acknowledgments

My debts in this project are great. First, I thank the many activists I interviewed from various movements and nongovernmental organizations (NGOs). They gave me extraordinary access to their viewpoints and files even as most accepted my offer to maintain their anonymity in this book. If I have achieved my goal of writing a realistic explanatory account of transnational networking, this is in large measure due to the openness of my sources. If my view is more skeptical of movements and NGOs than is most existing scholarship, this is a tribute to their highly strategic approaches. I believe that transnational movements and NGOs offer valuable counterpoints to a global politics dominated by state and corporate interests. Yet to help these alternative actors reach their promise, one must take an unsentimental view of their operations. It is not enough to extol them as "moral" forces while refusing to scrutinize their interactions with each other and the public. I seek to offer a critical yet constructive perspective that not only illuminates these important interactions for scholars but also helps the local movements seeking aid and the NGOs distributing it.

Friends and mentors contributed much to this project. At the Massachusetts Institute of Technology, where the book started as a doctoral thesis, I thank the late Myron Weiner for his enthusiasm and broad learning, Stephen Van Evera for his generative skepticism and championship of clear writing, and, most important, Daniel Kryder for his encouragement, strategic advice about theses, books, and jobs, and knowledge of the social movements literature. All of them read early versions of the manuscript and gave me detailed comments. Friends and faculty members also provided generous feedback and encouragement when the book was in its earliest stages. I thank Karen Alter, Eva Bellin, Amy Gurowitz, Brian Hanson, Richard Joseph, Daniel Lindley, Richard Samuels, Frank Schwartz, Taylor

Seybolt, and Steve Wilkinson. For allowing me to stay with them during a research trip to London, I thank Norman Letalik and my great aunt Lottie Levy. At the John F. Kennedy School of Government, I received not only office space and computer equipment but also new viewpoints (and job interview tips) from Sean Lynn-Jones, Steven Miller, Michael Brown, and Samantha Power. In addition, I thank two anonymous reviewers at Cambridge University Press and one at Cornell University Press for their incisive and helpful criticisms.

At Duquesne University, I have benefited greatly from the friendship and support of faculty in the Political Science Department and the Graduate Center on Social and Public Policy. The McAnulty College and Graduate School of Liberal Arts and the university as a whole have backed my research with grants from the Wimmer Family Foundation Faculty Development Fund and the Presidential Scholarship Fund. Faculty who have been particularly helpful include Charles Rubin, Richard Colignon, and Sharon Erickson Nepstad. Students in my graduate and undergraduate classes have also contributed to my thinking. Beyond the bounds of my institutional affiliations, other scholars have generously offered encouragement, ideas, and in some cases close readings over the many years of this project's gestation. Among them are Rogers Brubaker, Alison Brysk, Jeffrey Checkel, Bernard Finel, Jonathan Fox, Thomas M. Franck, Betty Hanson, Daniel Lev, John Markoff, Jackie Smith, Sidney Tarrow, Paul Wapner, and Michael Watts. In addition, I thank Thomas Olesen for permission to use a portion of an interview from his book *International Zapatismo*.

My research has appealed to audiences across the narrow bounds of academic disciplines, not only in political science but also in sociology, communications, and public policy. I have therefore had the privilege of presenting my arguments at diverse conferences and workshops where pointed comments broadened my perspectives and renewed my interest in the project. In addition to regular disciplinary gatherings in political science, international affairs, and sociology, I am particularly grateful for invitations to speak at the Cornell University/Syracuse University Workshop on Transnational Contention, the University of Connecticut Human Rights Initiative, Duke University's Comparative Politics Workshop, the University of Pittsburgh's Social Movements Forum, the University of California, Santa Cruz's conference on "Human Rights, Globalization and Civil Society Actors," the University of California, Irvine's conference on "Globalization and Human Rights," and Smith College. Of particular help was the Social Science

Acknowledgments

Research Council/American Council of Learned Societies conference on "Rethinking Social Science Research on the Developing World in the 21st Century."

Foreign Policy magazine published a brief version of my arguments under the title "Merchants of Morality" as the cover story in its March/April 2002 issue. In their zeal to market the magazine, however, the senior editors distorted the article's argument with cover photographs and language, as well as a summary blurb in the table of contents, that I had no hand in writing or designing. These did not reflect my findings, most importantly by implying that local movements "bull[y]" their way to international support. I was informed of the cover less than a week before the issue began circulating and did not see the blurb until I received a printed copy of the magazine. The issue was later one of three that *Foreign Policy* submitted in winning a 2003 National Magazine Award for Editorial Excellence. Ironically, then, the editors' "spin" on my arguments may have helped the magazine win this prestigious award. I hope this book will clarify my views.

The financial support of several institutions has been critical to the completion of this project. I thank the Smith Richardson Foundation International Security and Foreign Policy Junior Faculty Program, the United States Institute of Peace, the John F. Kennedy School of Government's Human Rights Initiative, the Albert Einstein Institution, the Harvard-MIT MacArthur Transnational Security Program, and the Social Science Research Council/American Council of Learned Societies.

Although my debts to these individuals and institutions are many, all of the views expressed here are my own, and I take full responsibility for errors.

Finally, my family has supported me wholeheartedly throughout the long years of graduate school training and writing this book. My mother, Renate Bob, and my late father, Murray Bob, have been an inspiration, with their warmth, generosity, intellectual curiosity, and skeptical attitude toward received wisdom. I only wish that I had completed this book in time for my father to see it. My in-laws, Ludmila Miles and the late Richard Miles, were also extremely helpful to me and my family over the years. My children, Alex and Natalie, have been a joy, providing endless fun and diversions as they have grown. Our skiing, biking, camping, and playing together refreshed me for the hard work of thinking and writing that went into this book. My wife, Joan Miles, deserves my special thanks. Early in our marriage, just after the birth of our first child, she supported my decision to leave the security of law practice for the vagaries of the academic world. Throughout my years of study and research, her humor, support, patience, and love have been essential. And without her cheerful willingness to move our young family from New York to Boston and then to Pittsburgh at the cost of her own job as a lawyer, I could not have finished my work. This book is dedicated to her.

The Marketing of Rebellion

1

Insurgent Groups and the Quest for Overseas Support

For decades, Tibet's quest for self-determination has roused people around the world. Inspired by appeals to human rights, cultural preservation, and spiritual awakening, thousands of individuals and organizations lend moral, material, and financial support to the Tibetan cause. As a result, greater autonomy for Tibet's five million inhabitants remains a popular international campaign despite the Chinese government's 50-year effort to suppress it.

But although Tibet's light shines brightly abroad, few outsiders know that China's borders hold other restive minorities: Mongols, Zhuang, Yi, and Hui, to name only a few. Notable are the Uyghurs, a group of more than seven million people located northwest of Tibet. Like the Tibetans, the Uyghurs fought Chinese domination for centuries, enjoying brief periods of independence twice during the twentieth century. Like the Tibetans, the Uyghurs today face threats from Han Chinese in-migration, centrally planned development policies, and newly strengthened antiterror measures. If, as the Dalai Lama has warned, Tibetan ethnicity, culture, and environment face "extinction," the Uyghurs' surely do, too. And, like the Tibetans, the Uyghurs resist Chinese domination with domestic and international protest that, in Beijing's eyes, makes them dangerous separatists. Yet the Uyghurs have failed to inspire the broad-based foreign networks that generously bankroll the Tibetans. No bumper stickers plead for East Turkestan's liberation. No Hollywood stars or corporate moguls write fat checks for the Uyghurs. No Uyghur leader has visited with a U.S. president or won the Nobel Peace Prize.

In their quest for external allies, the Tibetans and Uyghurs are far from unique. In armed and unarmed conflicts throughout the world, challengers confronting powerful opponents seek support outside their home states – from international organizations, nongovernmental organizations (NGOs), the media, and the broad public. But although many clamor for assistance, few draw the external backing won by the Tibetans. Instead, most remain as isolated as the Uyghurs. Whereas the world now knows about East Timor, similar insurrections in Indonesian Aceh and West Papua remain far less celebrated. Among environmental conflicts, a small number of cases, such as the Brazilian rubber tappers' efforts to save the Amazon, the conflict over China's Three Gorges dam, and the fight over the Chad–Cameroon pipeline, have gained global acclaim. But many similar environmental battles, such as the construction of India's Tehri dam, the logging of Guyana's rainforests, and the laying of the Trans Thai–Malaysia gas pipeline, are waged in anonymity. Whole categories of conflict, such as landlessness in Latin America and caste discrimination in South Asia, likewise go little noticed.

How and why do a handful of local challengers become global causes célèbres while scores of others remain isolated and obscure? What inspires powerful transnational networks to spring up around particular movements? Most basically, which of the world's myriad oppressed groups benefit from contemporary globalization?

Since the end of the Cold War, many have touted the emergence of a "global civil society" composed of formal and informal organizations with constituencies, operations, and goals that transcend state boundaries. Some believe that growing transnational interactions have fundamentally changed world politics, creating an alternative political space distinguished by sympathy and cooperation rather than the anarchy, self-interest, and competition that mark relations among states. In this rosy view, the media act as all-seeing eyes, pinpointing places in gravest distress. New technologies permit early warning of emerging conflicts. And compassionate organizations selflessly throw their services to the neediest cases. Emblematic of this brave new world are two entities: NGOs, private organizations operating across borders whose primary goals are political, social, or cultural; and "transnational advocacy networks" (TANs), loosely formed groupings of NGOs, activists, foundations, journalists, bureaucrats, and others, all of whom are bound by "shared values, a common discourse, and dense exchanges of information and services."[1] Both NGOs and TANs are frequently heralded

---

[1] Margaret E. Keck and Kathryn Sikkink, *Activists beyond Borders: Advocacy Networks in International Politics* (Ithaca, NY: Cornell University Press, 1998), 2; Ann M. Florini, ed. *The Third Force: The Rise of Transnational Civil Society* (Tokyo: Japan Center for International Exchange; Washington: Carnegie Endowment for International Peace, 2000); Thomas Risse, Stephen

as "principled" forces in an amoral international system. For some scholars, such as Richard Falk, the recent proliferation of these ethical actors is creating a cosmopolitan democracy of "humane governance" and human solidarity.[2] In this vision, cross-border activity holds special promise for domestic movements combating unresponsive or repressive states. In Margaret Keck and Kathryn Sikkink's influential metaphor, harried movements generate transnational support "boomerangs."[3] Using new technologies, they leap borders to contact the growing ranks of NGOs abroad. In turn, NGOs and the TANs they anchor altruistically adopt distant causes, volunteering aid, publicizing injustices, and pressuring foes. Ultimately, no local struggle goes unnoticed, "empowering the have-nots of the world."[4]

From the perspective of activists in the developed world, this interpretation may appear sound. There are multitudes of worthy causes on which to lavish attention – so many that picking clients can present a quandary. But for social movements in the developing world – groups for whom international linkages are not just a calling, a career, or a diversion – contemporary international politics has a different feel. New technologies, actors, and institutions promise much but deliver little. As Moses Werror, a leader of Indonesia's Free West Papua Movement, complained on the group's Web site, "We have struggled for more than 30 years, and the world has ignored our cause."[5] Or as a displaced person in war-torn southern Sudan recently

---

C. Ropp, and Kathryn Sikkink, eds., *The Power of Human Rights: International Norms and Domestic Change* (Cambridge: Cambridge University Press, 1999).

[2] Richard A. Falk, *On Humane Governance: Toward a New Global Politics: The World Order Models Project Report of the Global Civilization Initiative* (University Park: Pennsylvania State University Press, 1995).

[3] Keck and Sikkink, *Activists beyond Borders*, 12–13. See also Sanjeev Khagram, James V. Riker, and Kathryn Sikkink, eds., *Restructuring World Politics: Transnational Social Movements, Networks, and Norms* (Minneapolis: University of Minnesota Press, 2002).

[4] Allen L. Hammond, "Digitally Empowered Development," *Foreign Affairs*, March/April 2001, 105. Others who take a generally optimistic view of an emerging "global civil society" include Paul Wapner, *Environmental Activism and World Civic Politics* (Albany: State University of New York Press, 1996); Ronnie D. Lipschutz, "Reconstructing World Politics: The Emergence of a Global Civil Society," *Millennium: Journal of International Studies* 21, no. 3 (1992): 389–420; Alison Brysk, "From Above and Below: Social Movements, the International System, and Human Rights in Argentina," *Comparative Political Studies* 26, no. 3 (1993): 259–85; James N. Rosenau, *Along the Domestic–Foreign Frontier: Exploring Governance in a Turbulent World* (Cambridge: Cambridge University Press, 1997).

[5] Free West Papua Movement, OPM (Organisesi Papua Merdeka), http://www.converge.org.nz/wpapua/opm.html (accessed June 1, 2004).

cried, "Why do so many Americans care about saving seals and whales but not us?"[6]

At stake is more than a global popularity contest. For many challengers, outside aid is literally a matter of life or death. NGOs can raise awareness about little-known conflicts, mobilize resources for beleaguered movements, and pressure repressive governments. External involvement can deter state violence and force policy change. It can bestow legitimacy on challengers who might otherwise have meager recognition. And it can strengthen challengers, not only materially, through infusions of money, equipment, and knowledge, but also psychologically, by demonstrating that a movement is not alone, that the world cares, and that an arduous conflict may not be fruitless.

With so much at risk, challengers compete fiercely for transnational patrons. This book probes the reasons certain groups prick the world's conscience whereas others do not. Contrary to most recent scholarship, I highlight the action, innovation, and skill of movements themselves. Too often, their unexpected renown is attributed to their location in a strategically important region or to intercession by third parties such as the cable news network CNN. This book places local groups at center stage, focusing on the risky and difficult strategies they deploy to galvanize external help in the face of domestic despotism and international indifference. First, movements seek simply to be heard, to lift themselves above the voiceless mass of the world's poor and oppressed. To do this, they tap the media to raise international awareness and lobby potential patrons directly. Second, insurgent groups magnify their appeal by framing parochial demands, provincial conflicts, and particularistic identities to match the interests and agendas of distant audiences. In this global morality market, challengers must publicize their plights, portray their conflicts as righteous struggles, and craft their messages to resonate abroad.

In taking this approach, I make five arguments. First, *winning NGO support is neither easy nor automatic but instead competitive and uncertain*. Scores of challengers strive for overseas recognition even within a single country or region. For distant audiences, however, the ferment is invisible. Journalists and academics focus on insurgencies that shine internationally. They seldom place these groups in a broader context – as rare stars in a universe of hapless aspirants. The efforts of the less fortunate are overlooked.

---

[6] Kate O'Beirne, "A Faraway Country... about Which We Know a Lot," *National Review*, March 5, 2001, 30.

Or, as international resources flow to the few, unsuccessful competitors direct their energies elsewhere, join forces with the most flourishing, shift to the opposition, or die out. This analytic blind spot, compounded by recent enthusiasm about the beneficent effects of globalization and the Internet, has made the growth of NGO assistance look deceptively simple.

Second, *the development and retention of support are best conceived not as philanthropic gestures but as exchanges based on the relative power of each party to the transaction.* On the supply side of this market are a small number of influential NGOs with no reason to choose one desperate movement over another. On the demand side are myriad local groups for whom international linkages hold the prospect of new resources and greater clout in their domestic conflicts. This disparity in need creates an unequal power relationship. As a result, movements must often alter key characteristics to meet the expectations of patrons. By contrast, in most cases, NGOs can be circumspect in picking clients and need not reinvent themselves to do so. To explain their choices only as the result of "morality" or "principle" affords little analytic bite when this larger context is considered. Certainly altruism plays an important role in these decisions, but given their organizational imperatives, NGOs have strong incentives to devote themselves to the challenger whose profile most closely matches their own requirements – not necessarily to the neediest group.

Third, *competition for NGO intervention occurs in a context of economic, political, and organizational inequality that systematically advantages some challengers over others.* These disparities, which insurgents have limited capacity to change, make it easier for certain movements – those with more resources, superior knowledge, and preexisting international standing – to promote themselves abroad and pigeonhole themselves into acceptable categories of protest. To put this in Keck and Sikkink's metaphor, many needy movements cannot afford a "boomerang" to petition for aid. Those that can have varying capacities, giving their appeals different reach, aim, and spin. As a result, many "boomerang throws" miss their mark, falling unheeded in inhospitable political, social, and cultural terrain.

Fourth, *despite these structural biases, the choices of insurgents – how they market themselves – matter.* Most analysts take a top-down approach, focusing on NGOs and suggesting that transnational networks form when intrepid activists in rich countries reach into the developing world to succor helpless "victims." In fact, however, local movements insistently court overseas backing, and their promotional strategies count. Although they have numerous variants, these strategies share two broad aims:

raising international awareness of the movement and enhancing its appeal to NGOs.

Finally, *because of this market dynamic, the effects of assistance are more ambiguous than is often acknowledged.* For many scholars and journalists, overseas activism is an unmitigated blessing. Reflecting a penchant to idolize NGOs, analysts confuse the apparently altruistic intent of support with its effects. But when the latent sources of aid are considered, one can more easily assess its costs. On one hand, local challengers must conform to the needs and agendas of distant audiences, potentially alienating a movement from its base. On the other hand, the organizational imperatives driving NGOs mean that even the most devoted can seldom make a particular insurgent its top concern. The result can be problematic or even deadly: challengers, tempted into attention-grabbing tactics or extreme stances, may find distant stalwarts absent or helpless at moments of gravest peril.

Implications

The foregoing arguments reject the view that challengers who attract major backing are simply the lucky winners of an international crap shoot. Although chance plays some part, much can be explained systematically. The marketing perspective also denies that there is a meritocracy of suffering, with the worst-off groups necessarily gaining the most help. Every challenger faced with bloody state crackdowns or simple political exclusion rightfully depicts its troubles as deserving of the world's concern. Yet typically there is little relationship between a group's degree of oppression and its level of external acclaim. Everyday violence against South Asia's estimated 260 million untouchables has never made it high on the international agenda despite the vigorous efforts of Indian activists. And the appeals of the Sudan People's Liberation Army went unheeded for decades despite horrific human rights violations costing millions of lives.

It should be clear from the importance I place on groups whose efforts are ignored by NGOs that I reject generalizations about the impacts of "globalization." By themselves, economic integration, technological advances, and media penetration cannot explain why some worthy groups spark action whereas a host of others, often from the same locales, do not. A quick check on the Internet reveals scores of liberation groups, from Burma's Arakan Rohingya National Organisation to Ethiopia's Oromo Liberation Front to Mexico's Zapatista Army of National Liberation. Countless environmental, labor, human rights, and other movements also dot the globe, some with Web sites but most others not. But in cyberspace as in physical space, only a fraction of contenders for the world's favor capture more than a niche following. New technologies dangle the prospect of internationalizing their causes before more groups than ever before, but these innovations by no means assure it.

Similarly insufficient to explain these disparities is the reputed rise of a new "global consciousness" and the more tangible explosion of "moral actors" on the world stage. The admonition to "think globally" has undeniable ethical overtones: that we are part of one world whose condition should concern us all. Although noble, this impulse runs into a hard reality. The scope of global suffering remains so great that even the virtuous must repeatedly choose among a multitude of deserving causes. Those who view NGOs primarily as ethical actors cannot explain how these choices are made, why a few supplicant groups are selected for major attention whereas most fall by the wayside. It is true that NGOs often act out of deeply felt moral conviction; many of their choices about issues to highlight and local movements to champion rest in part on these principles. Yet a little-studied strategic element also plays a central role. Given the context of scarce resources in which NGOs operate, omitting this element leaves analysts with no reliable means of explaining behavior.

More generally, many who think about these issues have been dazzled by an explosion of new actors at the international level. It is true that, in the final analysis, an editor at the BBC or a manager at Amnesty International can make the difference between international obscurity and celebrity for a movement. But focusing on these powerful players illuminates only the last phase of a complicated strategic process. It reduces the role of challengers, painting them as secondary figures in the formation of their own international networks. At best, it portrays them as "poster children" for the larger agendas of distant NGOs; at worst, it depicts them as passively awaiting third-party attention and resources. Yet movements aggressively pursue external aid, orchestrating their own international networks. Using sophisticated approaches, they seek to influence the media, NGOs, and broader publics. In this, of course, insurgents do nothing more than their opponents – governments, multinational corporations, and international financial institutions with huge resources and privileged access to the international press. But where the powerful buy the world's best public relations machines, challengers must bootstrap themselves to the fore.

Most fundamentally, focusing on the suppliers of transnational support misses the hallmark of all markets, competition. Challengers scramble for scarce resources in a setting thick with similar aspirants. Despite its promise, today's "global civil society" is for many a Darwinian arena in which the successful prosper but the weak wither. At any one time, there is room for only a few challengers on any issue. Tacitly and at times openly, needy groups vie with one another for the world's sympathy, elevating themselves above their competitors and differentiating themselves from similar causes.

Definitions and Plan of the Book

In Chapter 2, I detail the marketing approach, explaining the development of NGO activism for "challengers," "insurgencies," and "movements." I use these terms interchangeably to embrace domestically based social currents and organizations that oppose governments, elites, and other powerful institutions chiefly using protest and pressure outside conventional political channels.[7] Although they have diverse foes, the movements I examine seek changes primarily in national rather than international policy. Such challengers vary widely in many respects. Beyond their obvious differences in goals, insurgents also span those that have widespread grassroots backing and those that do not. With regard to strategies, movements may deploy peaceful, "conventional" protest or violent, transgressive action.

"Activism," "support," and "adoption" mean sustained and substantial transfers of money, matériel, and knowledge by a foreign NGO or NGO network to a challenger, as well as provision of publicity, advocacy, and lobbying on its behalf.[8] These actions may benefit the group *directly*, by strengthening it, or *indirectly*, by weakening its opponent, for instance through notoriety, opprobrium, or sanctions. (Excluded from this definition is media reporting; although it may alert NGOs to conflicts and serve as a tool of activist networks, journalism seldom has aid as its principal aim.) There is tremendous diversity among NGOs and the networks they form, but in this study I focus on two broad types, "advocacy" and "solidarity."[9] The latter, for instance today's "Free Burma" coalition or the Spanish Civil War's Abraham Lincoln brigade, openly take sides in distant conflicts, backing challengers because of ideological, religious, or other deeply felt

---

[7] See Sidney Tarrow, *Power in Movement: Social Movements and Contentious Politics*, 2nd ed. (Cambridge: Cambridge University Press, 1998), 4.

[8] Most challengers are nongovernmental, whereas most NGOs are organized manifestations of broader movements. But for clarity I use the term "NGO" to refer to the foreign organizations giving aid rather than the domestic "movements" receiving it.

[9] Keck and Sikkink, *Activists beyond Borders*, 82, 95.

affinities. Although they differ from diaspora organizations, which have blood ties to challengers in their ancestral homes, solidarity organizations nonetheless identify closely with their clients, and their members often form tight personal bonds with insurgents. By contrast, advocacy organizations, exemplified by human rights NGOs such as Amnesty International, champion principles, procedures, or policies rather than parties. In practice, however, the two categories of NGOs and networks often overlap. In the heat of conflict, it is difficult for advocacy NGOs to separate adherence to ideals from endorsement of groups. In addition, many "principles," such as those concerning environmental causes, are more political than moral. Conversely, solidarity NGOs wrap their partisanship in rhetoric that simultaneously upholds tenets such as democracy or human rights. Thus, the two types of networks are best viewed as different points along a continuous spectrum of support. (Although I do not examine diaspora organizations here, the marketing perspective probably also explains their behavior toward coethnics in their homelands.)

Chapter 2 describes the size, character, and dynamics of the transnational market, including both the "demand side," movements searching for patronage, and the "supply side," the NGOs that provide it. Illustrating my points with numerous examples, I identify common strategies as well as underlying structural factors that lift certain movements over others. Thus, the book presents both a causal argument explaining the growth of activism (or lack thereof) and a "cookbook" for movements and NGOs. Social scientists may quibble that the argument is too complex. I plead guilty with mitigation: In the real world of transnational networking, many overlapping factors play a role. Any comprehensive explanation of a particular case will therefore be "messy." To build broader insights, however, I emphasize the fundamental forces at work: power, exchange, and competition.

The book's empirical chapters use this framework to analyze several recent insurgencies that have electrified activist networks, comparing them with similar movements from the same states operating at approximately the same time that have *failed* to do so. Unavoidably, these comparisons are not fully balanced because there is more information about groups that have become causes célèbres than about those that have not. But, to the extent possible, each chapter focuses on the strategic and organizational differences between transnational winners and losers.

Measuring support precisely is difficult because it requires collecting large amounts of information about informal relationships from dispersed private organizations around the world. There are also conceptual impediments. In principle, assistance may be gauged along two dimensions: breadth and depth.[10] "Breadth" refers to the number of NGOs a movement draws, with wider patronage presumptively more desirable than narrower support. Much depends on the nature and power of the actors composing a transnational network, however. A small number of major NGOs may be more effective than a large number of weak and obscure ones. "Depth" refers to the amount of backing NGOs provide, with "more" of one type seemingly better than "less." As is the case between direct and indirect forms of aid, however, among different types within each form, it is often difficult to rank their values. Finally, there are trade-offs. Convincing an NGO to deepen its aid may require an insurgent group to make commitments that alienate other potential patrons. Despite such caveats, these indicators are useful, at least as heuristic devices, and they point to rough methods of comparison both for a single movement over time and between matched movements at a single time.

The comparative case study approach I use here is unabashedly qualitative. This methodology is not appropriate to all questions in the social sciences, but in seeking to grasp the motivations and strategies of two or more sets of political actors, particularly as they interact with one another, qualitative analysis is superior to quantitative or statistical methods. Using the fine-grained insights available through immersion in and comparison between cases, I have constructed a broad theoretical framework applicable to a diversity of movements and NGOs. In addition, I demonstrate its usefulness in explaining transnational relationships in important recent cases.

A word about the movements I examine in the empirical chapters is in order. The processes of concern here are most visible in "unlikely" cases, where unknown movements suddenly vault to prominence. Such groups may not gain the "most" international acclaim of any insurgency worldwide, but their surprising achievements illustrate causal mechanisms in stark outline. Accordingly, I focus on groups that at the outset of their quest for external backing seemed highly unlikely to gain it – small, remote, and weak groups. By probing such cases, and particularly by doing so in comparison with matched groups whose international quests failed, I reveal a diversity of factors and strategies affecting the rise of support. Not surprisingly given these purposes, the groups I examine come from states in the

---

[10] Stephen M. Saideman, "Discrimination in International Relations: Analyzing External Support for Ethnic Groups," *Journal of Peace Research* 39 (2002): 27–50.

developing world and seek help primarily from NGOs based in the developed world. The scope of the marketing perspective is broader, however. With minor adjustment, the concepts of power and exchange at its heart should apply to movements in the developed world that also seek foreign connections – from the American civil rights movement in the 1950s to Spain's contemporary anti-dam movement to Japan's Burakumin minority.

In Chapter 3, I examine Nigeria's Niger River Delta, a region rife with ethnic, political, and environmental conflict. Out of this ferment, a small movement among the Ogoni people won major support in the mid-1990s, particularly among advocacy NGOs in the environmental and human rights sectors. Simultaneously, but far less successfully, similar movements among other Niger Delta minorities, such as the Ijaw, sought friends overseas. Chapter 4 discusses insurgency in Mexico, focusing on the Zapatista Army of National Liberation (the Ejército Zapatista de Liberación Nacional, or EZLN) in the southern state of Chiapas. This group, one of numerous insurgencies and indigenous movements in recent Mexican history, stands out because, shortly after its first public appearance in 1994, it galvanized advocacy and solidarity activists worldwide. Two years later, a similar rebel group in southern Mexico, the Popular Revolutionary Army (the Ejército Popular Revolucionario, or EPR), flopped in its attempt to duplicate its predecessor's success.

The chapters on Nigeria and Mexico aim both to explain the rise of overseas activism and to demonstrate the utility of marketing theory more broadly. Although these goals are in tension to some extent, I seek to do justice to both. To trace the development of support, I use information gathered from the local movements and their overseas followers. In the chapter on Mexico, I rely primarily on contemporaneous insurgent and NGO documents as well as media interviews. In the chapter on Nigeria, I use the foregoing along with retrospective interviews of movement leaders and NGO principals.[11] On a methodological note, although the internationally successful and failed groups in each country had limited interactions with one another, they pursued assistance separately and therefore may be treated as independent observations for analytic purposes.

In each chapter, I include two forms of comparison. First, I analyze the Ogoni and Zapatista experiences historically, highlighting how changing marketing strategies affected NGO involvement. Second and more briefly, I contrast each movement with its matched "failure" cases – the Ogoni

---

[11] For more about my interviewing techniques, see Appendix 2.

with the Ijaws and other Niger Delta minorities and the Zapatistas with the EPR – revealing the influence both of strategic decisions and of underlying organizational factors. In the two chapters, other potentially important factors remain constant. First, because both sets of movements sought help at about the same time, international variables such as NGO numbers, institutional setting, dominant ideologies, and technological development are nearly uniform. Second, the domestic context – state structures and leaders, societal groupings and attitudes, economic development and change – is almost the same for the two sets of movements. Indeed, in Chapter 3 and to a lesser extent Chapter 4, the challengers I examine come from the same region of their respective countries. Finally, in each chapter, the matched movements had similar grievances and comparable constituencies.

Despite these many background similarities, it is worth underlining that each movement, like all other social phenomena, is unique. Unsurprisingly, then, the Ogoni and the Zapatistas vary in important respects. Within their home societies, the most striking difference involves tactics, with the Zapatistas at least initially deploying force against the state, whereas the Ogoni used peaceful protest. The two movements also adopted different overseas strategies. For one thing, they framed distinct aspects of their causes. In addition, at the outset, they employed contrasting means to alert the world to their needs. The Ogoni directly lobbied NGOs, whereas the Zapatistas relied on diffuse international consciousness-raising, mostly by orchestrating media and Internet reports. They also attracted different kinds of backers, for the Ogoni primarily (though not exclusively) advocacy groups and for the Zapatistas a combination of advocacy and solidarity NGOs. Finally, although both groups moved from isolation to acclaim, the success of the Zapatistas' early media strategies meant that their main problem involved retaining activist interest; for the Ogoni, by contrast, initially gaining assistance was a lengthy and difficult process. Despite these superficial dissimilarities, the two cases share fundamental features, including marketing approach, factors driving it, and supporters' motivations. On this basis, I build a unified model of transnational marketing and draw broader conclusions.

Of course, the Ogoni and Zapatistas by no means exhaust the diversity of challengers worldwide. But the fact that such different movements used parallel strategies – and that similar factors explain their successes, whereas their absence explains the failures of their counterpart movements – buttresses the marketing approach. These facts also indicate the model's range. Viewed beforehand, the Ogoni and Zapatistas (as well as their matched movements) were representative of numerous challengers world-wide seeking a diversity of goals and using a variety of tactics. Despite the individuality of every such movement, what unites them and what justifies my examination is that they were initially unknown and isolated outside of their home countries – like every other challenger at some point in its history. Only in retrospect do these two movements appear exceptional due to the strong backing they attracted. Thus, the marketing approach applies to insurgents using both conventional and transgressive tactics, having both significant and limited domestic acceptance, seeking any number of goals, and attracting advocacy, solidarity, or both types of supporters.

In the Conclusion, I first compare the Ogoni and Zapatista cases. Although both challengers won significant overseas backing, the differences in its composition further illuminate the role of strategic and organizational factors as well as "structural" differences between the movements' opponents. This cross-regional comparison does not include the same controls as the earlier analysis, but it extends and deepens the marketing approach. The Conclusion also considers the effects of international support on movements, NGOs, and conflict outcomes while suggesting ideas for reducing some of the transnational marketplace's more problematic aspects. Finally, the Conclusion draws out the argument's implications for theories of world politics.

2

Power, Exchange, and Marketing

To gain support, challengers must persuade overseas audiences with little at stake in a conflict to take a sustained interest and make sacrifices for the cause. They do so under unfavorable circumstances: pressed by powerful opponents; in competition with a host of other worthy movements; and in the face of limited attention and resources. Still, the promise of assistance attracts many local insurgents to the international realm. There they find an environment less receptive than many imagine. Certainly sympathy and concern about distant issues distinguish NGOs from profit-hungry multi-national corporations and power-driven states. As their central missions, NGOs promote ideas, principles, or policies. Their recent proliferation has brought novel perspectives to global issues, enriching debates, widening choices, and improving outcomes. Taking action on behalf of the distressed is often one of their core values. And most NGO staff care deeply about the causes they champion. Yet NGOs at their root are organizations – with all the anxieties about maintenance, survival, and growth that beset every organization. In the formation of transnational relationships, these realities create frictions. No matter how cohesive their networks, local movements and transnational NGOs have distinct objectives, constituencies, and approaches, operate in disparate political settings, and are motivated by divergent needs.

Given this dualism, movement–NGO interactions are best seen as exchanges. The concept of exchange has long been used in social analysis, but its insights have not been plumbed by those who study transnational networks.[1] In this context, domestic insurgents stand on one side, seeking

[1] Peter M. Blau, *Exchange and Power in Social Life* (New Brunswick, NJ: Transaction Books, 1964); Sidney R. Waldman, *Foundations of Political Action: An Exchange Theory of Politics*

money, matériel, information, legitimacy, and access to aid them in their conflicts with powerful opponents. On the other side are NGOs impelled by their missions but constrained by their interests. By supporting local movements, NGOs do more than help the needy and more than meet their principled or political goals – however worthy these achievements. They also gain important nonmaterial resources. Chief among these is a raison d'etre, legitimation for the NGO's international activism and proof that its agenda remains unfulfilled. Often as well, movement clients provide their NGO patrons with symbols for broader campaigns, with prestige among their own support base, and with information or strategies useful in other struggles. Moreover, the right client can save an NGO scarce material and nonmaterial resources that can be employed in other operations and struggles.

This mutuality of interest creates a market for transnational support, but one with a heavy imbalance between supply and demand. On the demand side, numerous challengers, pushed by desperation or pulled by the prospect of resources and opportunities, vie for aid. Although there is no compendium of domestic challengers, various indicators give a rough idea of the numbers involved. Major NGOs receive a steady stream of appeals from around the world by e-mail, fax, telephone, and in person. Another indicator are insurgent Web sites on the Internet, one of whose chief functions is to alert the world to activists' claims. Hundreds of these sites have sprouted in recent years.[2] Local challengers also participate in international

(Boston: Little, Brown, 1972); Sidney Tarrow, *Power in Movement: Social Movements and Contentious Politics*, 2nd ed. (Cambridge: Cambridge University Press, 1998). Theorists from Keohane and Nye to Keck and Sikkink have noted that various types of exchanges occur in transnational political interactions, but the implications of this fact have not been explored. See Robert O. Keohane and Joseph S. Nye, Jr., eds., *Transnational Relations and World Politics* (London: Cambridge University Press, 1971); Richard W. Mansbach, Yale H. Ferguson, and Donald E. Lampert, *The Web of World Politics: Non-State Actors in the Global System* (Englewood Cliffs, NJ: Prentice-Hall, 1976); Peter Willetts, ed., *Pressure Groups in the Global System: The Transnational Relations of Issue-Oriented Non-Governmental Organizations* (New York: St. Martin's Press, 1982). Only recently has an organizational perspective begun to be applied to transnational networking. See Susan K. Sell and Aseem Prakash, "Using Ideas Strategically: The Contest between Business and NGO Networks in Intellectual Property Rights," *International Studies Quarterly* 48, no. 1 (2004): 143–75; Alexander Cooley and James Ron, "The NGO Scramble: Organizational Insecurity and the Political Economy of Transnational Action," *International Security* 27, no. 1 (2002): 5–39.

[2] See, for example, movements linked at such Web sites as Homelands, "Autonomy, Secession, Independence and Nationalist Movements," http://www.visi.com/~homelands (accessed May 15, 2004); NativeWeb, "Resources for Indigenous Cultures around the World," http://www.nativeweb.org/hosted/ (accessed May 15, 2004); and Unrepresented

meetings on issues ranging from the environment to racism to human rights. There has been a dramatic increase in nongovernmental presence at U.N.-sponsored conferences over the last 30 years, prompting the creation of special conclaves, often with their own screening procedures.[3] Even regular annual meetings of such low-level U.N. bodies as the Working Group on Indigenous Populations attract scores of dissident groups. These gatherings serve multiple functions, but networking is one of the most important.

Notably, the foregoing indicators understate the demand for support. For one thing, they do not measure the amount of aid challengers desire. Insurgent goals may entail major policy shifts by multinational corporations, international financial institutions, or governments – everything from unionizing a plant to halting a dam to partitioning a country. Indeed, if their aims were easily achieved, movements might not seek outside help. Of course, savvy insurgents are careful not to overwhelm their prospects, instead calibrating their "asks" to the capacity, interest, and donation record of potential backers. But, although they may not admit it openly, challengers usually seek large and continuing commitments.

The sources just discussed also undercount the number of groups wanting support. Those who start a Web site or attend a conference already stand above a multitude of groups who have not reached even these modest milestones. Finally, the foregoing indicators say nothing about latent demand. Among desperate populations, the sudden prospect of outside resources may conjure up a host of supplicant organizations. In the environmental field, Carrie Meyer has described the rapid growth of local ecology organizations in Ecuadorean villages when international actors suddenly made funds available.[4] At a more abstract level, sociologists argue that increases in "political opportunities," such as the availability of money and allies, lead social movements to mobilize.[5] Thus, challengers may spring into being

Nations and Peoples Organisation, "Members of the UNPO," http://www.unpo.org/members_list.php (accessed July 15, 2004).

[3] Ann Marie Clark, Elisabeth Friedman, and Kathryn Hochstetler, "The Sovereign Limits of Global Civil Society: A Comparison of NGO Participation in UN World Conferences on the Environment, Human Rights, and Women," *World Politics* 51, no. 1 (1998): 1–35.

[4] Carrie A. Meyer, "Opportunism and NGOs: Entrepreneurship and Green North-South Transfers," *World Development* 23, no. 8 (1995): 1277–89. See also Eric Bjornlund, "Democracy Inc.," *Wilson Quarterly*, Summer 2001, 18–24.

[5] Tarrow, *Power in Movement*; Doug McAdam, *Political Process and the Development of Black Insurgency, 1930–1970*, 2nd ed. (Chicago: University of Chicago Press, 1999); J. Craig Jenkins and Charles Perrow, "Insurgency of the Powerless: Farm Worker Movements (1946–1972),"

or expand their demands as outside resources become more accessible – whatever their actual local "needs."

Of course, not every group challenging powerholders in the developing world will move to internationalize its cause. Autarkic beliefs or nationalist ideologies argue against bringing in the outside world. This is one reason Peru's Shining Path made few forays abroad and seemingly cared little about its international image. Other insurgents find adequate resources and allies within their home states. Some of India's smaller ethnic groups have succeeded in carving their own states out of existing ones by amassing support at the national rather than the international level. Eschewing external help also may be a strategic decision given the realities of domestic politics. Internal opponents of the Castro regime in Cuba, for instance, refuse open aid from U.S. sources. In Malaysia as well, civil society organizations keep their distance from sympathetic foreigners because the country's top politicians have denounced NGOs as foot soldiers of Western imperialism. Notwithstanding these caveats, as political scientist E. E. Schattschneider argued decades ago, "the basic pattern of all politics" is expansion, and large numbers of challengers frustrated in achieving their goals at home chase scarce assistance abroad.[6]

On the supply side of the transnational support market stand activists and organizations based for the most part in the North. NGO numbers and budgets have grown significantly in recent years.[7] Yet even the most prominent of these organizations complain that they cannot meet local needs. Human Rights Watch, one of the world's largest human rights organizations, states that it "simply lacks the capacity to address" many serious human rights

American Sociological Review 42, no. 2 (1977): 249–68; John D. McCarthy and Mayer N. Zald, "Resource Mobilization and Social Movements: A Partial Theory," *American Journal of Sociology* 82, no. 6 (1977): 1212–41.

[6] E. E. Schattschneider, *The Semisovereign People: A Realist's View of Democracy in America* (Hinsdale, IL: Dryden Press, 1960), 2 (emphasis omitted). As Lipsky described it, "the essence of political protest consists of activating third parties" whose involvement in a conflict can change the balance of power between the main contestants. See Michael Lipsky, "Protest as a Political Resource," *American Political Science Review* 62, no. 4 (1968): 1153.

[7] Kathryn Sikkink and Jackie Smith, "Infrastructures for Change: Transnational Organizations, 1953–93," in *Restructuring World Politics: Transnational Social Movements, Networks, and Norms*, Sanjeev Khagram, James V. Riker, and Kathryn Sikkink, eds. (Minneapolis: University of Minnesota Press, 2002), 24–44; Jackie Smith, "Characteristics of the Modern Transnational Social Movement Sector," in *Transnational Social Movements and Global Politics: Solidarity beyond the State*, Jackie Smith, Charles Chatfield, and Ron Pagnucco, eds. (Syracuse, NY: Syracuse University Press, 1997), 42–58.

violations.[8] Similarly, the International Foundation for Election Systems, based in Washington, D.C., reports "an overwhelming demand" for democracy and governance assistance.[9] In the development field, the scope and depth of poverty dwarf NGO resources.[10] And among environmental organizations such as the International Rivers Network, continuous threats to critical ecosystems force selectivity in adopting causes.[11]

Even while their resources fall short of local needs, NGOs face stiff competition of their own for scarce funding from government sponsors, foundation donors, or individual members. Although many new NGOs have sprung up in recent years, scores of others have died out.[12] Rivalry among NGOs leads them to differentiate, for instance by focusing on particular problems or specializing in specific tactics. Across issues and despite the unique niches NGOs come to fill, however, one can distinguish several roles crucial to support networks. Central to network formation are *gatekeepers*, whose decisions to back a movement activate other organizations and individuals across the world. In part, this stems from gatekeepers' reputations for credibility and clout, reputations earned through years of work in a field. Just as important, these organizations have the capacity to project information widely. Typically they enjoy access to other NGOs, journalists, and government officials. Even if gatekeepers do not communicate concerns directly to other network members, their choices have powerful demonstration effects, signaling that certain movements are important and certifying them for support.[13] For most issues, gatekeepers are

---

[8] Human Rights Watch, "Introduction," in *Human Rights Watch World Report 2001*, http://www.hrw.org/wr2k1/intro/index.html (accessed May 18, 2004).

[9] International Foundation for Election Systems, "Mission and Goals," http://www.ifes.org/mission.htm (accessed July 15, 2004).

[10] World Bank Group, *World Development Report 2000/2001: Attacking Poverty* (Washington, DC: World Bank, 2000).

[11] International Rivers Network, "About International Rivers Network," http://www.irn.org/index.asp?id=/basics/about.html (accessed July 17, 2004).

[12] Although not yet applied to transnational NGOs, "organizational ecology" techniques have been used to measure births and deaths of other organizations. Virginia Gray and David Lowery, *The Population Ecology of Interest Representation: Lobbying Communities in the American States* (Ann Arbor: University of Michigan Press, 2000). See generally Debra C. Minkoff, "Macro-Organizational Analysis," in *Methods of Social Movement Research*, Bert Klandermans and Suzanne Staggenborg, eds. (Minneapolis: University of Minnesota Press, 2002), 260–85.

[13] McAdam, Tarrow, and Tilly define "certification" as "the validation of actors, their performances, and their claims by external authorities." See Doug McAdam, Sidney Tarrow, and Charles Tilly, *Dynamics of Contention* (Cambridge: Cambridge University Press, 2001), 145.

easy to identify. Among human rights organizations, Amnesty International and Human Rights Watch play this role, and in the environmental field, Greenpeace, Friends of the Earth, and other major organizations serve similar functions.

Follower NGOs rely heavily on gatekeepers' analyses and recommendations. Often organizations with primarily national missions, followers usually do not investigate insurgent claims themselves for lack of sufficient resources, expertise, or desire to cross cultural divides. Indeed, they usually have limited contact with the movements they back. As an official at the U.S.-based Sierra Club stated in explaining his group's reliance on gatekeepers in internationally oriented campaigns: "We don't have field offices or staff abroad. So we rely heavily on the Human Rights Watches and the Amnesty Internationals, the World Wildlife Fund and other international environmental groups that feed us information."[14]

Despite their pivotal role in galvanizing broad support networks, gatekeepers may not be an insurgent group's earliest supporter. Instead, movements often make initial contacts with less prominent *matchmakers*, who promote the group to powerful NGOs. Individuals with strong ties to a local movement for a variety of unique reasons – missionaries or academics, for instance – may play this role on an ad hoc basis. Indeed, American anthropologists have formally recognized the practice of "action anthropology," one of whose main goals is saving threatened indigenous peoples, in part by making their plight known to the world. Some NGOs also serve as professional matchmakers and marketing consultants, helping local movements connect with more powerful external actors and suggesting approaches to arouse international audiences. As one example, Nigeria's Kudirat Initiative for Development (KIND) has a program specifically designed to foster linkages between domestic civil society organizations and appropriate NGOs.[15] More broadly, local "regranting" organizations have become common vehicles for connecting foundation donors with needy local communities.

Two caveats are in order concerning the foregoing roles. First, their existence does not imply that support networks form only in a single way or that there is a directive force behind networks. As the name suggests, networks are loosely tied agglomerations of autonomous groups in which

---

[14] Interviewee 28 (Sierra Club manager), telephone interview by author, April 27, 2001.

[15] Kudirat Initiative for Development, "KIND's Vision: Our Work," http://www.kind.org/work.php3 (accessed September 15, 2004).

leadership, although sometimes agreed to by consent of the members, is often absent. Second, a particular NGO does not fill the same role in every support network. In recent years, this has been especially true as support networks cross traditional issue lines and gatekeepers in one issue area become followers in another.

Power and Exchange

In the transnational support market, the discrepancy between vast local needs and limited international resources produces sharp differences in power. Much of the literature on transnational relations acknowledges such gaps but conceives of them narrowly, as the result of imbalances in material resources between the two parties. In this context, however, strength is not related simply to budget size or number of protesters mobilized. More fundamentally, the relative power of each party to the exchange hinges on two factors: the *value* of each party to the other reduced by the *need* of each party for the other.[16] Value means the extent to which one party benefits from establishing a relationship with the other. An NGO is valuable to an insurgent group if it has the resources and connections to bolster the insurgency's campaign; an insurgent group is valuable to an NGO if support will advance the NGO's agenda. Need means the extent to which each party requires a relationship with the other to reach its goals. An insurgent group needs external support if it can tap few domestic resources or institutions to reach its goals; an NGO needs an insurgency if its core mission is to provide aid or if it requires clients to exemplify aspects of a broader agenda. Notably, because they are difficult to gauge and are seldom measured consistently or comparatively, both value and need are as much subjective perceptions as objective facts. Nonetheless, in deciding whether to support an insurgent group, NGOs often attempt to evaluate both the group's predicament and the utility of adopting it.

In most cases, value and need considerations heavily favor NGOs. Their support has great significance for hard-pressed movements, yet NGOs, despite their principled missions and political goals, have little reason to back any particular challenger. Faced with a plethora of suffering in the world, NGOs select among potential clients and choose the one that best suits their own requirements. For most challengers, the tables are

---

[16] For a similar formulation in a different context, see Gadi Wolfsfeld, *Media and Political Conflict: News from the Middle East* (Cambridge: Cambridge University Press, 1997), 16.

turned. Faced with few alternatives, they approach all who will listen. Yet among foreign audiences, ignorance and indifference about conditions in distant countries are endemic. Even for NGOs that care about the issues, any single movement will have little to recommend it. Given this asymmetry, NGOs usually have the upper hand in these exchanges. Their concerns, tactics, and organizational requirements create a loose but real structure to which needy local insurgents must conform to maximize their chances of gaining support. The asymmetry also fuels competition between challengers. Just as in the world economy, where local contractors must meet the demands of multinational corporations, local insurgents, vying against one another for scarce international assistance, must satisfy NGO expectations.

But these considerations also suggest a more complicated picture, in which challengers may have significant value even if they also crave support. In rare instances, NGOs may flock to an indigent insurgent that enjoys high value, perhaps because of spectacular mobilizations or a celebrity leader. In other cases, NGOs may search for a group whose difficulty illustrates the need for an NGO's solution to a broader problem.[17] There are also fashions for causes just as for products. As a result, fortunate challengers may suddenly come into vogue. Sudan's Christian-dominated People's Liberation Army, at war with the Muslim-controlled government for decades, suddenly became a cause célèbre in the late 1990s. Benefiting from the growth of a new Christian fundamentalist human rights movement in America and Europe, Sudan's profile rose as the conflict found unexpected traction not only among religious conservatives but also among African American politicians distressed by Muslim enslavement of black Sudanese.

The power perspective also suggests a rough hierarchy of value and need among insurgents and NGOs. In choosing clients, NGOs tacitly (and at times explicitly) rank the many groups that request help by their value (i.e., their match with the NGO's broader organizational attributes and interests). At times, this metric may correspond with the relative needs of groups seeking support, but in deciding where to act, NGOs consider their own organizational exigencies as well. For their part, savvy insurgents engage in parallel grading of NGOs by power and influence. Much of the social science literature has treated NGOs in undifferentiated fashion. Scholars have focused on organizations with high profiles and substantial

---

[17] Deborah Stone, "Causal Stories and the Formation of Policy Agendas," *Political Science Quarterly* 104, no. 2 (1989): 281–82.

resources – the Greenpeaces and Amnesty Internationals of the world – while paying little attention to the broader structure of the NGO sector. Yet there are clear hierarchies among NGOs, with top organizations having the deepest pockets, the best staffs, and the greatest credibility, often in a single package. Not surprisingly, then, perceived NGO pecking orders affect the behavior of shrewd insurgents. Given a choice, they will pursue the most valuable supporters they can attract.

The parties' needs also play a role here. More desperate movements will be less picky in targeting potential patrons, even while the costs of seeking support will limit the scope of their appeals. While hoping to attract a powerful NGO, they will also look for assistance even from those with little clout and few resources. Indeed, the neediest and least knowledgeable may inadvertently associate themselves with an NGO whose reputation or ideology may alienate wider backing. For its part, the needier an NGO, the lower its standards and the more likely it is to back an insurgency of lesser value – that is, one that squares more awkwardly with the NGO's organizational profile. For instance, if an NGO suddenly requires a particular kind of client, perhaps to serve as an exemplary case in a broader campaign, its adoption standards will decline, and it may adopt a distant movement after only cursory fact-gathering.

Given the usual structure of the transnational support market, however (vast local needs but scarce transnational resources and concern), most challengers face serious difficulties attracting support from distant NGOs. To improve their chances, they follow two broad marketing strategies: raising NGO awareness about themselves; and framing their causes to match key NGO characteristics. Challengers undertake these strategies in various ways (Table 2.1), which I discuss in the following two sections of this chapter.

Table 2.1. *Movement Strategies for Attracting NGO Support*

A. Raising NGO awareness through:
    1. Targeted lobbying
    2. Diffuse consciousness-raising (primarily using the media)
B. Framing to "match" NGO's:
    1. Goals
    2. Culture
    3. Tactics
    4. Ethics
    5. Organizational needs

It should be noted that in this discussion I seldom touch on the moral aspects of movement–NGO interactions. Principle, sympathy, and altruism provide an important context throughout, but to clarify the understudied strategic element – the element that typically makes the difference between a movement's support and isolation – I generally omit the former. This may sometimes make movements appear more opportunistic and NGOs more cold-blooded than they in fact are. In reality, opportunism and principle mingle throughout the parties' relationship, but from an analyst's standpoint, highlighting movement strategies is essential to understanding success and failure in the support market. In the discussion that follows, I also focus on insurgents' specifically *transnational* strategies. Yet overseas marketing occurs in a context of ongoing conflict between a movement and its domestic foes; indeed, it is often constrained by, entwined with, or subordinate to national interactions. For greater analytic precision, however, I generally omit this context, although I examine it in Chapters 3 and 4. Finally, it is worth noting at the outset that both a movement's ability to undertake these broad strategies and its success at them are affected by relatively fixed "structural" factors, underlying characteristics of the movement and its opponents, which I discuss in the section on "who wins support."

Raising International Awareness

Although insufficient to clinch support by itself, international awareness is clearly necessary. Local movements recognize that achieving such awareness is their first hurdle. To clear it, they spend much time simply boosting name recognition among distant audiences. As one East Timorese activist stated in explaining his movement's lack of preparedness for independence in 1999, "We have been so focused on raising public awareness about our cause that we didn't seriously think about the structure of a government."[18]

Movements raise awareness in two ways: targeted lobbying of prospective supporters; and diffuse consciousness-raising. The first involves direct personal contact, often in the prospect's home country. The second uses intermediaries, usually the international press, to spread word about the movement's activities. Each method has its pros and cons. Lobbying reaches only limited numbers, but these may be NGOs with real political

---

[18] Constancio Pinto, interview by Colum Lynch, "Timor Fears Trojan Horse in Indonesia Independence Offer," *Boston Sunday Globe*, February 7, 1999, A3.

clout, gatekeepers that hold the key to broader support. Although targeted lobbying may occur through e-mail or over the telephone, direct personal contact with NGO principals offers clear advantages. By putting a face on a movement, lobbying makes abstract conflicts concrete. Personal lobbying also serves an important secondary function: market research. Even failed lobbying offers opportunities to gauge audience reactions and probe reasons for rejection. Most importantly, personal lobbying permits insurgent groups to maintain control over their message. On the other hand, this very control can raise questions about the reliability of an insurgent's claims. Unless backed by objective evidence, a movement's appeals may be dismissed as propaganda by prospective supporters.

Targeted lobbying occurs in various settings. International conferences, whose numbers have risen in recent decades, have become frequent sites for forging global linkages. Describing one such meeting, a *New York Times* correspondent called it "half bazaar and half Speaker's Corner," where thousands "on too tight a budget . . . set up booths or [find] corners to distribute homemade tracts and pamphlets alerting those more powerful to the injustices they feel."[19] The insurgent tour is also a venerable method of heightening awareness and building support. Early in the twentieth century, Sun Yat Sen roamed the world raising money to overthrow the Manchu dynasty. When the revolution finally came, Sun found himself in Denver, where he learned of it from an American newspaper. Today, lobbying trips and "solidarity tours" have become routine. Sponsors such as San Francisco–based Global Exchange introduce their charges to government officials, foundation staff, and international prize committees, schedule news conferences and interviews, and provide intimate forums, in college seminar rooms and church sanctuaries, for insurgent marketers to plead their cases directly to receptive audiences.

Wealthier insurgents station representatives in New York, London, and other key capitals. These quasi-diplomatic offices counter foreign ignorance and home state disinformation. The Washington, D.C.–based Uyghur Information Agency, for example, aims to raise overseas awareness of the Uyghur and their problems, starting with the most basic information – the "correct spelling of our ethnic name – Uyghur," rather than "all other forms of wrong spelling including 'Uighur', 'Uigur', 'Uiger', 'Uygur' or

---

[19] Barbara Crossette, "Why the U.N., Became the World's Fair," *New York Times*, March 12, 1995, Section 4, page 1.

'Weiwuer'.[20] Recently, many local movements have established Web sites replete with documents, flags, maps, and contribution buttons. These serve as beachheads for disseminating carefully screened information to a world audience. But since the unaware are unlikely to stumble on an insurgent's home page, such Web sites are most useful for movements that already have a high profile or existing support base.

In addition to directly lobbying potential supporters, movements use the media to raise awareness. Journalistic reporting has unparalleled reach, and a compelling account in a reputable outlet can alert uninformed audiences to a distant conflict. On the other hand, journalistic norms cut two ways. Most reporters follow professional standards of newsworthiness and objectivity. As a result, for a challenger to rely on media promotion is risky and uncertain. The media spotlight often shines elsewhere; although David and Goliath stories make good copy, journalists need more compelling reasons to focus on any particular David. Just as important, in using the press, insurgents risk losing control over their arguments and image. Indeed, media definitions of a story may lead to damaging revelations about a movement. It is true that some reporters have recently adopted a "humanitarian" perspective, making them highly sympathetic to local challengers.[21] In most cases, however, a movement's message filtered through journalistic lenses will not represent an insurgent group's view of the issues.

To counter these problems, movements time their media campaigns to dovetail with predictable and well-publicized events such as politically charged anniversaries or meetings of major international organizations. Insurgents use press releases and trained spokesmen to promote their viewpoints. And wealthier challengers employ public relations firms to sprinkle information about their movement among the press and key foreign audiences. In the 1967–70 Nigerian Civil War, for instance, the Biafran government employed PR firms, including Burston-Marstteller, to promote its cause. While famine and battle raged in Nigeria, the firm fought a public relations skirmish against the powerful promotional outfits hired by

---

[20] Uyghur Information Agency, "Media Advisory," http://www.uyghurinfo.com (accessed July 17, 2004). Thus far, this aim has not been achieved, as major media and academic sources continue to use the spelling "Uighur."

[21] Jo-Anne Velin, Human Rights Internet, and International Centre for Humanitarian Reporting, *Reporting Human Rights and Humanitarian Stories: A Journalist's Handbook* (1997), http://www.hri.ca/doccentre/docs/handbook97/ (accessed July 17, 2004).

the Nigerian government.[22] In recent years, American supporters of the Sudan People's Liberation Army also footed the bill for a high-powered Washington PR firm.

Most local movements, having far fewer resources, labor alone to attract media coverage. For them, a frequent and relatively cheap strategy is political "spectacle," a major, highly visible, sometimes novel event. Common forms include strikes, mass marches, and land invasions. Violence and terror, which often attract the media more effectively than peaceful events, may also be considered forms of spectacle. Whether violent or nonviolent, however, the key is action grabbing media attention and dramatically encapsulating a challenger's identity, grievances, and demands. Without such spectacle, the likelihood of sustained and substantial media attention is small. Even then, however, the vagaries of the media make the press a fickle means of arousing NGOs.

Matching NGO Expectations

Whether an insurgency raises awareness through direct lobbying or media promotion, support is not assured. Obscure challengers pleading their causes at international conferences exemplify groups whose efforts at consciousness-raising have not attracted backing. Guerrilla movements that fascinate the press but disgust the public – Peru's Shining Path, Uganda's Lords Resistance Army, or Sierra Leone's Revolutionary Popular Front – illustrate the gulf between overseas attention and support.

To explain when an insurgent group will attract overseas backers, I view both parties abstractly, as having five critical attributes: substantive goals, customary tactics, ethical precepts, cultural attitudes, and organizational needs. The greater the match between transnational actor and local movement on these five attributes, the greater the likelihood of adoption. Underlying this dynamic is the fact that both parties to any support relationship are distinctive organizations and must look to their own survival and growth as their first priority. For insurgent groups, this simple fact drives the quest for outside aid. For NGOs, it means that questions of costs and benefits are important, particularly in initial decisions on supporting a movement. Again, this is not to say that organizational considerations foreclose altruistic motives. When deciding on support, NGOs follow their missions and assess

[22] Morris Davis, *Interpreters for Nigeria: The Third World and International Public Relations* (Urbana: University of Illinois Press, 1977).

26

a movement's needs. Yet "need" itself hinges on interpretations and comparisons often done rapidly, secondhand, and inevitably with the NGO's own interests in mind. In a context of scarce resources, sharp power imbalances, and subjective decision making, altruism mixes with self-interest, benevolence with exchange.

The importance of matching on these five attributes means that movements whose characteristics happen to fit with those of NGOs enjoy an advantage. The interaction is highly strategic, however, with insurgents framing their causes to match the interests and concerns of transnational actors. "Framing" generally refers to a movement's portrayal of its goals to resonate with those of third parties.[23] But, as we shall see, the concept can be extended to the four other attributes outlined earlier, and NGO support hinges on projection of a total movement "package." Several general aspects of framing bear emphasis. First, framing is dynamic and mutual. Both insurgent groups and NGO patrons reshape themselves in interaction with one another. As discussed previously, however, in the transnational support market, NGOs usually have more power than insurgent groups and therefore have less need to adapt themselves. Accordingly, my focus here is framing by movements. Nonetheless, it bears emphasis that matching usually involves some accommodation by both sides, and, as I show in Chapters 3 and 4, even powerful NGOs may be changed by their interactions with seemingly weak insurgent groups.

Second, the real contours of a conflict circumscribe framing's extent and direction. Although new frames are sometimes surprising, they are not boundless.[24] The issues at a conflict's root, the nature and reaction of opponents, and the identities of constituents all limit a movement's freedom to reinvent itself. Ethical and ideological precepts also impose self-controls on movement framing. In addition, NGOs familiar with how movements sculpt themselves to fit patron preferences screen out the most extreme recastings. Thus, as social movement scholars have long recognized, a successful frame blends realistic and opportunistic elements.

[23] David A. Snow, E. Burke Rochford, Jr., Steven K. Worden, and Robert D. Benford, "Frame Alignment Processes, Micromobilization, and Movement Participation," *American Sociological Review* 51, no. 4 (1986): 464–81; David A. Snow and Robert D. Benford, "Master Frames and Cycles of Protest," in *Frontiers in Social Movement Theory*, Aldon D. Morris and Carol McClurg Mueller, eds. (New Haven, CT: Yale University Press, 1992), 133–55.

[24] As a result, movements with broad and vague goals enjoy greater scope for framing than those with narrower and more specific aims; cf. F. G. Bailey, *Humbuggery and Manipulation: The Art of Leadership* (Ithaca, NY: Cornell University Press, 1988), 58–59.

Third, framing by certain movements establishes models that others mimic, albeit with individual twists. More generally, "master frames," such as the concept of "rights," establish prototypes that many movements embrace.[25] In the end, the frame used by a movement is constructed and polished through interactions with supporters, opponents, and the media. Along with predictions about the resonance of an approach must come facility at adjusting one's presentation. This is a matter of maneuver rather than position; of observing and responding to one's audience rather than blindly making one's case; of stress and form as much as content; of seizing opportunities and capitalizing on accidents as much as preplanning. Much depends on the information obtained about potential patrons. For most movements, such data are incomplete and imperfect, far from what a business would collect before launching a new product. Yet the greater its knowledge of its target's key characteristics, the more likely that a challenger's appeals will resonate.

Once successfully deployed, frames often congeal into "brands," with movements constantly reemphasizing distinctive elements that capture distant imaginations. The hope, in the words of one activist supporting India's Dalits (Untouchables) in internationalizing their cause, is to make Dalit a "household word, invade popular culture with it ultimately, in a lot of the same ways as the anti-Apartheid movement did."[26] Branding typically involves goals, tactics, and ethics but also extends to more symbolic movement elements. Yasir Arafat's kaffiyeh and stubble, the Dalai Lama's saffron robes, and Subcomandante Marcos's mask all have helped create and perpetuate insurgent brands.

Substantive Matching

A threshold issue in the development of transnational linkages is overlap between the parties' substantive aims. A potential supporter will devote scarce time and resources only to a client whose grievances and goals jibe with the NGO's central mandate. A few major NGOs cover broad issues such as human rights, democratization, or the environment. Smaller NGOs occupy narrower niches, focusing on a distinct subissue, a singular client identity, a specific region, or even a particular topographic feature. But

[25] Snow and Benford, "Master Frames."

[26] Interviewee 39 (Ford Foundation program officer), telephone interview by author, May 16, 2001, audiotape.

28

even the largest and most comprehensive NGOs must limit their purview, often by subtle criteria such as establishing a geographically or topically "balanced" client portfolio, which may slight needy groups in a desperate region or recurrent predicament.[27]

Today's dominant issue areas and their thriving niches reflect broad agreement among powerful publics in the developed world about today's most important social problems. This consensus gradually changes, often through the activism of particular social movements, even, on rare occasions, movements from the developing world. But at any one time, a particular set of problems dominate. Notably, the internationally ascendant view often deviates from what local groups see as their primary needs. A significant issue in one part of the world may be an accepted and unproblematic fact in another. To take a recent example, female genital mutilation (FGM) has become a rallying cry for international women's rights groups in recent years, yet many African and Middle Eastern women still accept it as a vital cultural practice.[28] Just as commonly, the dominance of particular social problems in the developed world may lead to neglect of other pressing issues. An important example is the long twilight of social, cultural, and economic rights within a "universal" human rights movement dominated by concern for civil and political rights.[29]

Local movements whose causes do not fit with the NGO consensus will find few friends and little understanding abroad – unless they frame themselves to conform with leading views. This helps explain Keck and Sikkink's observation that advocacy networks form most easily around issues involving threats to bodily integrity and equality of opportunity.[30] Today, these values prevail among NGO constituencies and underwriters – the powerful and prosperous of the developed world – and their violation easily excites the press. Local movements with grievances outside these dominant concerns therefore have fewer chances of winning NGO allies. Yet there is nothing necessary or permanent about the orientation of today's NGOs. Communism exercised similar power over important overseas constituencies for

---

[27] Human Rights Watch, *World Report 2001*.

[28] Yael Tamir, "Hands off Clitoridectomy: What Our Revulsion Reveals about Ourselves," *Boston Review*, Summer 1996, http://bostonreview.net/BR21.3/Tamir.html (accessed July 17, 2004).

[29] Balakrishnan Rajagopal, *International Law from Below: Development, Social Movements, and Third World Resistance* (Cambridge: Cambridge University Press, 2003).

[30] Keck and Sikkink, *Activists beyond Borders*, 27.

long stretches of the twentieth century and evoked a similar response, with local groups adopting socialist ideology, often for instrumental reasons or simply out of fashion-consciousness.[31] Today, contrary orientations flourish, too, although usually out of view of Northern audiences. Thus, Islamist democracy movements in the Middle East and Central Asia, shunned by the West because of their illiberal politics, find support among transnational Muslim organizations.[32]

Given this preexisting structure of issues and NGOs, savvy local insurgents begin their quest for aid by "segmenting" the market, directing their appeals to potential supporters whose identity and goals approximate their own. (More desperate insurgents often begin with a blunderbuss approach, issuing a volley of vague grievances in the hope that some might stick.) Even then, movements must frame themselves to boost their chances of support. Local disputes, although vital at home, often appear puny, parochial, or perplexing abroad. To counter these perceptions, movements follow several tactics. They simplify and universalize their conflicts, finger and demonize prominent opponents, embrace voguish rhetoric, and appeal to the self-interest, as well as the sympathy, of distant audiences.

As a first step, movement activists strip their conflicts of complexity and ambiguity, projecting a stark picture of virtuous struggle against a villainous foe. In doing so, they tap into Manichean images readily grasped by distant audiences – even if these obscure the actual ambiguities of conflict. They link their plight to well-known and emotionally charged events, hoping thereby to vanquish the indifference of distant audiences. Thus, ethnic leaders flaunt their group's own "Holocaust," labor activists their members' enslavement.[33] At a deeper level, movements tap into cultural motifs having wide and perhaps universal appeal, such as good guy versus bad guy or underdog versus bully. In alluding to these myths, movements avoid simply being classified as victims. While they play up their repression, movements emphasize both their organizational coherence and their courage, rather

---

[31] Forrest D. Colburn, *The Vogue of Revolution in Poor Countries* (Princeton, NJ: Princeton University Press, 1994).

[32] Fiona Adamson, "The Diffusion of Competing Norms in Central Asia: Transnational Democracy Assistance Networks vs. Transnational Islamism." Paper presented at the 2003 Annual Meeting of the American Political Science Association, Philadelphia, PA, August 27–31, 2003.

[33] Samantha Power, "To Suffer by Comparison?" *Daedalus: Proceedings of the American Academy of Arts and Sciences* 128, no. 2 (1999): 31–67.

than their helplessness. As a result, they argue tacitly or overtly that a third party's support is not mere charity.

Movements also emphasize the universalistic aspects of parochial conflicts. Thus, on the world stage, local land disputes may appear as environmental issues and ethnic clashes as battles for rights and democracy. A problem's overseas recognition makes a difference, and insurgent groups therefore stress their status as victims of international law violations. Finally, savvy movements highlight trendy political and cultural currents. Consider the recent expansion in the concept of "indigenous" peoples. In the 1970s and 1980s, Indian activists in the Americas augmented and rode a cultural wave romanticizing nature and the "primitive."[34] In doing so, they animated the formerly moribund indigenous category, prompting the World Bank, United Nations, and major NGOs to redirect resources and concerns. More recently, Asian and African minorities have reinvented themselves as indigenous peoples despite the original concept's awkward fit in these nonsettler societies.[35] In addition, in recent years, many indigenous movements have latched onto ecological concerns, finding the latter issues more attractive in the developed world. As a result, "indigenous" groups have won greater repute than those who portray themselves merely as "poor."

As another strategy, movements target internationally notorious enemies rather than nameless domestic foes. Just as in interstate power politics, where "the enemy of my enemy is my friend," a local movement that finds such an opponent has a leg up in interesting NGO allies. The familiarity of the enemy raises emotions and forges connections, motivating action even when the challenger itself is little-known. "Rogue" states and despised leaders make particularly useful opponents. Thus, in explaining the Kosovar leadership's ambivalence toward Slobodan Milosevic in the 1990s, historian Miranda Vickers argues that "Unless Serbia continued to be labeled as profoundly evil – and they themselves, by virtue of being anti-Serb, as the good guys – they were unlikely to achieve their goals. It would have been a disaster for them if a peacemonger ... had restored human rights, since this would have left them with nothing but a bare political agenda to change

---

[34] Chris Tennant, "Indigenous Peoples, International Institutions, and the International Legal Literature from 1945–1993," *Human Rights Quarterly* 16, no. 1 (1994): 1–57.

[35] Andrew Gray, "The Indigenous Movement in Asia," in *Indigenous Peoples of Asia*, Robert H. Barnes, Andrew Gray, and Benedict Kingsbury, eds. (Ann Arbor, MI: Association for Asian Studies, 1995), 35–58; Crispin Bates, "'Lost Innocents and the Loss of Innocence': Interpreting Adivasi Movements in South Asia," in ibid., 103–19.

borders."[36] On the other hand, a challenger whose primary enemies are local power holders or a state that has a sterling reputation will have greater difficulty attracting outside sympathy. Although insurgencies are stuck with their home states and few face pariahs like Milosevic, they have flexibility in identifying other opponents. Given the reach of economic globalization, many local issues have international dimensions. Highlighting these helps a movement overseas. Multinational corporations make particularly inviting targets, especially if they are vertically integrated, with production and attendant impacts in the developing world and consumer sales in the developed world. In recent years, multinationals and international financial institutions have repeatedly served as stand-ins for obscure local enemies. Even when a movement itself is little-known, it can project an effective (if sometimes misleading) snapshot of its claims by identifying itself as the anti-McDonald's movement, the anti-Nike movement, or the anti-Unocal movement. By targeting enemies that they share with NGOs, insurgents make support serve double duty as a new front in an NGO's ongoing conflict with a mutual foe. Blaming a villain who is accessible in the developed world also creates the possibility for overseas activists to take direct action at home, fortifying their solidarity with distant movements.

Finally, movements appeal to the self-interest of potential supporters. During the Cold War, insurgencies framed themselves as pro- or anti-communist to gain the support of the United States or Soviet Union. Angola's Jonas Savimbi, for one, made repeated ideological pirouettes to maintain support – from someone. Today, insurgents playing on supporters' self-interest must frame themselves around other issues that transcend borders. Thus, movements attach their causes to universal "public goods," such as environmental quality or cultural diversity, from which everyone ostensibly benefits. In doing so, they portray themselves as "stewards of nature" or "canaries in a global coal mine," their plight serving as a warning sign of broader trouble for all. Conversely, they argue that refusing support will foster international public "bads" such as terrorism, "hot zone" diseases, or "ethnicide" ("killing" a culture without physically harming its individual members). However weakly, these pleas implicate the self-interest of distant audiences for whom a movement's moral appeals may hold little sway. As Amnesty International USA's Executive Director, William Schulz, has written, "What we need to make the human rights 'sale'... are compelling

[36] Miranda Vickers, *Between Serb and Albanian: A History of Kosovo* (New York: Columbia University Press, 1998), 268.

practical reasons why respect for human rights is in the best interests of the United States . . . framed, to the extent possible, in the language of realpolitik."[37] The same goes for local movements marketing themselves to Amnesty International and other NGOs.

None of this is to say that these issues and enemies are simply invented by insurgent groups. Most conflicts, even in far corners of the world, have multiple causes and international dimensions. For insurgents to garner NGO support, these broader linkages must be highlighted and local issues, sometimes those at the heart of a conflict, swept into the shadows. It is also important to emphasize that, in framing their conflicts, insurgent strategies mirror their opponents' rhetoric and action. States wave sovereignty as a bar to outside activism while charging intervenors with neo-colonialism. Multinational corporations argue that they are caught in purely local or national disputes. International financial institutions seek to channel input from communities affected by development projects into tightly controlled dispute-resolution procedures. Viewed in this broader context, insurgent groups that frame their conflicts for international audiences do nothing more or less than their opponents.

Cultural Matching

Whatever their goals, local movements reflect cultural patterns dominant in their home communities. Yet those same patterns may be inappropriate or unacceptable in the developed world, where most NGOs have their core constituencies and funding sources. As one example, gender equity remains rare in much of the developing world. Yet "progressive" NGOs, even those not specializing in women's rights, often reward local groups that exhibit awareness of gender issues. Predilections for like-minded organizations are particularly evident in grant, prize, and workshop competitions, where sponsors use written applications requesting information about diversity issues. Such subtle preferences, often based as much on the personal backgrounds of NGO staff as on formal screening standards, pervade NGO decisions, advantaging movements led by those who look and act most like NGO staff – often articulate, college-educated, well-traveled leaders.

More broadly, most NGOs prefer to deal with local groups whose organizational culture resembles their own – groups with a director, a staff,

[37] William F. Schulz, *In Our Own Best Interest: How Defending Human Rights Benefits Us All* (Boston: Beacon Press, 2001), 7.

an office, a mission statement, regularized fund-raising procedures, and written strategy documents. This tendency extends even to such niceties as a group's computer software, with many local movements feeling pressure to adopt the same programs used by major patrons in the developed world.[38] Such customary accouterments provide NGO staff with familiar organizational toeholds even as they foster confidence in a movement's competence. Less professionalized grassroots movements, unversed in international standards of organizational structure and procedure, may appear inept and unqualified. They may even seem disingenuous if they present information in the exaggerated, histrionic tones they sometimes use at home.

Northern NGOs also pay lip service to democratic internal governance – even if few NGOs, with their checkbook memberships and unelected leaders, actually implement these procedures themselves. Movements sophisticated enough to leaven their goals (whatever they may be) with the rhetoric of democracy benefit. Such cultural biases help explain why most democracy-assistance NGOs operating in the Middle East funnel support to familiar-looking "civil society organizations" while avoiding Islamist organizations, despite the latter's importance in indigenous democratization movements.[39] Movements that understand NGO dispositions can take steps to meet them; less worldly insurgents, often representing more isolated, poorer, and needier constituencies, cannot. Those adhering to indigenous values suffer, whereas those that adjust themselves, sincerely or through politically correct front men (and women!), prosper.

Tactical Matching

Even assuming substantive and cultural matching, an NGO's usual method of operation may not meet a challenger's needs. NGOs distinguish themselves by the ways in which they seek their goals and help clients, most basically by whether they provide material or rhetorical support (or both). Further tactical differentiation is usually present. Some NGOs specialize in researching conditions on the ground, others in targeting institutions such as the United Nations or World Bank, and still others in using

---

[38] Simson Garfinkel, "The Free Software Imperative," *Technology Review*, February 2003, 30.

[39] Imco Brouwer, "Weak Democracy and Civil Society Promotion: The Cases of Egypt and Palestine," in *Funding Virtue: Civil Society Aid and Democracy Promotion*, Marina Ottaway and Thomas Carothers, eds. (Washington, DC: Carnegie Endowment for International Peace, 2000), 45; Mustapha Kamel Al-Sayyid, "A Clash of Values: U.S. Civil Society Aid and Islam in Egypt," in ibid., 68–69.

mobilization techniques such as letter-writing, dramatic action, or disciplined protest. For certain issues, particular techniques dominate, pushing alternative methods and ideas to the wayside. Major human rights NGOs have long taken a legalistic approach. Local groups whose needs cannot be reduced to an advocate's brief or who lack knowledge of the law may therefore be overlooked – as may whole issues, such as poverty, that arguably create a climate in which rights violations thrive.[40]

Contacting an NGO whose tactics are inappropriate to a group's needs can be costly and sometimes fruitless. As one example, when Sri Lankan human rights activist Tharmalingam Selvakumar sought protection from threatened abuses in 1993, he tapped Amnesty International and other mainstream human rights NGOs working in the country. But his request fell outside these groups' standard actions, publishing reports and urgent action messages. As a result, Selvakumar endured months of continued peril before winning support from Peace Brigades International, an organization specializing in protective accompaniment for people at risk of violence.[41] To avoid this experience, movements with access to and knowledge of multiple NGOs target the groups that can help them most, sometimes NGOs with broad approaches but other times those with more specialized procedures. In either case, they ask for assistance that a potential backer regularly provides, thereby reducing costs and increasing their likelihood of winning aid. Movements also target distant foundations that provide forms of support such as grant money or training that can be used for multiple purposes. Similarly, insurgents favor support that is unrestricted or loosely monitored, even as NGOs prefer to retain control over their aid. Although grantors usually control these matters, the relative power of the parties affects the balance between fungibility and specificity, discretion and oversight, in any form of support.

Ethical Matching

NGOs are most likely to support insurgencies that use "acceptable" means in pursuit of their goals. Following standard practices in their European and North American bases, advocacy NGOs issue press releases, lobby

---

[40] Kathryn Sikkink, "Restructuring World Politics: The Limits and Asymmetries of Soft Power," in Khagram, Riker, and Sikkink, eds., *Restructuring World Politics*, 310; Rajagopal, *International Law from Below*.

[41] Patrick Coy, "Cooperative Accompaniment and Peace Brigades International in Sri Lanka," in Smith, Chatfield, and Pagnucco, eds., *Transnational Social Movements*, 81–100.

representatives, file lawsuits, build consensus, and support candidates. They value peaceful protest as a necessary tool of political struggle but shun violence. By contrast, most insurgent groups live in far rougher neighborhoods, and their methods must be correspondingly tough. Although sophisticated NGOs recognize these different political contexts, their ethical standards may prevent them from supporting movements with radically different rules of engagement.

This is particularly important when it comes to a crucial divide – between violence and nonviolence. Whereas diaspora and solidarity groups have fewer qualms about supporting an armed insurgency, for advocacy NGOs such clients are anathema. Thus, local movements using nonviolent tactics increase their likelihood of gaining the support of advocacy NGOs. Where violence has erupted, movements seeking the support of such NGOs depict themselves – often with good reason – as victims of opponents' repression. Or where movement constituents themselves take up arms, leaders dismiss them as agents provocateurs or as an irresponsible and uncontrollable fringe. Finally, where movements openly use force, they portray it as legitimate self-defense against the disproportionate attacks of ruthless foes. In a vicious setting, a local movement's relative restraint may be enough to spark ties even with NGOs that generally espouse nonviolence. None of this is to impugn the integrity of all challengers – only to suggest that the structure of NGO expectations creates incentives that shape the ways in which movements act and present their behavior. Reciprocally, of course, states and other opponents seek to portray movements in the darkest light. In the post-9/11 world, for instance, governments around the world have leaped to label movements seeking greater autonomy as terrorists – often with little justification.[42]

For challengers, the importance of ethical matching presents a dilemma. Although advocacy NGOs prefer their clients to be peaceful, violence attracts media attention more effectively. As a result, remaining passive in the face of oppression may mean remaining isolated. For much of the 1990s, Ibrahim Rugova's League for Democratic Freedom (LDK) waged a campaign of nonviolent civil disobedience against Milosevic's Serbia. Carefully gauging the likely response of the Yugoslav regime to more open confrontation, Rugova chose to avoid direct confrontation. The LDK thus

---

[42] Human Rights Watch, "Opportunism in the Face of Tragedy: Repression in the Name of Anti-Terrorism," http://www.hrw.org/campaigns/september11/opportunismwatch.htm (accessed August 3, 2004).

built a parallel society that quietly enabled Kosovar Albanians to avoid the worst of Serbian discrimination, even if it did not permit them to throw off Yugoslav control. Yet external attention to Kosovo remained sparse and Kosovar ambitions for independence unfulfilled. Only in 1998, as frustrated Kosovars resorted to arms under the leadership of the Kosovo Liberation Army (KLA) and the Yugoslav army predictably responded with bloody repression, did the issue rise on the international agenda. The KLA may have had few NGO friends, but unlike the LDK, it managed to raise the conflict's profile, propelling powerful NGOs and states into actions supportive of the Kosovar Albanians.

Organizational Matching

A final area of matching relates to organizational issues. NGOs are most likely to adopt movements that will not harm and may in fact help them. In that sense, they make cost/benefit calculations, albeit in an overall context of sympathy and support. Of course, the "bottom line" for an NGO is more complicated and ambiguous than dollars and cents. Costs are often measured in lost trust or reputation, benefits in fulfillment of goals or missions. Yet ultimately an NGO's interest in its own maintenance and survival will affect its adoption of client groups.

The cost of support has four aspects: the direct and immediate expense of backing a movement; the long-term risk of associating with it; the transaction cost of deciding on support; and the opportunity cost of selecting a particular client rather than others. Of these aspects, the *direct costs* are the most easily planned and measured. NGO budgets, both in money and time, can be estimated with some accuracy. Although the length of a campaign may be uncertain, NGOs may limit commitments beforehand or make continuation contingent on a local movement's achievement of milestones. What this means, however, is that NGOs, particularly in the advocacy mold, will be reluctant to support movements who seem unlikely to benefit from the help or whose overall chances of success appear slim. As one NGO staffperson put it, "We consider our own reputation. We don't want to fail; we want to have some successes."[43] Moreover, advocacy NGOs in particular will prefer to support groups involved in issues that appear to have the greatest potential to leverage social change beyond the particular conflict

---

[43] Interviewee 45 (International Foundation for Election Systems manager), telephone interview by author, June 10, 2002.

site.[44] For solidarity NGOs and especially for diaspora groups, such considerations are less important. Intent on achieving the goals of their ideological or ethnic comrades, they are more willing to make longer-term sacrifices for the movement. Even for the most committed, however, backing a hopeless cause carries high costs. In such circumstances, solidarity support also may fade.

NGOs' concerns over direct costs pose special difficulties for newly formed movements. Although such groups need to emphasize the depth of their grievances and the immediacy of their peril, they must also show that support will not be pointless – that victories are possible. This may encourage movements to undertake spectacular actions demonstrating their opponents' vulnerability, actions that usually entail danger to the movement itself. Insurgents in repressive states face an acute dilemma: take actions that run a high risk of violent response, or remain internationally isolated.

Similarly, groups riven by dissent will have more difficulty gaining support than their more unified competitors. NGOs, unwilling to squander resources on internecine disputes, will look elsewhere. Smaller, more cohesive movements, those dominated by a single leader, and those managed by professional staffs therefore gain an advantage. Conversely, more conflictive, grassroots movements – often more democratic as well – suffer unless they can project an image of unity. This dynamic has secondary effects, encouraging insurgent groups to highlight their victories and the role of third-party support in achieving them. (For this reason, insurgent assessments of the efficacy of third-party support are unreliable.) Just as important, insurgent groups have strong incentives to lower expectations about the prospects of final success. Instead, they emphasize its difficulty (but not impossibility) and the importance of lesser achievements along the long road to victory.[45]

The *long-term risks* of support also strongly influence an NGO's decision about adopting a client. An NGO may incur significant costs if adoption is later found unwarranted or if claims about the client prove untrue. These costs, primarily the loss of reputation and prestige, are intangible but potentially severe. For advocacy NGOs, credibility and reliability constitute organizational capital amassed over years, easily lost, and difficult to restore. In an NGO's own promotional efforts among the media and

---

[44] See, for example, International Rivers Network, "About International Rivers Network."

[45] Mark I. Lichbach, *The Rebel's Dilemma* (Ann Arbor: University of Michigan Press, 1998), 197–200.

governmental actors, as in their fund-raising among major foundations and the public, these assets are precious. Protecting them therefore has high priority. Greenpeace took years to recover from the black mark it received for opposing the 1994 sinking of the *Brent Spar* oil rig with little scientific justification. The heated international controversy surrounding David Stoll's recent critique of Rigoberta Menchú demonstrates the large organizational (and personal) investments that solidarity supporters made in the Guatemalan Indian leader – investments these groups were anxious to protect.[46] Because they know the risks of error and the likelihood that local movements will market themselves aggressively, NGOs cross-check claims and seek third-party confirmation. On the other hand, every NGO has individual standards based on its own organizational culture, power, and need for clients. Although no NGO wants to be "spun" by a client, some can be credulous, taking a supplicant's words at face value or willfully believing statements that mesh with their own preconceptions and interests.

In assessing the risks of adoption, NGOs have two primary concerns: the reality of a challenger's grievances and the challenger's legitimacy among its claimed constituency. For advocacy organizations, information about grievances is particularly important. Amnesty International, Human Rights Watch, and other front-line human rights NGOs routinely send researchers to the field for months of painstaking investigation. Their reports, detailing victims' names and abuses, are written to withstand scrutiny by hostile governments eager to leverage minor inaccuracies into wholesale refutations. For other issues, grievances are less concrete or more speculative, making confirmation of insurgent assertions more difficult. Predictions of future environmental harms, for instance, are less verifiable than claims of past rights violations.

The legitimacy of local challengers is another consideration, particularly for NGOs in the solidarity mold but also for those that maintain organizational (and emotional) distance. Major NGOs receive frequent appeals from individuals and organizations claiming to represent aggrieved constituencies in faraway locales. Before adopting a group, NGOs seek to verify the bona fides of these representatives: Who are they? Do they in fact enjoy support on the ground? Today, when "democracy" has become a basic international norm, assuring that one's client has at least a modicum

---

[46] David Stoll, *Rigoberta Menchú and the Story of All Poor Guatemalans* (Boulder, CO: Westview Press, 1999); Larry Rohter, "Tarnished Laureate: Nobel Winner Finds Her Story Challenged," *New York Times*, December 15, 1998, A1.

of such credentials has become an important concern. For their part, opponents frequently call these issues into question and sometimes take more devious tacks, prying cracks in movements or planting media stories about dissension.

The *transaction costs* of gathering and evaluating information about potential clients also affect NGO decisions. Information is critical to transnational campaigns. This is true not only when networks target opponents, as Keck and Sikkink have shown; it is equally true as networks form and operate. Before lending support, NGOs cut through a thicket of self-serving information produced both by movements and their opponents. Savvy insurgents seek to reduce patrons' transaction costs by providing media reports, videotapes, eyewitnesses, and other objective evidence to substantiate claims. They tap respected and seemingly unbiased vouchers – journalists, scientists, missionaries, and others. And they approach powerful gatekeeper NGOs first, knowing that the conversion of these groups may serve as proof to follower NGOs unable to investigate fully themselves. (Followers enjoy reduced transaction costs since earlier supporters have already vetted a movement.) To cultivate patrons, sophisticated recipients document how NGO resources have helped achieve concrete goals. In these efforts, movements emphasize their virtues while eliding their faults. Of course, seasoned NGO staff are not naïve; they know that needy supplicants and current clients strive to present themselves in the best possible light. If they have the resources, NGOs seek independent confirmation of insurgent claims using their own evidence and sources. Nonetheless, movements that lower NGO transaction costs will have an advantage in attracting aid.

Given NGOs' limited resources, adopting a new cause entails substantial *opportunity costs*. As a result, NGOs avoid commitments to unknown and low-status insurgencies. Movements that attract support block others suffering similar problems but coming slowly to the international scene. Although latecomers may benefit indirectly – for instance, through NGO spotlighting of an obscure region or issue – they seldom attain the prominence of their more precocious competitors. For analogous reasons, NGOs flock to prominent movements. When a challenger wins gatekeeper support and media attention, follower NGOs benefit from supporting the insurgency and incur costs for *not* doing so. Gains include publicity deriving from the fame of the insurgency; losses may encompass constituent support if the NGO does not "take a stand" concerning a cause célèbre in a relevant area. As a result, transnational bandwagons may develop, with NGOs piling onto a fortunate challenger. As bandwagons grow, they exert an ever-stronger pull because the organizational advantages of joining them attract NGOs even if other aspects of a match are weak. Unfortunately, however, bandwagons may deprive equally worthy causes of support.

Because support exacts costs, its potential *benefits* weigh heavily in an NGO's decision. In the language of social movement scholars, NGOs act in a "structure" of threats and opportunities presented by opponents, allies, and client movements. Their principles are always important, but NGOs are apt to back causes that appear relevant, important, and understandable to their constituents or funders. As we have seen, this means insurgents whose goals, tactics, ethics, and culture overlap with the NGOs'. A local group that can serve as a "test case" for an NGO's larger mission provides clear benefits. Similarly, well-known clients confer important benefits on their patrons. NGOs burnish their images by demonstrating their sympathy and kinship with a courageous local movement, even as they also help the client and meet their own missions. The "Tibet brand," with its connotations of nonviolence and spirituality, has these effects. By contrast, movements that are unique or strange will provide few such advantages, making adoption less likely. The relative foreign isolation of China's Falun Gong may stem in part from this problem.[47]

Strategy and Support

The foregoing discussion has analyzed each of five strategies separately, although in actual campaigns local movements deploy multiple strategies simultaneously, adapting them to fit audience responses and ultimately concentrating on ones that work. As noted earlier, these strategies help explain how unknown and isolated movements gain support. In addition, they illuminate how movements retain assistance over the long term. Given the usual structure of the transnational market, with its excess of demand over supply, even those challengers who win scarce backing remain in danger of losing it. They must therefore be proactive. Of course, having broken through initially, they have real advantages over their competitors. For one thing, they have solved the difficult initial problem facing all movements – anonymity. Moreover, having found a niche with major NGOs, they are in a good position to maintain it. Nonetheless, even well-supported groups face endemic pressures. Many NGOs, caught in their own pursuit of funding and support, restlessly move from issue to issue. At a more abstract level,

[47] Richard Madsen, "Understanding Falun Gong," *Current History*, September 2000, 243–47.

scholars have long noted an "issue-attention cycle" in which particular social problems first rise and then fall in public consciousness whether or not
they are "solved."[48] To delay such a decline, local movements must follow
strategies analogous to those they used to attract support initially. First,
they must remain visible internationally. Second, they must cultivate their
supporters and other potentially receptive audiences, monitoring changing interests, showing appropriate results, and framing themselves suitably.
Radical new frames may not be credible, but more subtle changes can keep
the group in line with an evolving international consensus on important
issues, appropriate tactics, and requisite procedures.

Skeptics might ask, despite the examples just given, whether movements
can really be so opportunistic and NGOs so hard-bitten. It is true that, in
any particular case, these elements may be difficult to discern, given the
sympathy and support involved where adoption occurs. Once contacts between NGO staff and clients deepen, respect, trust, and affection can also
bind the two parties. Moreover, the entire relationship occurs in a context
mixing NGOs' moral and political goals with their organizational interests.
Principles clearly do count, and in the overall support relationship, NGOs
often act altruistically. Yet broadening the analytic lens reveals the importance of highly rationalistic factors. In the context of the scarce NGO resources and vast insurgent needs that typically characterize the transnational
support marketplace, pragmatic assessment of organizational interests and
regular deployment of marketing strategies are in fact critical to determining which groups do or do not gain support. (And, for scholars, these considerations explain far more about variations in NGO assistance than one can
learn simply by acknowledging the altruistic aspects of the relationships.)

Although the specific criteria they use in selecting clients may be unwritten, NGOs that face frequent requests for support sometimes formalize
them. (See Appendix 1 for several samples.) With a set of criteria in mind or
on paper, NGO staff triage the many local groups seeking their help. Typically these decisions are made independently of one another as new groups
appear seeking support. In such circumstances, competition among local
movements is indirect but real. NGO staff, particularly those at key gatekeepers, compare a movement's claims with those of others heard in the past
and expected in the future. In this necessarily approximate and uncertain
way, NGO principals choose clients for major support while sending other

---

[48] Anthony Downs, "Up and Down with Ecology: The 'Issue-Attention Cycle,'" *Public Interest*
28 (Summer 1972): 38–50.

groups away with little more than advice or good wishes. In other cases, such as foundation grants and training programs, such decisions are made in head-to-head competitions among local groups who submit formal requests. Even then, picking "winners" is often a close and ambiguous matter. Consider how Human Rights Watch chose African participants for its Fellows Program. Based on written applications, a manager roughly sorted prospects into three "tiers": well-established local advocacy groups with the expertise to benefit from the program – and to prepare a competent dossier; emerging grassroots groups with neither skill; and groups who fell somewhere in between. Only those placed in the first group made the cut.[49]

Who Wins Support?

Although the typical structure of the transnational marketplace requires movements both to project their causes overseas and to match themselves with potential NGO supporters, not all movements are equally capable of deploying these strategies. Their ability to do so is strongly influenced by underlying "structural" factors that movements have little ability to control. One set of these factors is historical: the general level of technological, legal, and moral development worldwide, such as the availability of rapid communication or transportation, the number of NGOs, and the degree of concern about conflicts across borders. At any particular time, these factors affect all insurgents equally. As such, they help explain differences in support for movements operating in different historical periods. By the same token, however, they are of little use in clarifying discrepancies among contemporaneous movements. In that case, two other sets of structural factors are of greatest importance, one concerning the insurgent group itself, the other its opponents (Table 2.2).

With regard to the first of these factors, if a challenger has high *international standing* – if it is well known abroad for preexisting, nonpolitical reasons – it will have enhanced access to gatekeeper NGOs and the media. Standing provides insurgents with a platform on which to launch appeals. It confers a presumption of legitimacy on insurgent claims, making it more likely that the group's presentation of the issues will pass NGO muster. Indeed, high standing may attract support even if the insurgency's goals are poorly understood – as Tibetan flags on rusted bumpers attest.

---

[49] Interviewee 27 (Human Rights Watch manager), personal interview by author, March 14, 2001.

Table 2.2. *Structural Factors Affecting Success of Movement Strategies*

A. Movement characteristics:
1. Standing
2. Contacts
3. Knowledge
4. Material resources
5. Organizational resources
6. Leadership
B. Opponent characteristics:
1. Identity
2. Reactions

Standing has many sources. Tibet's fame rests not just on a massive marketing campaign but also on the centuries-old Western fascination with Shangri-La and on more recent interest in Eastern spirituality.[50] Insurgent leaders may also achieve recognition due to personal achievements in non-political fields from literature to sports. Standing also has shallower roots. Humanitarian awards such as the Nobel Peace Prize, the Goldman Environmental Prize, the Robert F. Kennedy Memorial Human Rights Prize, and the Right Livelihood Prize confer name recognition, as well as money. Similarly, attracting a celebrity to one's cause – a Princess Diana or a Richard Gere – builds stature through reflected glory. Finally, major international support itself raises standing. If a movement has won sustained backing previously, later attempts to revive or enhance it will be easier.

Closely linked to standing are preexisting *contacts* with international gatekeepers or matchmakers. Contacts may stem from the fame of a celebrity leader, but they also have humbler sources. For instance, key activists may retain important contacts as a result of prior educational or work experiences in the developed world. An active diaspora in a global city can also make a major difference, alerting NGOs and the media to events in the homeland and providing a base of operations for visiting lobbyists. Chechnya's lack of such a diaspora may have retarded external concern in the early 1990s, although more recently its exile population has become larger and more active.[51]

[50] Donald S. Lopez, Jr., *Prisoners of Shangri-La: Tibetan Buddhism and the West* (Chicago: University of Chicago Press, 1998).
[51] Gail Lapidus, "Contested Sovereignty: The Tragedy of Chechnya," *International Security* 23, no. 1 (1998): 5–49.

Various forms of *knowledge* also make insurgent marketing campaigns more effective. A rudimentary understanding of NGO identities and expertise is basic. Better yet, a grasp of NGO hierarchies enables challengers to contact well-linked gatekeepers while avoiding those whose poor reputations or dubious methods may poison attempts to gain wider support. Something as simple as a leader's fluency in English or another world language enables NGO staff or journalists to appreciate insurgent claims. An understanding of public relations techniques, permitting a movement to project a coherent and pleasing image, can subtly influence hardened NGO professionals. The ability to write a grant proposal and budget sheet often helps in meeting a patron's organizational needs. And insurgent knowledge of the international zeitgeist – or better yet a target NGO's organizational culture – can make for effective and resonant framing. All of these skills help groups from countries most affected by an expanding "world culture" encompassing social, economic, political, and technological aspects.[52] Groups fronted by sophisticated, well-educated representatives are most effective at using this knowledge. In the case of Papua New Guinea's secessionist Bougainville Interim Government (BIG) in the 1990s, this meant choosing spokesmen knowledgeable about both "Western culture and our Melanesian way of life." As its "U.N. representative," BIG therefore chose an Australian citizen long resident on Bougainville island because, according to an indigenous leader, "as a white person he can handle himself in a way some of us cannot. Language, mentality – because he's a white man he can think like a fellow white man. . . . It's to our advantage having that kind of person there."[53]

Insurgents with large *monetary resources* also hold clear advantages in projecting their causes abroad. Although not huge, the costs of foreign lobbying trips can be overwhelming for small, remote, or impoverished groups. Similarly, developing the evidence to meet even minimal NGO demands for proof of claims is costly. And buying the services of a professional public relations firm can be hugely expensive. Of course, as among oppressed groups, economic differences may be slight. But even a single wealthy and dedicated individual among an otherwise impoverished population may be the source of crucial funds.

---

[52] John Boli and George M. Thomas, eds., *Constructing World Culture: International Nongovernmental Organizations since 1875* (Stanford, CA: Stanford University Press, 1999).

[53] Interviewee 30 (Bougainville Interim Government official), personal interview by author, July 13, 1996.

Organizational resources, such as a movement's unity, coherence, and leadership, also make a major difference. Most basically, organizational resources permit movements to focus on externally directed mobilization rather than internal upkeep. Effective political spectacle requires a high level of coordination and planning – to pull protesters into the streets, guide their activism, and interpret its meaning to outsiders.[54] In addition, such resources make it more likely that a movement will be able to present a coherent image, whether by squelching or hiding dissent. The importance of organizational resources also suggests a broader insight about the groups most likely to gain support: Many will fail to coordinate effectively, and larger groups representing more diffuse interests will have more difficulty living up to their organizational potential than smaller groups representing narrower interests.[55]

The foregoing factors relate closely to one another, and their frequent correlation advantages certain movements over others. Groups that fall behind in the competition find it all the harder to mobilize support once a competitor gains an edge in funding, knowledge, or contacts. By themselves, however, these factors do not animate a movement's quest for external aid. The most successful movements are also directed by "charismatic" *leaders*. Scholars often downplay the role of individuals, instead highlighting historical or economic trends as key sources of change. But the world's best-known "local" movements are instantly associated with personalities – the Dalai Lama, Aung Saan Suu Kyi, Subcomandante Marcos, and Chico Mendez, to name only a few. And, as little-known Guatemalan guerrilla Rigoberta Menchú found when her semiautobiographical book became a best-seller, obscure individuals may also be thrust into leadership roles through outside acclaim.

Whatever their origins, such leaders are often the primary face of a movement for foreign audiences. Many crisscross the globe, drumming up aid. Others magnetically attract supporters to remote command centers. They combine the knowledge, contacts, and resources that elevate movements to prominence. They have impressive communication skills, capable of firing culturally diverse audiences in diverse locales worldwide. They forge emotional bonds with distant backers, making it harder to sever ties

[54] William A. Gamson, *The Strategy of Social Protest*, 2nd ed. (Belmont, CA: Wadsworth Publishing, 1990).

[55] Mancur Olson, *The Logic of Collective Action: Public Goods and the Theory of Groups* (Cambridge, MA: Harvard University Press, 1965).

in the future. They come to embody insurgent "brands," the suffering and risk they bear enhancing the movement's mystique. Given the importance of these "heroes," it is not surprising that their loss can spell doom for a movement.

What transforms insurgent marketers into international icons? For NGOs and other supporters, it is often easier to identify with a single person than a large movement. In that sense, NGOs (and the media) are primed to apotheosize individuals who then come to personify a movement. In this, a leader's eloquence, energy, courage, and single-mindedness undeniably help. But "charisma" also hinges on a host of pedestrian factors that are nonetheless unusual among oppressed groups. Fluency in a key foreign language, especially English, an understanding of Western protest traditions, familiarity with international political trends, and expertise in media and NGO relations are all important for a leader's ineffable qualities to shine through. Would the Dalai Lama appear as charismatic in translation? Without the ability to communicate directly to NGO principals and larger audiences, material support, let alone emotional ties, will seldom flower.

Most of these prosaic characteristics are learned, not innate. Groups long exposed to the developed world, with educated middle classes and large expatriate communities, are likeliest to produce adept exponents. Early NGO supporters may also act as international Henry Higginses to insurgent Eliza Doolittles, enlightening callow leaders about key institutions and disciplining them to unfamiliar expectations. Much of this occurs informally, as local movements absorb, for instance, that gender equity and ethnic tolerance are today expected by prospective patrons in the developed world. Some NGOs also provide formal "capacity building" programs, preening their charges for exposure to broader audiences and weaning them for the day when support will end. (Of course, most of the groups that gain admission to such programs already enjoy significant advantages over their less fortunate competitors.) Such programs teach everything from international legal principles to diplomatic etiquette to press relations. The Unrepresented Nations and Peoples Organization (UNPO), based in The Hague, regularly holds media training sessions for its member "nations," preparing spokesmen through role plays and mock interviews. According to an UNPO staffperson: "Part of it is emphasizing words like 'peaceful protest' instead of just 'protest,' or 'peaceful demonstration,' instead of just a 'demonstration.' ... You have to make it exciting, which sounds awful.... You need words that sound exciting, and that telegraph the story.... 'We have been fighting and are oppressed': When [an UNPO member] say[s] that, they bring up a negative connotation. Then the audience says, 'Oh they've been fighting, they must be incredibly violent.' It's all in the words that you use. If a member says, 'They've killed people in 5 neighboring villages,' it's much better than 'We've been fighting.' "[56]

One of the most elaborate programs is the Washington, D.C.-based International Human Rights Law Group's two-year Advocacy Bridge Program, which aims to "increase the skills of local activists to amplify their issues of concern globally" and to "facilitate their access to international agenda-setting venues."[57] What do NGO consultants seek to create by grooming their clients in these ways? Typically, it is a balance between cosmopolitan savvy and indigenous authenticity. To counter slick attacks by powerful opponents, NGOs build the sophistication of their client groups while maintaining "local color." Epitomizing this fine line is an UNPO staffperson's account of an incident involving their West Papuan member:

West Papua is a ghastly situation: it is very hard to get visual images out. I kept seeing the same image – men running around in penis sheaths and the Indonesian Ambassador saying, "These people can't be taught, can't count." Then the next night, we went to Leonie, a young articulate West Papuan woman who said, "Utter rubbish: I'm intelligent, I'm educated, I'm just like you." It was absolutely ludicrous – on one hand, here's this guy saying they're sub-humans almost; then a very articulate woman speaking for the West Papuan people; dressed in a West Papuan T-shirt. Luckily she happened to be wearing that when they flew her over. Traditional garb is fabulous too. Flags are also good, though you have to be careful about that; people associate it with nationalism.[58]

Internationally successful insurgent leaders therefore look surprisingly similar to the supporters they chase and quite different from their downtrodden domestic constituencies. Indeed, in notable cases they are outsiders, either members of the group with long exposure to the outside world or foreigners. Burmese democracy leader Aung Saan Suu Kyi spent decades outside the country, and Ecuador's indigenous Cofanés spokesman Randy Borman is the son of missionaries.[59] These are individuals with one foot in the local realm and another in the transnational one. In many cases, a

---

[56] Interviewee 13 (UNPO manager), personal interview by author, July 11, 1996.

[57] International Human Rights Law Group, "Advocacy Bridge Project," http://www. hrlawgroup.org/site/programs/Adbridge.htm (accessed July 17, 2004).

[58] Interviewee 13 (UNPO manager), July 11, 1996.

[59] Alison Brysk, *From Tribal Village to Global Village: Indian Rights and International Relations in Latin America* (Stanford, CA: Stanford University Press, 2000), 274.

leader's "charisma" stems as much from the needs and preferences of global audiences as from special personal qualities.[60] In that sense, receptive audiences make causes célèbres as much as the latter promote themselves. NGOs look for a figure that neatly embodies their own ideals or fulfills romantic Western notions of rebellion – in short, a leader who seems to mirror their own central values. Other leaders, deaf to the international vogue, too closely tied to the local milieu, or simply unwilling to adapt, remain friendless and underfunded.

Beyond the characteristics of insurgents, the *identity and reactions of opponents* strongly affect the success of a movement's marketing campaign. The media and many NGOs pay disproportionate attention to large, economically important, or strategically located states.[61] Insurgents from these states, as well as movements in conflict with powerful and well-known multinational corporations or financial institutions, have a structural advantage in attracting media reporting. By contrast, those insurgents from international backwaters or fighting obscure local battles must struggle simply to be heard – unless they frame their conflict around a more notorious foe. As one NGO staffperson noted: "Sometimes going into a smaller country . . . it is easier to have an impact. We can make a difference – and be seen to have made a difference. On the other hand, we can't go into some that are too small; of course it would be politically incorrect for me to say which those would be."[62] Similarly, opponent identities help explain geographic variations in support. Thus, a movement opposing a state in the developing world will often gain disproportionate attention and support from NGOs based in the country's old colonial ruler. Contemporary ties to a movement's target also explain differences in response to the same insurgency among countries. If a multinational corporation is a primary movement target, for instance, NGOs in its headquarters state take a special interest.

Given NGOs' organizational imperative to back successes, insurgents facing opponents that appear to be potentially malleable have some advantage over those confronting implacable enemies. Movements whose gripe is with entities having institutionalized dispute-resolution procedures probably also have an advantage over those facing adversaries without such mechanisms. International financial institutions may therefore be preferred

---

[60] Douglas Madsen and Peter G. Snow, *The Charismatic Bond: Political Behavior in Time of Crisis* (Cambridge, MA: Harvard University Press, 1991).

[61] Wolfsfeld, *Media and Political Conflict*, 18–19.

[62] Interviewee 45 (International Foundation for Election Systems staffperson), June 10, 2002.

foes for movements opposing intransigent dictatorships. As one example, the World Bank's environmental and indigenous peoples policies may make the Bank more responsive to pressure than many foreign governments. Knowing this, local movements facing multiple opponents highlight the more accessible and tractable one, even if it is not necessarily the main culprit.[63]

An opponent's reaction to insurgent protest also affects the NGO response. For one thing, where a home state exercises effective control over a conflict site, challengers will have greater difficulty promoting their plight to third parties. Even in the age of the Internet, miniature video recorders, and satellite communication technology, states remain capable of limiting insurgent access to the international community. In the 1990s, for example, the government of Papua New Guinea did just that on Bougainville Island, site of a bloody separatist struggle that cost 15,000 lives, or roughly 10 percent of the island's population. During an eight-year blockade (1989–97), foreign journalists could enter the island only under government guard, while the rebels could dispatch emissaries abroad only at great risk. India has used similar tactics in Kashmir, prohibiting independent human rights monitors from entering the territory and seizing passports of activists seeking to plead the Kashmiri case before the United Nations General Assembly. At times during its decades-long civil war, Sudan kept foreigners from entering the country's vast southern region.[64] And even today, inaccessibility and danger can greatly reduce a conflict's international profile, as was the case in the late 1990s during the "world war" that wracked the eastern Congo or more recently in the genocide that enveloped Sudan's Darfur region.

---

[63] For a possible example of this dynamic, see Pieter Bottelier, "Was World Bank Support for the Qinghai Anti-Poverty Project in China Ill-Considered?" *Harvard Asia Quarterly* 5, no. 1 (2001), http://www.fas.harvard.edu/~asiactr/haq/200101/0101a007.htm (accessed August 3, 2004). Meyer and Staggenborg make the analogous point that movements suffering defeats in one venue shift their activities to other, more amenable sites. David S. Meyer and Suzanne Staggenborg, "Movements, Countermovements, and the Structure of Political Opportunity," *American Journal of Sociology* 101, no. 6 (1996), 1628–60. On venue shifting, see also Keck and Sikkink, *Activists beyond Borders*, 18; Frank Baumgartner and Bryan Jones, "Agenda Dynamics and Policy Subsystems," *Journal of Politics* 53, no. 4 (1991): 1049.

[64] Steven Livingston, "Suffering in Silence: Media Coverage of War and Famine in Sudan," in *From Massacres to Genocide: The Media, Public Policy, and Humanitarian Crises*, Robert I. Rotberg and Thomas G. Weiss, eds. (Cambridge, MA: World Peace Foundation, 1996), 68–89.

Conclusion

Assuming there is access to a conflict site, an opponent's treatment of an insurgent group affects international concern. In this situation, repression of a movement may increase media and NGO attention. Social movement scholars have long noted that a government crackdown may increase third-party sympathy and concern for the insurgency.[65] By making martyrs, particularly of well-known movement leaders, repression may inadvertently inflame once passive bystanders. Aware of this dynamic, movement leaders sometimes take the risky tack of goading their opponents into violence. By dramatically encapsulating chronic, low-level repression in a single bloody and clearly unjust incident, insurgents can gain publicity and sympathy for an issue that might otherwise be overlooked by distant audiences. In the 1960s, American civil rights leaders took this strategy, protesting in cities where they expected hot-headed local authorities to counter nonviolent actions with violent suppression.[66] Similarly, journalists have documented the willingness of Tiananmen Square protest leaders to provoke state repression to gain outside attention and support.[67] Although this risky strategy is difficult to control, modern insurgents may conclude, like Gandhi, that "the willing sacrifice of the innocent" is not only a "powerful answer to insolent tyranny" but also the best way to galvanize jaded overseas audiences.[68]

Conclusion

The marketing perspective presents a dynamic view of today's transnational politics. Numerous local movements involved in diverse struggles

---

[65] Gene Sharp, *The Politics of Nonviolent Action* (Boston: Porter Sargent Publishers, 1973); Lee Smithey and Lester R. Kurtz, "We Have Bare Hands: Nonviolent Social Movements in the Soviet Bloc," in *Nonviolent Social Movements: A Geographic Perspective*, Stephen Zunes, Lester R. Kurtz, and Sarah Beth Asher, eds. (New York: Blackwell Publishers, 1999), 96–124. Conversely, a ruthless local insurgency may foster sympathy for the state it opposes, as the Shining Path did for Peru in the 1990s. See James Ron, "Ideology in Context: Explaining Sendero Luminoso's Tactical Escalation," *Journal of Peace Research* 38, no. 5 (2001): 569–92.

[66] David J. Garrow, *Protest at Selma* (New Haven, CT: Yale University Press, 1978), 227–28; McAdam, *Political Process*, 178–79.

[67] *Frontline*, "The Gate of Heavenly Peace," show no. 1418 (Boston: WGBH Educational Foundation, 1996).

[68] Mahatma Gandhi, *The Collected Works of Mahatma Gandhi*, vol. XXVI (Delhi: Publications Division, Ministry of Information and Broadcasting, 1958), 141. Stacy Sullivan documents this dynamic in *Be Not Afraid, for You Have Sons in America: How a Brooklyn Roofer Helped Lure the U.S. into the Kosovo War* (New York: St. Martin's Press, 2004). See also Alan J. Kuperman, "Humanitarian Hazard: Revisiting Doctrines of Intervention," *Harvard International Review* 26 (Spring 2004): 64–68.

reach outside their states for support while transnational activists, NGOs, and networks offer succor and seek clients. In these interactions, issues of power – of the relative value and need of the parties – are fundamental. And asymmetries in power are endemic, forcing the weaker party to the transaction, usually a local challenger, to pursue backers based in the developed world. Although altruism, sympathy, and principles move NGOs, insurgents improve their chances overseas if they adjust their rhetoric and behavior to meet NGO expectations, with variations in the parties' relative power affecting the amount of change necessary. Of course, NGOs and networks are not rigid; they evolve, sometimes through interaction with their clients, and they are often open to new ideas. But at any particular time, NGOs have stable practices and agendas, making them more receptive to challengers who appear to fit their organizational needs.

Control over information is critical to this interaction. The most successful movements simultaneously seek information about their targets while managing facts about themselves. On the one hand, if a movement understands a potential supporter's key interests and concerns, its proficiency at tapping and persuading the target will grow. On the other hand, if a movement limits undesired news about itself – from opponents, the media, or even loose-lipped members – while producing positive and credible data, it will enjoy greater appeal. Successful movement framing highlights issues having international resonance, whether or not they are centrally important to the underlying conflicts. As such, framing may reshape a challenger, altering its goals and tactics. Nonetheless, framing has its limits. NGOs are not naïve about the incentives movements face. Thus, they investigate movements' claims both to protect themselves and to assure the effectiveness of their support. Notwithstanding altruistic missions, NGOs operate – indeed must operate – with their own interests always in mind. How else can they carry on the good fight than by mixing the morally charged goals they present to external audiences with pragmatic or even skeptical attitudes toward potential clients?

At times, such considerations jibe nicely with the exigencies facing local movements. More often, they sit uneasily with desperate dissidents and vast needs. Local movements gain support when they convince NGOs of overlapping goals and tactics, of parallel ethics and culture, and of benefits greater than costs. All of this requires effective marketing, including everything from raising awareness among distant audiences to deciphering the preferences of prospective supporters to constructing an attractive frame. Yet insurgents vary greatly in these skills because of "structural" factors affecting both themselves and their opponents. These factors are not immutable; indeed, through outside support, insurgents hope to affect them. Yet, compared with their strategies, the structural factors facing insurgents are more difficult to change either because they are rooted in historical circumstances or because they are largely under the control of other parties.

It would be going too far to claim that the marketing perspective can foretell whether a particular challenger will gain major transnational support. The variety of factors, the importance of individual leadership skills, and chance all play a role, which makes such a prediction risky. Most importantly, movements act strategically, changing their consciousness-raising techniques and altering their frames as opponents, the media, and potential supporters react. The results can be surprising – even to movement marketers themselves. Nonetheless, in explaining why some causes ignite the world's concern whereas others do not, the marketing perspective illuminates processes that recur across regions and issues. In Chapters 3 and 4, I demonstrate its utility in explaining the transnational successes of two important recent movements, Nigeria's Ogoni ethnic movement and Mexico's Zapatista Army of National Liberation, respectively. As I discuss, both won significant overseas backing, while similar movements from the same countries failed to do so. Only the marketing approach can explain these differences. In doing so, the approach also clarifies the shape and character of contemporary world politics, challenging optimistic visions of a "global civil society" with a more cautious and realistic account.

3

From Ethnic to Environmental Conflict

NIGERIA'S OGONI MOVEMENT

In the summer of 1995, in a stifling courtroom in Port Harcourt, Nigeria, Ken Saro-Wiwa and nine other members of the Movement for the Survival of the Ogoni People (MOSOP) stood on trial for their lives. Led by Saro-Wiwa, MOSOP had for five years sought political autonomy for the Ogoni minority group while protesting ethnic discrimination, economic exploitation, and environmental destruction by the Nigerian government and Royal Dutch/Shell, the major oil producer in the region. Now, accused on flimsy evidence of incitement to murder four rival leaders, the MOSOP members faced a military tribunal hand-picked by the country's brutal dictator, General Sani Abacha. As the kangaroo court plodded forward that summer, MOSOP members, supported by major NGOs, fanned out to world capitals. Enlisting heads of state from Bill Clinton to Nelson Mandela to John Major, the Ogoni network pressured the Nigerian government but to no avail. On November 10, 1995, only days after the tribunal's long-predicted guilty verdict, Saro-Wiwa and eight others were marched to the gallows and their bodies dumped in unmarked graves.

Saro-Wiwa's killing was a severe blow to the Ogoni. But in a few short years, the man and his small movement had scored remarkable successes on the international stage against one of the world's most repressive governments and one of its largest corporations. Most basically, MOSOP lifted the Ogoni out of historical anonymity to widespread support. As late as 1992, the Ogoni, an impoverished group numbering perhaps 500,000 and living in a 400-square-mile corner of an expansive country with more than one hundred million people, were almost unknown abroad.[1] For decades both

---

[1] Although widely cited, these Ogoni population figures, deriving from MOSOP itself, should be treated cautiously. Ken Saro-Wiwa, *Genocide in Nigeria: The Ogoni Tragedy* (Port Harcourt,

before and after Nigeria's independence in 1960, they opposed the central government over political, economic, and environmental issues. Dwarfed by disputes among Nigeria's three major ethnic groups and shrouded in international indifference to African affairs, Ogoni grievances festered outside the limelight. As late as 1990–92, major NGOs rejected the group's pleas for help in their quest for autonomy. Yet, by 1995, MOSOP had propelled the Ogoni to the front ranks of activism on two fronts, human rights and the environment. Among the many NGOs that assisted the Ogoni were Amnesty International, Human Rights Watch, Greenpeace, Friends of the Earth, and the Sierra Club. And despite Saro-Wiwa's execution, MOSOP and its international followers had important though limited effects on Nigerian politics and society – a major achievement given the group's minuscule size and the government's great power. In addition, the transnational Ogoni campaign spurred Shell to attend to its operations in the region and its human rights and environmental record worldwide.

The Ogoni rise to international prominence tells us much about the difficulties and dangers faced by local activists seeking foreign support. The pattern of NGO responses – initial rejections during 1990–92, adoption by a panoply of NGOs during 1993–95, and slow decline since 1995 – is particularly useful for uncovering insurgent and NGO strategies. The story is even more revealing when set in a broader context. The Ogoni are one of dozens of minorities living in the country's Niger River Delta that faced similar threats in both colonial and independent Nigeria. Organizations representing groups such as the Ijaw, Ikwerre, Itsekiri, Urhobo, and others sought external support during the early 1990s both before and after MOSOP's rise. As late as 1992, little seemed to distinguish the Ogoni from these other minorities. Yet, within two years, MOSOP eclipsed them all on the international scene, often overshadowing even the nationwide Nigerian democracy movement. Even today, few outside Nigeria know of the Niger Delta's far larger Ijaw ethnic group, Nigeria's fourth largest, with an estimated population of 13 million. Groups closer in size to the Ogoni are even less visible. If they sometimes gain recognition today, much of the credit goes to the Ogoni, whose actions illuminated the troubles plaguing the entire Niger Delta.

How did this obscure Nigerian minority stir the world's conscience? Why did it succeed when similar groups in the region did not? This

Nigeria: Saros International, 1992); Ken Wiwa, *In the Shadow of a Saint* (Toronto: Alfred A. Knopf Canada, 2000), 68–69.

chapter highlights MOSOP's unusual ability to project its cause abroad, emphasizing various advantages that the Ogoni had over other Niger Delta minorities. But this alone was insufficient to attract outside aid. The Ogoni gained backing only after their struggle came to match the preferences and predilections of key NGO gatekeepers. This resulted in part from MOSOP's strategic decision to deemphasize long-standing ethnic grievances while highlighting important but previously secondary issues involving Shell's environmental record in the group's homeland. In addition, the conflict itself changed, as Nigeria's military dictators cracked down hard on a movement challenging critical ethnic and economic policies. Together, these shifts brought the Ogoni international media attention and NGO support but also overshadowed their core minority rights claims.

Roots of the Niger Delta Conflict

The Niger River Delta, in Nigeria's south, is a densely populated area long marginalized in the country's politics. Since the formation of British Nigeria in 1914, and especially since independence in 1960, its assorted ethnic minorities, today constituting approximately 15 percent of the country's population, have feared domination by the three largest groups, the Hausa-Fulani, located primarily in the north (currently estimated to be about 29 percent of the population), the Yorubas in the southwest (21 percent), and the Igbos in the southeast (18 percent).[2] To avoid this fate, the minorities have sought more control over their territories, greater input into regional and national politics, increased central state revenues, subsidies, and development assistance, and preservation of their distinct cultures and languages. Much of this agitation has come in the form of demands for ethnically based regional or local governments that would allow the various groups to consolidate their power, manage indigenous resources, and exploit opportunities provided by the central government. As one of many examples from the colonial era, in 1946 pressure from Ogoni leaders resulted in the formation of a single local administrative district encompassing all Ogoni through which, it was hoped, the group's interests could be

[2] Central Intelligence Agency (CIA), *The World Factbook* (Washington, DC, 2003), http://www.odci.gov/cia/publications/factbook/geos/ni.html (accessed July 17, 2004); Rotimi T. Suberu, *Federalism and Ethnic Conflict in Nigeria* (Washington, DC: United States Institute of Peace Press, 2001), 168. Ethnic population figures in Nigeria are unreliable and contentious due to measurement problems and political manipulation.

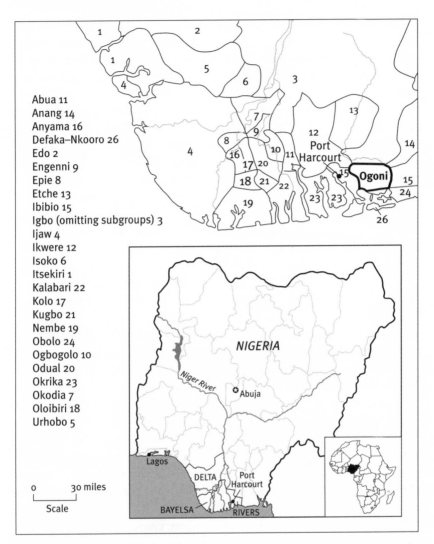

Abua 11
Anang 14
Anyama 16
Defaka–Nkooro 26
Edo 2
Engenni 9
Epie 8
Etche 13
Ibibio 15
Igbo (omitting subgroups) 3
Ijaw 4
Ikwere 12
Isoko 6
Itsekiri 1
Kalabari 22
Kolo 17
Kugbo 21
Nembe 19
Obolo 24
Ogbogolo 10
Odual 20
Okrika 23
Okodia 7
Oloibiri 18
Urhobo 5

Map 3.1   Selected Ethnolinguistic Groups of the Niger River Delta. Adapted by permission from Christopher Moseley and R. E. Asher, *Atlas of the World's Languages* (London: Routledge, 1994), Map 106.

better articulated. As the British prepared Nigeria for independence in the 1950s, the Ogoni and other Delta minorities, as well as minorities elsewhere, came to fear their subordination in the new country. Under the 1954 Lyttelton Constitution, the colonial administration nonetheless created a federation of three regions, each dominated by one of the major ethnic groups. In 1957, a royal commission, charged with inquiring into the continuing "fears of minorities and the means of allaying them," heard many, including the Ogoni, plead for their own states or some other more decentralized form of political administration.[3] But these calls went unmet, and at independence, the Niger Delta remained within the Igbo-dominated Eastern Region.

Since independence, calls for more states and local government areas have grown throughout the country. Initially, many of these claims were based on cultural arguments – that minorities faced repression, even "extinction," unless their territories were excised from units dominated by other groups. More recently, most such calls have been grounded in struggles for scarce revenues controlled by a powerful, often autocratic, central government ruling over a poor society with few economic opportunities in the private sector.[4] In sometimes violent competitions with one another, both minority and majority groups have demanded new governmental units, each of which typically entails the creation of political and bureaucratic posts; the allocation of new funds for roads, hospitals, schools, and other infrastructure; and the distribution of scholarships, contracts, and loans. But in a society where ethnic loyalties dominate over national ones, new states generate additional aggrieved minorities, fueling further demands for states or local government areas.

In the Niger Delta, minority grievances turned to violence soon after independence with Isaac Boro's declaration of the Niger Delta Republic in 1967. Although crushed within days, this revolt indicated the depth of minority opposition to the structure of the new country. Later that year, some Delta populations, including many Ogoni, acquiesced in the Igbo-led Biafran secession. The resulting war killed over one million people and displaced millions more before ending in 1970. In addition, the Biafran crisis triggered the abolition of the country's regions. In their stead, 12 less powerful states were created, including one in the Niger Delta, Rivers State, that grouped many of the minority peoples outside Igbo control. Yet the smaller minorities remained dissatisfied in part because of Ijaw predominance in Rivers State. In 1974, the Ogoni and other Rivers State

---

[3] Colonial Office, *Nigeria: Report of the Commission Appointed to Enquire into the Fears of Minorities and the Means of Allaying Them* (*Willink Commission Report*) (London: Her Majesty's Stationery Office, 1958; reprint, Port Harcourt, Nigeria: Southern Minorities Movement, 1996).

[4] Suberu, *Federalism and Ethnic Conflict*, 80–81.

minorities called in vain for excision of a Port Harcourt State free of Ijaw domination. In 1976 and 1987, these and other demands for new states in the Delta went unheard even as states were created elsewhere, bringing Nigeria's total to 19, then 21.

Minority discontents deepened after oil drilling began in the Delta in 1957. Production increased slowly during the 1960s, then leaped during the 1970s. Today, the country is one of the world's largest crude oil producers and has a growing natural gas business, with almost all of both resources found in or around the Niger Delta. Major multinationals, including Royal Dutch/Shell (Shell), ExxonMobil, ChevronTexaco, ENI/Agip, and TotalFinaElf, operate joint ventures with the state-owned Nigerian National Petroleum Corporation (NNPC) to drill for petroleum, most of which is shipped to the United States and Europe. In the Ogoni area, Shell was the primary producer during the early 1990s, with its subsidiary, Shell Petroleum Development Corporation (SPDC), the lead foreign company in a joint venture with Chevron, Elf, and the NNPC.[5] Before their shutdown in 1993, SPDC's Ogoni operations included five major oil fields, which produced abut 30,000 barrels per day, accounting for about 1.5 percent of Nigeria's oil production. In Nigeria as a whole, SPDC produced about 40 percent of total crude oil output (800,000 barrels per day). For Shell, Nigerian oil accounted for about 14 percent of its global production.[6]

During the 1970s, petroleum quickly became Nigeria's most valuable export. Although the precise figures vary from year to year depending on world petroleum demand and prices, about 90 percent of Nigeria's annual foreign exchange earnings and 80 percent of its revenues came from oil during the 1990s. Yet the Niger Delta minorities who sit atop the oil fields have little to show for this bonanza. Instead, in Nigeria's highly centralized, notoriously corrupt, and ethnically riven political system, the country's leaders, both military and civilian, have siphoned most of the revenue

---

[5] Shares in the joint venture were divided as follows as of late 1995: NNPC 55%; Shell 30%; Elf 10%; and Agip 5%. Shell International Petroleum Company, Group Public Affairs, "Shell in Nigeria," Shell Briefing Note (London: Shell International Petroleum Company, December 1995), 1, Gumberg Library Archive, Duquesne University [hereafter Gumberg Library].

[6] Shell International Petroleum Company, Group Public Affairs, "Operations in Nigeria," Shell Briefing Note (London: Shell International Petroleum Company, May 1994), 2, Gumberg Library; World Bank, Industry and Energy Operations Division, West Central Africa Department, Africa Region, *Defining an Environmental Development Strategy for the Niger Delta* (Washington, DC: World Bank, 1995), Vol. 1, p. 4.

to projects serving their communal kin, primarily in the country's north. In practical terms, this occurred through bitterly disputed policies concerning "vertical" distribution of revenues among the hierarchy of governmental units and "horizontal" distribution of the share accruing to state and local bodies. With respect to the first issue, the national government has greatly expanded its taxing authority, with petroleum profit taxes a core prerogative, fostering state and local dependency on a national Federation Account. Beginning in the late 1970s, federal, state, and local authorities were to receive 55 percent, 35 percent, and 10 percent of the account, respectively.[7] The country's military dictators, General Ibrahim Babangida (1985–93) and General Sani Abacha (1993–98), however, diverted billions of dollars for various special projects or to themselves, depriving states and localities of about half their share.[8]

The horizontal distribution of these remaining shares has also been highly contentious. During the 1950s and 1960s, the "derivation principle" allotted the Eastern Region and successor states 50 percent of mining rents and revenues from their territories, a figure reduced under pressure from the non-oil regions to 45 percent in 1970 and 20 percent in 1975.[9] With oil revenues from the Delta exploding even while the larger economy languished, and with the oil states' population accounting for only a small share of the country's total, the derivation portion was curtailed in 1981 to 2 percent, a figure reduced to 1 percent during 1989–99. Instead, funds were distributed primarily on the basis of interstate parity, population, and, to a lesser extent, need, criteria that benefited large, resource-poor states, particularly in the country's north. Moreover, even the funds designated for the oil states frequently failed to advance the minority populations living in petroleum production areas. Much was pocketed by corrupt officials or distributed to the larger ethnic groups who administered the funds at the state level. In an attempt to address these problems, the 1981 Revenue Allocation Act established a special federal fund for the development of mineral-producing areas. In 1992, this fund was converted to a permanent federal agency, the Oil Mineral Producing Areas Development Commission (OMPADEC), and its funding bumped from 1.5 percent to 3 percent

---

[7] The figures changed marginally in 1990, with a decline in the state share and rise in the local. See Suberu, *Federalism and Ethnic Conflict*, 53–55.

[8] Ibid.

[9] Nigeria's large offshore oil revenues were vested in the federal government beginning in 1971.

of mineral revenues in the Federation Account. However, both the fund and OMPADEC were severely criticized for improper allocation of funds, misguided development projects, and failure to include legitimate community representatives from the oil-producing regions.

The upshot for the Niger Delta has been that although a few state officials and local leaders have prospered from ties to the oil industry, most of the Delta's people remain mired in some of Nigeria's worst poverty. Malnutrition, disease, and unemployment are rampant, while roads, hospitals, and schools remain scarce. The result is deep grievances, with the minorities arguing that "their" petroleum riches are being stolen by the country's largest ethnic groups and the multinational oil companies. Even jobs in the oil fields often go to individuals from Nigeria's larger groups thanks to the Nigerian principle of "federal character," which provides, among other things, that employment in state-owned enterprises such as the NNPC must reflect the country's overall ethnic composition.

To make matters worse, the Delta bears the brunt of oil production's social and environmental costs. Migrant workers and security personnel disrupt economic and social relations. Stark contrasts between the poverty of local villages and the luxury of oil company enclaves heighten the minorities' sense of injustice. Oil production also causes environmental problems. Above-ground pipelines snake across the landscape, crossing fields and villages. Air and water pollution from fires, blowouts, and day-to-day operations poisons fishing grounds and blackens the landscape. Light and noise pollution from constant natural gas flaring causes continuous disturbances. And Nigeria's courts have failed to compensate or protect local communities and individuals from oil-related accidents and damage.[10] According to a 1995 World Bank study, oil production has not been the largest source of environmental problems in the Delta; urban pollution plays that role. But oil contributes significantly. Corrosion and equipment failure have been the most frequent sources of spills and other accidents, although vandalism of pipelines and flow stations has sometimes played a role. With the multinationals' salience in the impoverished Delta, local communities perceive them as the primary culprits for the region's environmental problems. Moreover, because state authority is weak – and because the government has spent little on the region – the Niger Delta minorities often see the

---

[10] Jedrzej Georg Frynas, *Oil in Nigeria: Conflict and Litigation between Oil Companies and Village Communities* (Munster: Lit Verlag, 2000).

companies as the most accessible authorities for a host of pressing needs from jobs to development.[11]

In the 1980s, as Nigeria lurched from democracy during the Second Republic (1979–83) to military rule for the rest of the decade and beyond, unrest in the Delta manifested itself in many forms. At the local level, some communities protested against oil development projects. Others filed lawsuits demanding greater compensation for pollution and land takings. In some areas, bands of "youths" – unemployed men of diverse age and education – sabotaged production equipment as leverage for claims against the companies. In many communities, tensions mounted between educated but poor youths and local leaders who benefited from the oil wealth. At the state and national levels, the minorities' political demands also intensified. This occurred in the midst of broader ferment in Nigerian society preceding the repeatedly promised, then postponed, democratic transition from General Babangida's military rule. In April 1990, for instance, an abortive coup against the Babangida government included participants from the Delta angry over ethnically based imbalances in the distribution of political power and economic resources. Like many other groups across the country, the Niger Delta minorities saw the endless transition as a time to organize and prepare for a more open society in which their relationship with the center might be renegotiated. In this context, minority political leaders agitated, formed coalitions, and proposed new states, localities, and a national convention to reconfigure the Nigerian federation. Central to their diverse demands was the quest for greater power vis-à-vis the federal government and the dominant ethnic groups.

The contemporary Ogoni movement began in August 1990 as a manifestation of these broad minority grievances and the group's own extensive history of activism. The Ogoni, a primarily Christian ethnic group, are composed of six linguistically distinct clans, or "kingdoms." For analytic purposes, I treat the group as unified, but since the early colonial period, conflicts with outside authorities occurred simultaneously with internal disputes over ethnic identity, boundaries, and authority.[12] MOSOP

---

[11] World Bank, *Defining an Environmental Development Strategy for the Niger Delta*; David Moffat and Olof Lindén, "Perception and Reality: Assessing Priorities for Sustainable Development in the Niger River Delta," *Ambio* 24 (1995): 534–36; Norimitsu Onishi, "Deep in the Republic of Chevron," *New York Times Magazine*, July 4, 1999, 26; Marina Ottaway, "Reluctant Missionaries," *Foreign Policy*, July/August 2001, 44–54.

[12] In 1968, for instance, Saro-Wiwa apologized to the Khana, Gokana, and Eleme people, who "will object to the name 'Ogoni' on the grounds that it is alien." See Ken Saro-Wiwa,

was founded not as an individual membership organization but as an umbrella encompassing both existing political, cultural, and religious groups
and new ones founded by the movement's leaders. Ogoni society was rife
with such organizations, whose leaderships, in the narrow confines of the
group's homeland, often interlocked.[13] Throughout its history, MOSOP
used nonviolent activism outside institutional channels rather than working
as a political party. The movement's initial leaders comprised two factions.
On one side were a group of Ogoni chiefs, many long active in Nigeria's party politics, then moribund because of Babangida's military rule. On
the other side was a set of educated, mostly younger Ogoni frustrated by
a lack of economic opportunity and the group's continuing marginalization in Nigerian politics. Many of these younger, educated Ogoni were
originally members of the Committee for Ogoni Autonomy (COA) and
the National Youth Council of Ogoni People (NYCOP), which at first
worked independently of MOSOP to educate and organize the Ogoni
masses.

Spanning the two camps and acting as MOSOP's guiding spirit was
Kenule Beeson Saro-Wiwa, an author, television producer, businessman,
and, from his youth, an ardent Ogoni nationalist. Born in 1941, Saro-Wiwa
published *The Ogoni Nation Today and Tomorrow* in 1968, urging his people
to regain "its lost dignity and honour." During the Biafran War, Saro-Wiwa
took the federal side because he feared that his group would suffer greater
repression at the hands of a smaller, less pluralistic new state dominated by
the Igbo. Escaping to the rump of Nigeria, he became administrator of the
important oil port of Bonny at age 28. When the war ended, Saro-Wiwa
first worked in government, then in business, founding a successful grocery
chain that expanded into a broad-based conglomerate, Saros International.
In the early 1980s, he turned to fiction writing and television, producing
one of Nigeria's most popular television shows, *Basi & Co.*, which lam-
pooned the lives of Nigeria's money-grubbing urban classes. Later in the
decade, he made a name for himself as an outspoken newspaper columnist
and political gadfly. By the end of 1990, he had been fired as an opinion

preface (1968) to *The Ogoni Nation Today and Tomorrow*, 2nd ed. (Port Harcourt, Nigeria:
Saros International, 1993), 3. See also Renate Wente-Lukas, *Handbook of Ethnic Units in
Nigeria* (Stuttgart: F. Steiner Verlag Wiesbaden, 1985), 139, 215, 290; Eghosa E. Osaghae,
"The Ogoni Uprising: Oil Politics, Minority Agitation and the Future of the Nigerian
State," *African Affairs* 94 (1995): 327–29; Wiwa, *Shadow of a Saint*, 68–69.

[13] MOSOP, *Constitution of the Movement for the Survival of the Ogoni People (MOSOP)*, 1993,
Gumberg Library.

writer for Nigeria's government-owned *Sunday Times* newspaper because of controversial columns on topics such as corruption, dictatorship, ethnicity, and "The Coming War in the Delta." By this time as well, he had developed a minor international reputation as a writer, leading to invitations to visit the United States, Soviet Union, and Europe. Saro-Wiwa's attitude toward Nigeria was ambivalent. Although he despised the country's anarchy and corruption, he found the chaos energizing and full of opportunity. Although he championed Ogoni culture and power, he believed that a unified, albeit restructured, Nigeria held the best hope for his people. Such a Nigeria would follow the vision of one of Saro-Wiwa's heroes, the Yoruba chief Obafemi Awolowo, who at independence argued unsuccessfully for a federation in which ethnic groups of every size would be treated equally.[14]

As a nationally recognized Ogoni figure, Saro-Wiwa was instrumental both in convincing more conservative leaders to form MOSOP and in pushing them to approve mass action in January 1993. At first, he took an unofficial position in the organization, acting as spokesman while deferring titular leadership to established Ogoni leaders. Nonetheless, as the moving force behind MOSOP, Saro-Wiwa often acted as the group's de facto head. As institutional politics reopened in 1993 and MOSOP faced increasing state repression, the more conservative leaders grew to oppose Saro-Wiwa's preferred tactics of open critique and mass mobilization. In June 1993, they left the movement and Saro-Wiwa took over as president. Meanwhile, the tactics that alienated the conservative leaders drew both educated insurgents and broader mass support.[15]

The seminal document in the Ogoni struggle, the *Ogoni Bill of Rights*, was adopted on August 26, 1990, even before MOSOP's formal launch. Written in English and signed by members of five of the six kingdoms, the *Bill of Rights* demanded "Political Autonomy to participate in the affairs of the republic as a distinct and separate unit," including the following:

a. political control of Ogoni affairs by Ogoni people;
b. the right to the control and use of a fair proportion of Ogoni economic resources for Ogoni development;

---

[14] Saro-Wiwa, *Ogoni Nation*, 22; Ken Saro-Wiwa, *A Month and a Day: A Detention Diary* (New York: Penguin Books, 1995), 63, 70.

[15] Saro-Wiwa discusses his side of internal Ogoni politics in Saro-Wiwa, *A Month and a Day*. For another perspective, see Ben Naanen, "Effective Nonviolent Struggle in the Niger Delta," http://www.iisg.nl/~sephis/ogonipeople.pdf (accessed July 30, 2004).

c. adequate and direct representation as of right in all Nigerian national institutions;

d. the use and development of Ogoni languages in Ogoni territory;

e. the full development of Ogoni culture;

f. the right to religious freedom;

g. the right to protect the Ogoni environment and ecology from further degradation.[16]

In the Nigerian context, these points went well beyond the usual claims for ethnically based states and had major implications. Ogoni ethnic autonomy even within Nigeria would have required redrawing administrative boundaries and retrenching elites. Local resource control would have reversed the existing ethnic power balance – to favor the Ogoni and other subordinated Niger Delta minorities that sit atop most of Nigeria's oil. The *Bill of Rights* pointed toward a radically reconstituted Nigeria, a "true federation" in which "all ethnic groups, irrespective of size, are treated equally" and have "full responsibility for [their] own affairs."[17] Ultimately, Saro-Wiwa's ambition was broader. He repeatedly attacked the "new black colonialists wearing the mask of Nigerianism" and hoped that the "Ogoni revolution" might "undo" the colonially determined boundaries of today's African states, serving as "a model for other small, deprived, dispossessed and disappearing peoples" of the Continent.[18]

"Knocking on Closed Doors": MOSOP's International Campaign, 1990–92

In the year following the issuance of the *Ogoni Bill of Rights*, MOSOP leaders sought to realize its objectives domestically. To alert the government, they sent a copy to President Babangida's Armed Forces Ruling Council and published it as an advertisement in a national newspaper. Saro-Wiwa also

---

[16] *Ogoni Bill of Rights*, reprinted in Saro-Wiwa, *A Month and a Day*, 67–70.

[17] Ken Saro-Wiwa, quoted in Theodore Ihejieto, "Minority Group Doubts Transition Programme," *Vanguard* (Ilorin), March 24, 1992, 3, 10; Ken Saro-Wiwa, foreword to *Ogoni Bill of Rights Presented to the Government and People of Nigeria October 1990 with an Appeal to the International Community* by Movement for the Survival of the Ogoni People (MOSOP) (Port Harcourt, Nigeria: Saros International, 1992), reprinted in *Fourth World Bulletin* 5, nos. 1–2 (1996): 17.

[18] Saro-Wiwa, *A Month and a Day*, 186, 134. See generally ibid., 183–94; Ken Saro-Wiwa, "Ethnic Energies Are Needed to Unscramble Africa: Guest Column," *Africa Analysis*, August 21, 1992, 15.

promoted Ogoni autonomy in speeches and newspaper articles nationwide. In early 1991, MOSOP undertook a brief public education campaign to explain the *Bill of Rights* to the Ogoni people, who had not formally voted on it. Organizing and consciousness-raising occurred, primarily through COA and NYCOP, but MOSOP mounted no protests to pressure the Nigerian state. Nonetheless, the *Bill of Rights* garnered media attention in Nigeria, as did continuing agitation for new states by other ethnic groups in the Niger Delta and elsewhere. Responding to pressure from the larger ethnic groups, especially the Igbo, the Babangida administration created nine new states in September 1991, bringing the country's total to 30. But the Niger Delta minorities got little, and Ogoni autonomy claims were ignored.[19]

This pan-Nigerian restructuring, which Saro-Wiwa portrayed as the Babangida regime at its "most insensitive and most bandit-like," spurred MOSOP to organize more vigorously at home and to seek support abroad.[20] In Saro-Wiwa's view, the government scorned MOSOP's demands because Nigeria's military and ethnic leaders wanted the oil revenues for themselves and because the Ogoni were too small to threaten the dominant groups. Moreover, the weakness of Nigeria's courts and the constitution's indifference to minority rights made judicial achievement of Ogoni goals impossible. Of course, rather than reaching beyond the country's borders, MOSOP might have allied with other groups having similar interests. In fact, Saro-Wiwa founded the Ethnic Minority Rights Organization of Nigeria (EMIRON) in March 1992 and appointed a journalist from another minority group as the organization's secretary. But EMIRON and its successor, the Ethnic Minority Rights Organization of Africa (EMIROAF), did not garner significant backing, and MOSOP avoided existing coalitions seeking multiethnic minority states in the Delta. Instead, fearing that their voices would be stifled in such new states, the Ogoni movement steadfastly pursued autonomy.[21]

With domestic avenues of limited use in this quest, the Ogoni turned overseas. There, Saro-Wiwa believed, Ogoni demands would find a receptive audience for several reasons: the end of the Cold War, increasing international concern for the global environment, and the "[h]istorical forces

---

[19] In partial response to Ijaw demands, Delta State was carved out of Rivers State, but its capital was placed in an Igbo-speaking region. See Suberu, *Federalism and Ethnic Conflict*, 100–101.

[20] Saro-Wiwa, *A Month and a Day*, 99.

[21] Saro-Wiwa, *Genocide in Nigeria*, 84, 87; Akpo Esajere, "Southern Minorities Plan Strategies for Third Republic," *Guardian* (Lagos), March 26, 1992, 1.

at work in the world [which] dictate that all multiethnic states become confederations of independent ethnic groups."[22] In Saro-Wiwa's striking terms, autonomy "is the path which has been chosen by the European tribes in the European community, and by the Russians and their neighbors in the new Commonwealth which they are now fashioning. The Yugoslav tribes are being forced into similar ways. The lesson is that high fences make good neighbors. The Ogoni are therefore in the mainstream of international thought."[23] To mark the formal inauguration of its efforts to attract international organizations interested in the "preservation of our nationality," MOSOP published the *Addendum to the Ogoni Bill of Rights* in August 1991. Under the banner "Ogoni Appeal to the International Community," the *Addendum* reiterated the group's political claims and specified for the first time that the Ogoni should control 50 percent of their economic resources.[24]

For 16 months after the revised campaign opened, MOSOP built a constituency at home but ventured no mass protests. Abroad, the campaign bore mixed results. On the one hand, MOSOP raised awareness, with Saro-Wiwa presenting the Ogoni case at conferences and making himself known to key staffpersons at major human rights and environmental NGOs. This in itself was a major achievement since the Ogoni and the wider problems of the Niger Delta were virtually unknown overseas at that time. In addition, this distinguished the Ogoni from other Niger Delta minorities who were less successful in projecting their movements. On the other hand, most of the NGOs that MOSOP contacted before 1993, and all of the most powerful ones, *rejected* MOSOP's overtures. Only beginning in early 1993, after the Ogoni shifted strategies, did they win broad support, including that of NGOs who had earlier rebuffed MOSOP's appeals.

To take the positive accomplishment first, why was MOSOP able to raise awareness and to promote the Ogoni overseas, even if at first fruitlessly? One factor was the Nigerian government's disinterest in the overseas activities of the Niger Delta minorities. Apparently believing that international lobbying posed little threat, the Babangida dictatorship did not block Saro-Wiwa's frequent trips and may in fact have encouraged them, perhaps

---

[22] Ken Saro-Wiwa, "Before the Curtain Falls," speech, Lagos, October 10, 1991, in Saro-Wiwa, *A Month and a Day*, 83.

[23] Saro-Wiwa, foreword to MOSOP, *Ogoni Bill of Rights*, 17.

[24] *Addendum to the Ogoni Bill of Rights*, August 26, 1991, in Saro-Wiwa, *A Month and a Day*, 89–92.

to slow MOSOP's domestic organizing.[25] In this permissive environment, other Niger Delta organizations also promoted their causes to foreign audiences. The Rivers Chiefs and Peoples Conference, an Ijaw group based in Port Harcourt, sent a delegation to the Earth Summit in 1992.[26] Other Ijaw leaders contacted the British-based "tribal peoples" support group Survival International during the early 1990s.[27] And a number of groups, including the Itsekiri and Omadino, featured in isolated international press reports during 1990–92. In the volume of lobbying and breadth of organizations contacted, however, Ogoni efforts dwarfed those of the other Niger Delta minorities. As a result, by the end of 1992, staff at several major NGOs were familiar with the Ogoni. Although some understood that the Delta's problems were wider than the Ogoni's, they knew little of these other struggling ethnic groups.

MOSOP's unusual ability to project its cause overseas hinged on several factors. First, it had substantial resources. Although small in population compared with other Delta minorities, the Ogoni were relatively advanced. For its size, the group had won a high number of appointments to state and federal offices, and there was a small but highly educated Ogoni elite.[28] Ogoniland's location, within about 20 miles of the major city of Port Harcourt, helps explain these past successes. Moreover, the Ogoni had another advantage: Ken Saro-Wiwa's personal wealth and willingness to spend it for the cause. Although the extent of his resources is unclear, Saro-Wiwa had sufficient means to send his children to expensive private schools in England, including Eton, and to purchase a house for his family outside London. In these respects, Saro-Wiwa was unusual but by no means unique among the elites of other Niger Delta minorities. The difference, however, was that by the early 1990s, Saro-Wiwa began devoting his wealth and time to MOSOP. He paid for printing the *Addendum to the Ogoni Bill of Rights* as an advertisement in Nigerian national newspapers, he self-published a book circulated to NGOs in 1992, *Genocide in Nigeria: The Ogoni Tragedy*,

[25] Saro-Wiwa, *A Month and a Day*, 109.

[26] Rivers Chiefs, "The Endangered Environment of the Niger Delta: An NGO Memorandum of the Rivers Chiefs and Peoples Conference, Port Harcourt, Nigeria for the World Conference of Indigenous Peoples on Environment and Development and UNCED, Rio de Janeiro, Brazil, 1992," memorandum, Gumberg Library.

[27] Interviewee 19 (Ijaw activist), personal interview by author, London, England, July 23, 1996; Stanley E. Eguruze, "The Federation of Ijaw Communities (FEDICOM): The Marketing of a Non-Governmental Organisation (NGO) in Nigeria," M.A. dissertation, School of Marketing, University of Greenwich, July 1996, Gumberg Library.

[28] Osaghae, "Ogoni Uprising," 331–32.

and he underwrote key preparations for the pivotal Ogoni Day march in January 1993. Nor did he hesitate to spend on lobbying trips to Europe and North America. Finally, Saro-Wiwa's costs went beyond money – to a troubled relationship with a family orphaned by a cause.[29]

Just as important as its financial resources was MOSOP's access to gate-keeper NGOs and the media, itself a result of Saro-Wiwa's modest but real international standing. Saro-Wiwa's writing and his presidency of the Association of Nigerian Authors had earlier won him recognition in British literary circles. He became an occasional commentator on contemporary African culture for the British Broadcasting Corporation's London-based Africa service and in that capacity repeatedly promoted the Ogoni cause.[30] As a result, he developed a handful of personal and professional contacts who helped him gain an entrée to key NGOs. This standing, although small compared with that of figures like the Dalai Lama, was nonetheless singular among the Niger Delta's minority leaders. Thus, on several occasions, Saro-Wiwa turned to his friend the well-known British novelist William Boyd for counsel about receptive NGOs to contact. In 1990, he won a trip to America, sponsored by the United States Information Agency, based on his achievements in fiction and nonfiction writing. During this visit, his host organization, the African-American Institute, set up meetings with groups he thought useful to the movement, including environmental organizations and oil companies.[31]

Finally, knowledge was critical to MOSOP's success at raising awareness overseas. MOSOP's top ranks were filled with public relations experts, lawyers, and politicians. Saro-Wiwa's own talents spanned his fluent and forceful command of English, his broad understanding of the NGO and media scene, and his experience in advertising, television, and journalism. Although Nigerian ways were not always appropriate abroad, on balance Saro-Wiwa's experience helped. Saro-Wiwa had great faith in public relations, remarking in 1990 that Nigeria's abysmal image was just "lousy PR" by the government.[32] In the Ogoni campaign, he constantly used his prior knowledge of "how to promote an idea or a product." According to

---

[29] See Wiwa, *Shadow of a Saint*.

[30] Interviewee 35 (British Broadcasting Company reporter), telephone interview by author, July 25, 1996.

[31] Saro-Wiwa, *A Month and a Day*, 88; United States Information Agency, International Visitor Program, "Mr. Ken Saro-Wiwa: National Itinerary," n.d.

[32] William Boyd, "Smile on the Face of the Niger," *Times* (London), December 15, 1990, http://www.lexis-nexis.com/ (accessed August 2, 2004).

Saro-Wiwa's son, Ken Wiwa, even his father's trademark pipe was meant to leave a "lasting image" in his audience's mind.[33]

Notably, in promoting the Ogoni overseas, Saro-Wiwa was the dynamic, central actor. During the early 1990s, he followed a dizzying schedule of trips between Europe, North America, and Nigeria. He was MOSOP's primary international link, adept in politicking both at home and abroad. Indeed, for most NGOs, he came to embody the movement. In retrospective interviews with NGO staff, most recalled him as a magnetic personality single-mindedly dedicated to the Ogoni cause. Although it is difficult to compare these qualities with those of other minority leaders, there is ample evidence of Saro-Wiwa's peculiar gifts. Foreign NGO staff have characterized no other Niger Delta leader in the same admiring terms. Saro-Wiwa's earlier success in Nigerian television, journalism, and letters was unique. And, paying tribute to his skills, other Niger Delta minorities eagerly sought his advice on how to further their own movements.

One illustration of the advantages Saro-Wiwa gave the Ogoni came in 1992, when the ethnic groups on the Delta were presented with an unprecedented opportunity to reach a national audience in the United Kingdom. An independent television production team commissioned by the British Channel Four network traveled to the Delta to shoot the Nigeria segment of a documentary concerning multinational oil operations in developing countries. The filmmakers, Glen Ellis and Kay Bishop, planned that the report would examine the Nigerian Mobile Police Force's October 1991 massacre of 80 ethnic Etche villagers peacefully protesting Shell operations in the village of Umuechem near Ogoni territory.[34] Prior to their visit to Nigeria, the filmmakers had not known of the Ogoni and had intended to focus their work on the Etche. Once Ellis and Bishop began background work in Port Harcourt, however, they quickly learned of Saro-Wiwa, who, with his English fluency and media talents, was "the most articulate spokesperson for any of the ethnic groups on the Delta at odds with Shell."[35] As a result, although the Etche appeared in the documentary, Saro-Wiwa featured

---

[33] Saro-Wiwa, *A Month and a Day*, 138–39, 58–59, 65, 118, 147, 152; Wiwa, *Shadow of a Saint*, 69.

[34] Nigeria, Rivers State, "Judicial Commission of Inquiry into Umuechem Disturbances Under the Chairmanship of Hon. Justice Opubo Inko-Tariah (Rtd.)," January 1991; Anyakwee Nsirimovu, *The Massacre of an Oil Producing Community: The Umuechem Tragedy Revisited* (Port Harcourt, Nigeria: Institute of Human Rights and Humanitarian Law, 1994).

[35] Interviewee 5 (filmmaker and Greenpeace International consultant), telephone interview by author, June 25, 1996.

prominently, and the Ogoni benefited most when *The Heat of the Moment* was screened in October 1992.

However, although broadcast of the film and MOSOP's previous promotional efforts raised the Ogoni's profile, MOSOP won few allies prior to January 1993, even among NGOs that might have been expected to back its cause. Saro-Wiwa, in "cavernous despair" that the Ogoni were "destined for extinction," lamented that he was "knocking on closed doors."[36] Why did major NGOs reject MOSOP's appeals at this time? Most importantly, the Ogoni cause as framed by MOSOP early in the campaign did not fit with the central missions of the NGOs. In addition, Ogoni pleas included too little evidence to substantiate their claims. In late 1991 and early 1992, MOSOP unsuccessfully sought assistance from environmental NGOs, including most prominently Greenpeace International and Friends of the Earth. Saro-Wiwa's interpretation of these rebuffs – the unfamiliar nature of the Ogoni problem – partially explains his failures. In approaching Greenpeace and Friends of the Earth, Saro-Wiwa discussed the Ogoni's environmental problems and Shell's role but also filled his presentations with the pressing political, economic, and cultural issues the group faced as a tiny minority within Nigeria. The federal government's dishonesty and the other ethnic groups' greed were particular concerns, as were the resulting poverty and underdevelopment of his people. As a solution, MOSOP's autonomy claim took center stage. In short, in its early NGO appeals, MOSOP presented its case in much the same terms it used in Nigeria. As a result, the Ogoni cause did not appear to fit the agendas of gatekeeper environmental NGOs based in the developed world.

In the case of Greenpeace, the rejection of MOSOP was a close and controversial decision pitting a few staffpeople moved by Saro-Wiwa's appeals against the NGO's leadership.[37] At the time, one of Greenpeace's four main campaigns focused on the environmental impacts of petroleum exploration and consumption, with a particular focus on the role of the world's largest multinational oil companies. Staff members in its "Oil Campaign" saw the Ogoni case as a potential symbol of multinationals' environmental

---

[36] Saro-Wiwa, *A Month and a Day*, 88–89.

[37] Sources for the information in this paragraph include Interviewee 1 (Greenpeace International communications officer), telephone interview by author, July 24, 1996; Interviewee 6 (Greenpeace International staffperson), telephone interview by author, July 16, 1996; Interviewee 9 (Greenpeace International staffperson), personal interview by author, July 14, 1996; Interviewee 14 (Greenpeace International consultant), telephone interviews by author, June 26, 1996 and July 24, 1996.

crimes in the developing world. But Greenpeace management was reluctant to become involved for several reasons. First, the organization had never previously worked in West Africa and had no Nigerian affiliate. Compounding its unfamiliarity with the region was the complexity of the Ogoni grievances and their overt ethnic nature. Because of the controversial "political" aspects of the Ogoni autonomy claim, management feared that aiding MOSOP would open Greenpeace to charges of "play[ing] the colonial role" in a developing nation.[38] Also weighing against MOSOP was Greenpeace's standard campaign method. Far from endorsing other organizations, Greenpeace typically made itself the center of attention by dramatically bearing witness to an environmental problem. Finally, Greenpeace managers feared that involvement would take scarce resources away from more tractable issues in the developed world. For those in a decision-making position in Greenpeace, aiding the Ogoni seemed to require significant time and personnel. In addition, such a commitment would require a long-term public education campaign quite unlike Greenpeace's more typical tactics, brief media-oriented actions designed to focus public attention on a discrete problem. Greenpeace managers permitted a few of their "Oil Campaign" staff to work with the Ogoni "on their own time" but refused to put the organization's name behind MOSOP in 1991.[39]

Amnesty International experienced no comparable dissent but found other reasons for rejecting Saro-Wiwa's appeals. Amnesty's mandate at the time was the prevention of a limited set of well-defined human rights abuses, most involving physical violence against individuals. As of MOSOP's initial contacts with Amnesty in 1991, such violations were not directed at the Ogoni, although they were occurring elsewhere in Nigeria. As an Amnesty staffperson told Saro-Wiwa, the NGO could not act because no Ogoni had been killed or jailed.[40] MOSOP leaders sought to convince Amnesty that the Ogoni were victims of genocide, but their definitions of the term were shifting and loose. Sometimes the Ogoni highlighted cultural "extinction" of the Ogoni people as a result of the state's neglect of Ogoni languages. At other times, claims of genocide hinged on the human health impacts of chronic environmental problems. These broad interpretations fell outside Amnesty's far stricter definitions. As Saro-Wiwa concluded, Amnesty was

---

[38] Interviewee 1 (Greenpeace International communications officer), July 24, 1996.

[39] Interviewee 6 (Greenpeace International staffperson), July 16, 1996.

[40] Information and quotations in this paragraph are from Saro-Wiwa, *A Month and a Day*, 88–89, and Interviewee 20 (Amnesty International staffperson), personal interview by author, July 17, 1996.

only interested in "conventional killings," whereas the Ogoni were being destroyed "in an unconventional way."[41]

For Survival International, different reasons explain their rejection of Saro-Wiwa's personal pleas. Like Greenpeace, Survival was unfamiliar with Nigeria. In addition, the apparent Ogoni advantage of having a sophisticated and urbane leader backfired given Survival's organizational culture. Ken Saro-Wiwa's 1992 visit to Survival's London office, accompanied by film producer Glen Ellis, was a fiasco – ironically because it convinced the organization's intake staff that the Ogoni had "their publicity in order" and therefore did not need help.[42] From Survival's perspective, the Ogoni appeared too advanced and insufficiently needy. They were very different from the NGO's usual clients, smaller, more remote groups with "minimal savoir-faire." According to the Survival International staff member who met Saro-Wiwa, "This is a comparative issue – many groups we deal with are completely lacking in media contacts.... This was not the case with Saro-Wiwa. Therefore, we decided that the Ogoni should not be a priority for us." MOSOP also received a skeptical reception from sectors of the international indigenous rights movement, which initially believed that the Ogoni could not be "indigenous" because they were not ruled by a white settler population remaining from the colonial period. In mid-1992, for instance, one Scandinavian NGO conditioned possible assistance on MOSOP's preparing an essay proving that the Ogoni met the internationally accepted definition of "indigenous."[43]

Organizational considerations also motivated NGO rebuffs. Critical to an NGO's decision about adopting a distant movement is independent verification of its claims and legitimacy. Yet when MOSOP contacted the NGOs during 1991–92, it presented little evidence to allay these concerns. Until early 1993, MOSOP conducted few public activities and no demonstrations in Nigeria, and the Nigerian government continued to ignore the group. One NGO staff member recalled Saro-Wiwa's accounts of Shell's "genocide" against the Ogoni as "sound[ing] a bit farfetched."[44] Another,

---

[41] Saro-Wiwa, *A Month and a Day*, 88–89.
[42] This and subsequent quotations concerning this meeting are from Interviewee 10 (Survival International staffperson), telephone interview by author, June 18, 1996; additional background information is from my personal meeting with this interviewee on July 22, 1996.
[43] Naanen, *Effective Nonviolent Struggle*, 23–24.
[44] Interviewee 3 (Unrepresented Nations and Peoples Organization (UNPO) staffperson), personal interview by author, July 18, 1996.

a staffperson at Friends of the Earth–Netherlands, also saw problems in Saro-Wiwa's initial presentation of the issues. "From the very beginning, Ken came here with this huge story about what was happening and nothing was written on paper, nothing was very factual, no research had been done at this moment. Everything was, if I had to believe him, . . . his own word. This is what happened. I sat down with him for a day and got all his stories out of him. He was a good story teller anyway. . . . It was very clear to him that probably I would believe him but that the rest of the Western world would never believe him if there was nothing on paper and nothing verified by independent sources."[45]

Equally troubling to this staff member and other NGO staff was the question of Saro-Wiwa's bona fides. Who were the Ogoni? Who was Saro-Wiwa? And did he in fact have constituents in Nigeria?

If somebody says he's representing the Ogoni, well everybody can. If you go to Nigeria, there will probably be a hell of a lot of government agents saying they represent MOSOP. So I had to verify all [Saro-Wiwa's] accounts of things, [using] personal contacts; Friends of the Earth in Ghana; journalists; researchers who I knew; people traveling through Africa, people I could trust; a couple environmentally aware people in Port Harcourt and Lagos, who I knew or heard of through the grapevine; . . . embassy people; even friendly people in Shell, on the ground people. That's very much how it goes; how I can sometimes not take up a case, because I don't have the information – *if* I don't have the information. Information is the bottom line. If you don't have a grasp politically of what's going on, then you don't know what you're going into.[46]

Without evidence or a well-known and reliable source vouching for the Ogoni, Saro-Wiwa's entreaties failed to persuade major environmental NGOs to lend their name, reputation, and resources to the Ogoni cause. Greenpeace and Friends of the Earth staff suggested ways for the Ogoni to bolster their cause – by developing proof of environmental pollution and MOSOP's mass base – but neither NGO threw its weight behind MOSOP until 1993.

Thus, at the start of its international campaign, MOSOP underestimated the documentation a major NGO would demand before adopting an unknown organization claiming to represent an obscure ethnic group making controversial claims against powerful foes. In retrospect, Saro-Wiwa's

---

[45] Interviewee 2 (Friends of the Earth International staffperson), personal interview by author, July 17, 1996.
[46] Ibid.

The Growth of NGO Support, January–June 1993

In 1993, MOSOP's limited NGO backing began to expand. This groundswell developed against a backdrop of domestic Ogoni activism and government suppression. The first half of 1993 was marked by growing tension and uncertainty preceding the country's first national election in ten years, scheduled for June 12. Anticipating the transition from military rule, leading Nigerian politicians demanded a Constitutional Convention to secure the civil and political rights that would establish a stable foundation for democracy. Less prominently, the Ogoni and other Delta minorities argued that these calls were premature. Before discussing "political" issues at a Constitutional Convention, they contended, the country must hold a National Convention aimed at rethinking the Nigerian federation, particularly the rights and responsibilities of its component ethnic groups.[54]

At home, MOSOP mobilized its constituents, beginning with the Ogoni Day march on January 4, 1993. During the following months, Ogoni leaders built on the march's success with a series of smaller actions. In February, Saro-Wiwa opened the One Naira Ogoni Survival Fund, seeking monetary contributions from every Ogoni. In March, MOSOP held a candlelight vigil, in coordination with the region's Christian churches, calling for deliverance from the multinational oil companies and the country's oppressive rulers. In late April and May, the movement publicized local rallies against a Shell contractor near Biara. Between these actions, MOSOP encouraged mass involvement through frequent, sometimes weekly, meetings of its component organizations. Finally, at Saro-Wiwa's insistence, MOSOP bucked the Nigerian democracy movement and boycotted the June election because it presupposed the legitimacy of the Nigerian federation.[55]

MOSOP's activities brought increasingly strong reactions from the state, especially after other Delta minorities began organizing and issuing their own proclamations modeled on the *Ogoni Bill of Rights*.[56] Although

---

[54] Peter Ishaka, "The Minorities' Agenda: A New Minorities' Consensus Sets High Stakes for the Presidential Election," *Tell* (Lagos), April 27, 1992, 12–15.

[55] Saro-Wiwa, *A Month and a Day*, 175–84; Naanen, *Effective Nonviolent Struggle*, 34–35; Tayo Lukula, "Ogonis Boycott Election," *Guardian on Sunday* (Lagos), June 13, 1993, A6; "Ogonis Boycott," *Sunday Sketch* (Ibadan), June 13, 1993, n.p.

[56] Nembe Creek Oil Field Community, *Letter to the Head of State*; N. B. C. Ineneji, "Urhobos and the National Question – A Call to Duty," Advertisement, *Guardian on Sunday* (Lagos), May 30, 1993, A12. Other similar declarations include the *Izon People's Charter* by the Movement for the Survival of the Izon (Ijaw) Ethnic Nationality in the Niger Delta (MOSIEND) and the *Charter of Demands of the Ogbia People*, by the Movement for the Reparation to Ogbia

---

NGO contacts attributed this mistake to different cultural practices in Nigeria. As one Greenpeace employee stated, "I wanted pictures, factual proof. If we have this material, we can get much more attention. But we did not get them because eyewitness oral reports have the same value as photographs in Nigerian culture. I always wished there would be more photos. But I understand the different cultural values."[47] When NGO staff directly questioned Saro-Wiwa about apparent hyperbole in his stories, his replies seemed to confirm this interpretation. To be noticed in Nigeria, he said, required exaggeration: "'If it was only six killed you couldn't get attention; it has to be 16.'"[48] For NGOs, on the other hand, accuracy is critical to maintaining public trust. This is particularly true for human rights NGOs, whose body counts and lists of victims are detailed and explicit. Even in the case of environmental NGOs, where there is often more room for prediction and speculation, reliable data are important, especially in battles for credibility played out in the media.

Explaining Ogoni failures with these seemingly natural NGO allies were the realities of power and powerlessness in the transnational realm. MOSOP's need for aid was great. It was a newly founded organization representing a small and impoverished minority group. Its grievances were many, its goals sweeping. Its opponents were a robust, dictatorial state and one of the world's largest corporations. And its potential domestic allies were unresponsive, even hostile. Not surprisingly, then, MOSOP sought the most valuable NGOs it could reach, among them major environmental and human rights gatekeepers. On their face, these organizations, with their political or moral agendas, appeared to be promising prospects. Yet, having limited resources and other pressing issues more closely fitting their missions, the NGOs had little need to boost the Ogoni. From the standpoint of the NGOs, the Ogoni also had low value. Prior to MOSOP's lobbying, the Niger Delta had garnered scanty media attention and its problems were little-known abroad. Moreover, in MOSOP's presentation of the issues, the conflict appeared to fit awkwardly with the NGOs' core agendas. For the NGOs, supporting a fledgling movement mired in a poorly understood but seemingly complex conflict also held significant risks, which MOSOP's muddy and unsubstantiated presentation of the issues did little to assuage. In this highly unequal power dynamic, the major NGOs turned

---

[47] Interviewee 6 (Greenpeace International staffperson), July 16, 1996.

[48] Interviewee 3 (UNPO staffperson), July 18, 1996. See also Interviewee 2 (Friends of the Earth International staffperson), July 17, 1996.

down MOSOP's appeals. This is not to say that the NGOs acted in unprincipled fashion. Rather, given their own needs and existing commitments, they quite rationally undertook a difficult moral triage that left the Ogoni isolated.

MOSOP's sole success during this period, with the Unrepresented Nations and Peoples Organization (UNPO), a small, recently founded, and low-profile NGO, underscores these points. Based in The Hague, UNPO has about 50 members comprised of "nations and peoples" who believe themselves to be unrepresented in international affairs.[49] Its members include organizations representing Australian aborigines, Chechens, Hawaiians, Lakota Indians, Taiwanese, and Tibetans. UNPO's primary mission is to help its members gain a "voice" in the international sphere. Depending on the member, this goal might be realized by participating in United Nations bodies and international conferences, gaining recognition of ethnic or indigenous rights within states, or winning outright independence (in which case UNPO membership lapses). To help its members reach their goals, UNPO provides assistance and training on such issues as international law, international organizations, diplomacy, and media relations. Established in 1991 with a grant from Doug Tompkins, founder of Esprit clothes and member of the Deep Ecology movement, UNPO is funded by member contributions and donations from corporations, foundations, and governmental entities.[50] Its small staff is entirely volunteer. In size, reach, and clout, UNPO pales by comparison with the major NGOs that had rejected MOSOP earlier. Its support nonetheless proved important to the Ogoni's later networking.

Saro-Wiwa first met UNPO's Secretary General, Michael van Walt von Praag, at the United Nations Working Group on Indigenous Populations

49 Information in this paragraph is from Unrepresented Nations and Peoples Organization, "About UNPO," http://www.unpo.org/news_detail.php?arg=01 & par=153 (accessed August 3, 2004); Unrepresented Nations and Peoples Organization, "The First Three Years," n.d. [1994?], Gumberg Library; Barbara Crossette, "Those Knocking, Unheeded, at U.N.'s Doors Find Champion," *New York Times*, December 18, 1994, Section 1, page 21. Additional information is from my interviews with UNPO staff in July 1996.

50 Cynthia Osterman, "Unrepresented Peoples Plan to Set Up Alternative U.N.," *Reuter Library Report*, February 4, 1991, http://web.lexis-nexis.com (accessed August 2, 2004). Among organizations that helped fund UNPO's Fourth General Assembly were Apple Computer Benelux B.V., European Human Rights Foundation, Interchurch Organization for International Development Cooperation, the City of The Hague, and the Royal Foreign Ministry of Norway. Unrepresented Nations and Peoples Organization, "General Assembly IV: Summary Report and Documentation, UNPO's 4th General Assembly, January 20–26, 1995, The Hague, The Netherlands," March 15, 1995, iii, Gumberg Library.

(UNWGIP) in Geneva in the summer of 1992. Impressed by Saro-Wiwa's speech, von Praag quickly offered MOSOP help in making its case there. By January 1993, UNPO had admitted MOSOP to membership and elected Saro-Wiwa Vice Chairman of the organization's General Assembly. In subsequent months and years, UNPO provided MOSOP with critical and wide-ranging support. Why did MOSOP succeed with UNPO when it failed with other NGOs? First, there was a substantial overlap of goals and interests. MOSOP's quest for political autonomy fit easily with UNPO's mandate. For UNPO, the existence of other issues – environmental and human rights – raised no red flags. Indeed, as one UNPO principal stated, "Almost typically, the suppression of a people is very linked to . . . exploitation of the natural environment."[51] MOSOP's peaceful organizing in Nigeria also meshed with UNPO's requirement that its members be nonviolent.

UNPO staff had initial questions about MOSOP's legitimacy and proof of its claims. But when MOSOP submitted its written application for membership, the Ogoni were admitted in record time. A key reason was an organizational balance of power: Both UNPO and MOSOP were young and unknown organizations, unlike the major NGOs that MOSOP had approached earlier. They shared similar organizational needs, increased name recognition and patronage, creating incentives for cooperation and exchange. As one UNPO staff member described it: "This was the beginning of a relationship between UNPO, Ken and MOSOP. What was agreed was that UNPO would become the distribution point for information coming out of Nigeria. It was a mutually advantageous agreement because what it meant was that UNPO could build its reputation for releasing information first from an area, at the same time that MOSOP could know they had to send it to one place and then it was internationally distributed. And communications with Nigeria were difficult at the best of times."[52] As Saro-Wiwa affirmed, "How could we make contact with the outside world without [UNPO]?"[53] Notably, however, UNPO's embrace of MOSOP did not extend to other groups in the Delta. Its many actions benefited the Ogoni directly but the other Niger Delta minorities only indirectly in the form of increased overseas attention to the region.

51 Interviewee 13 (UNPO manager), personal interview by author, July 11, 1996.
52 Interviewee 3 (UNPO staffperson), July 18, 1996.
53 Guido de Bruin, "Human Rights: Unrepresented Peoples' Forum 'Coming of [...], Press Service, February 5, 1993, http://www.lexis-nexis.com/ (accessed Augus[...]

government officials met with MOSOP leaders on January 9 and May 13, 1993, coercion grew in the spring. On April 3, Saro-Wiwa was detained and "deported" from a neighboring state, Delta, where he had been scheduled to address a gathering of students from another oil-producing minority. On April 18 and April 23, Saro-Wiwa was taken into custody again, each time for several hours. On April 30, 11 Ogoni were injured when government forces opened fire on a peaceful local protest against a Shell contractor in Biara. Then, on May 6, the Babangida regime announced the "Treason and Treasonable Offences Decree," making it a capital offense for Nigerians to "conspire with groups within or outside the country, and profess ideas that minimise the sovereignty of Nigeria."[57] Although the decree was so vague and broad that it threatened all forms of political expression, one of its chief targets was the MOSOP leadership.[58] On June 14, 1993, the Nigerian authorities confiscated Saro-Wiwa's passport as he was about to fly to Vienna to address the U.N.-sponsored World Conference on Human Rights. Finally, on June 20, the government jailed Saro-Wiwa and two other MOSOP leaders, sparking Ogoni riots in the town of Bori.[59]

Internationally, support for MOSOP mushroomed during this period, starting slowly in early 1993 and then expanding rapidly by the middle of the year. First, environmental organizations, including several that had previously rejected Ogoni pleas, came to MOSOP's aid. Greenpeace International and Friends of the Earth International became active, particularly in Europe and North America. By summer, Greenpeace staff had begun working so closely with the Ogoni that MOSOP press releases referred those seeking further information both to the NGO's communications

---

(MORETO). Other Niger Delta ethnic groups that organized protests around this time included the Ikwerre, Igbide, Irri, and Uzere. See Human Rights Watch/Africa, "Nigeria: The Ogoni Crisis: A Case-Study of Military Repression in Southeastern Nigeria," *Human Rights Watch/Africa Report* 7, no. 5 (July 1995): 33.

[57] Camillus Eboh, "Demand for Ethnic Autonomy Now Treason," *Guardian* (Lagos), May 7, 1993. The decree was not officially published and was "set aside," though not rescinded, on May 22, 1993, after broad public criticism. See Claude E. Welch, Jr., *Protecting Human Rights in Africa: Strategies and Roles of Non-Governmental Organizations* (Philadelphia: University of Pennsylvania Press, 1995), 250–51.

[58] Okey Ekeocha, "A Cry for Justice – Or Drum Beats of Treason?" *African Guardian*, May 17, 1993, 21.

[59] For a more complete account of state actions against the Ogoni during this period, see Civil Liberties Organisation, *Ogoni: Trials and Travails* (Lagos, Nigeria: Civil Liberties Organisation, 1996); Human Rights Watch/Africa, "Ogoni Crisis"; Claude E. Welch, Jr. and Marc Sills, "The Martyrdom of Ken Saro-Wiwa and the Future of Ogoni Self-Determination," *Fourth World Bulletin* 5, nos. 1–2 (1996): 5–16.

office in London and to UNPO.[60] At Friends of the Earth's Amsterdam office, a staffperson became one of the central figures in the Ogoni's international network. By mid-1993, other environmental groups, such as the U.S.-based Sierra Club and Rainforest Action Network, began aiding the Ogoni, and the "campaigning corporation" The Body Shop made the Ogoni a major cause, eventually underwriting MOSOP-United Kingdom's London office.[61] Beginning in 1993, human rights NGOs also issued lengthy reports documenting the violations, designated MOSOP leaders "prisoners of conscience," and lobbied their home governments for action against Nigeria. With a growing awareness of the conflict thanks to increasing NGO and media interest and with UNPO taking care of administrative details, Saro-Wiwa was able to meet foreign ministry officials in the Netherlands, Switzerland, and the United Kingdom as well as officials at the United Nations Human Rights Commission and the International Commission of Jurists.[62]

What explains this broadening and deepening in MOSOP's support? Three factors were critical: MOSOP's strategic deployment of an environmental frame demonizing Shell, its demonstration of organizational legitimacy, and the rise of serious state-sponsored human rights abuses.

The Environmental Frame

The new frame had its intellectual roots as early as December 1990, when Saro-Wiwa, traveling on a United States Information Agency program, visited an environmental group in Colorado that impressed him with its lobbying of government and businesses. For decades, Shell's operations had concerned the Ogoni community on environmental and economic grounds, but Saro-Wiwa's trip to the United States suggested to him that ecology should be a "strong plank" in his burgeoning movement.[63] MOSOP's early approaches to major NGOs had combined such grievances with the group's

---

[60] MOSOP, "Shell's Genocide Against Ogoni People," Briefing Note, August 1993, Gumberg Library.

[61] Interviewee 11 (MOSOP-UK leader), personal interview by author, July 23, 1996.

[62] Saro-Wiwa, *A Month and a Day*, 174; Naanen, *Effective Nonviolent Action*, 18–33. Many other NGOs in Europe and North America also played important roles in the Ogoni support network. I focus on these particular NGOs because they were the Ogoni's earliest and most prominent supporters and because their pioneering actions set the stage for broader NGO support.

[63] Saro-Wiwa, *A Month and a Day*, 80.

minority rights focus. By mid-1992, however, MOSOP began highlighting ecological issues and playing the "Shell card" to demonstrate "what a demon [the] model corporate citizen was" in Nigeria.[64] MOSOP never abandoned its earlier political claims, but for foreign audiences the new stress overshadowed the *Ogoni Bill of Rights'* core demand for autonomy. In turn, media and NGO interest in Shell's record encouraged the Ogoni to further emphasize environmental and corporate malfeasance issues.

A first example of this dynamic occurred in the summer of 1992 at the United Nations Working Group on Indigenous Populations (UNWGIP), a low-level United Nations organization where Saro-Wiwa gave a fiery speech denouncing the "disaster" created by oil company operations. Reversing the logic of Ogoni demands over past decades, Saro-Wiwa stated: "Incidental to and indeed compounding this ecological devastation is the political marginalization and complete oppression of the Ogoni and especially the denial of their rights, including land rights."[65] International media coverage was limited to only a single Reuters report. But this story magnified MOSOP's reframing, highlighting Saro-Wiwa's charges that "environmental degradation" was a "lethal weapon in the war against" the Ogoni. Exaggerating this focus, the story omitted the issues of political rights and oil revenue allocation discussed at length in Saro-Wiwa's speech.[66] In later media coverage and NGO promotion, the pattern recurred: MOSOP sharpened its appeal by stressing issues of environmental degradation and Shell's villainy. NGOs and journalists unversed in Nigerian politics seized on these familiar, seemingly clear-cut issues and downplayed the minority rights issues.

Another example of this dynamic began on October 8, 1992, with the British television broadcast of the Channel Four documentary *The Heat of the Moment*, which highlighted the evils of oil company activity in Nigeria. That day, the *Guardian*, a British national newspaper, ran a companion article focusing on Shell's responsibility for the Umuechem massacre and mistakenly identifying the victims as Ogoni.[67] Adding to the attention

---

[64] Naanen, *Effective Nonviolent Struggle*, 30.

[65] Ken Saro-Wiwa, "Statement of the Ogoni People to the Tenth Session of the Working Group on Indigenous Populations, Palais des Nations, Geneva, July 1992," July 28, 1992, Gumberg Library.

[66] Robert Evans, "Australian, Nigerian Minorities Seek U.N. Support," *Reuter Library Report*, July 30, 1992, http://www.lexis-nexis.com/ (accessed August 2, 2004).

[67] Paul Brown, "80 Nigerians Killed in Shell Oil Protest; Cover-up Charge as Villagers Demand Compensation," *Guardian* (London), October 8, 1992, 10.

generated by these media reports, Shell publicly defended its record in a press release aiming "to set the record straight."[68] The media reports and Shell's counterattacks drew the attention of several small but dynamic organizations in the English environmental community: the London Rainforest Action Group, the Oxford Rainforest Network, Earth First!, and Reclaim the Streets. Through personal ties to filmmaker Glen Ellis, key activists met Saro-Wiwa in the fall of 1992. During these encounters, Saro-Wiwa sparked further commitment with his personal charm and vivid portrayals of Shell's environmental crimes. On November 24, 1992, a handful of activists demonstrated at Shell's London office, threatening an international campaign unless Shell agreed to compensate local communities for the impacts of its operations on the Delta.[69]

To build on this modest but unprecedented overseas interest, MOSOP quickly developed several new strategies. Two days after the Channel Four documentary, Saro-Wiwa met with another MOSOP official to plan a mass action in the Ogoni heartland on January 4, 1993. To be coordinated with the start of the United Nations' International Year of the World's Indigenous People, the event would be called Ogoni Day. MOSOP took several steps to increase Ogoni Day's impact at home and abroad. First, it strengthened ties between the leadership and grassroots groups, with Saro-Wiwa and others making frequent visits to Ogoni villages starting in mid-November. The march would be the first regionwide protest in Ogoni history, and MOSOP relied on the local community organizations under its umbrella to make it succeed. In addition, MOSOP appointed six march coordinators for each Ogoni kingdom and four for each village. To build mass excitement and solidarity, movement leaders frequently used the Ogoni anthem, "Arise, Arise Ogoni People," written years before by Saro-Wiwa.[70]

Second, on December 3, 1992, MOSOP sent letters to Shell, Chevron, and the NNPC giving them 30 days to cease operations in Ogoni territory unless they met three demands: $10 billion in royalties and reparations for the companies' 30 years of operation there; a halt to environmental

[68] Shell International Petroleum Company, Group Public Affairs, '*The Heat of the Moment*', Information Brief (London: Shell International Petroleum Company, October 1992), 1.

[69] London Rainforest Action Group to Richard Tookey, Head of Public Affairs, Shell Petroleum Company, November 24, 1992, Gumberg Library.

[70] Saro-Wiwa, *A Month and a Day*, 102–17, 129.

destruction; and immediate negotiations over continued production.[71] Timed to expire just before the January 1993 demonstration, the demands added drama to grassroots preparations for Ogoni Day. They also had important strategic purposes outside Nigeria, attracting the interest of environmental NGOs. Flying to England in mid-December 1992, Saro-Wiwa lobbied environmental groups to send observers to the march, which he touted would attract 300,000 protesters. Shelley Braithwaite, an activist from the small London Rainforest Action Group, readily agreed to travel as Saro-Wiwa's guest. Saro-Wiwa had more difficulty convincing Greenpeace, where some argued again that the NGO had never acted as a mere observer to another organization's protests. Ultimately, however, "Oil Campaign" staff convinced managers to make a minimal commitment, sending a lone photographer, Tim Lambon.[72]

Ogoni Day was a watershed event marking the public unveiling of a major local social movement. Although the number of marchers is uncertain – Nigerian media estimates ranged from 100,000 to 500,000 – there is no doubt that this was the largest mobilization ever in Ogoni territory.[73] MOSOP's groundwork kept the march peaceful and fixed on internationally resonant issues. Protesters carried twigs as a symbol of environmental issues and English-language banners attacking Shell and proclaiming the group an indigenous people. Aware of the impact of visual images, MOSOP hired its own video team and escorted the Greenpeace photographer to pollution hot spots. Saro-Wiwa's speech at the main rally in the Ogoni capital of Bori capped the day by declaring Shell persona non grata in Ogoniland and urging other Delta minorities to rise up to fight for their rights. Although Ogoni Day garnered no contemporaneous media coverage outside

---

[71] MOSOP to Managing Director, Shell Petroleum Development Company of Nigeria, November 30, 1992, Gumberg Library; MOSOP, "Ogoni People Give Notice to Oil Companies," Press Release, December 1, 1992, Gumberg Library.

[72] Interviewee 4 (Rainforest Action Group activist), personal interview by author, July 19, 1996; Interviewee 9 (Greenpeace International staffperson), July 14, 1996.

[73] Two Nigerian newspaper accounts give a figure of 500,000 marchers, although the reliability of these estimates is questionable. Cyril Bakwuye, "Ogonis Protest Over Oil Revenue: Want Self Determination," *Daily Sunray* (Port Harcourt), January 6, 1993, [1?]; Kenneth Ezea, "Day Ogonis Cried for Reprieve," *Guardian on Sunday* (Lagos), January 17, 1993, A13. A third Nigerian periodical estimated 100,000 participants. "Exploitation: Stung by Alleged Neglect, Ogoni Community Takes Case to UN, Fights for Reparation and Control of Oil," *Newswatch* (Lagos), January 25, 1993, 9. None of these sources indicate the method used in estimating crowd size.

Nigeria, Saro-Wiwa screened the videotapes at the UNPO General Assembly in The Hague at the end of January. Just as important, his speeches attacking Shell won him notice in the Netherlands, Shell's home country. Attracted by the controversy, *CNN International* and *Time* also reported on the Ogoni's conflict with the oil company in late January 1993.

The emerging environmental frame had several aspects, all rooted in Ogoniland's serious and long-standing problems. One set of accusations concerned Shell's dirty and substandard operations in the Delta. In press releases, articles, books, and reports, MOSOP accused Shell of ravaging the Niger Delta through air, water, and noise pollution. Photographs of huge gas flares in the midst of Ogoni villages and oil blowouts coating farmlands in mucky crude all lent credence to a damning portrait: one of the world's richest corporations despoiling the pristine environment of an impoverished community. While continuing to call their ethnic group "indigenous," MOSOP used the term as much to highlight the Ogoni's assumed links to nature as to establish a basis for political rights. In Saro-Wiwa's words, Ogoni culture promotes a "deep awareness of the importance of the environment and the necessity to protect and preserve it."[74] Most pointedly, MOSOP accused Shell of double standards, showcasing clean facilities in the First World to cover antiquated, inferior, and dangerous operations in the Delta. As one MOSOP activist asserted, average life expectancies for those born in Ogoniland had fallen to 47 years, ten years below even Nigeria's already-low standard.[75] These accusations raised another potent line of attack, Shell's environmental racism, its operational practice that "what is good for the whites must not be good for blacks."[76] Finally, MOSOP internationalized the Delta's environmental problems, arguing that gas flaring contributed to global warming and that the international community – both Shell shareholders in America, Europe, and Japan and buyers of the Ogoni's "stolen property" – bore responsibility for the group's suffering.[77]

Accusations about the company's collusion with Nigeria's military dictators also leaped to the fore. Reversing the logic of the *Ogoni Bill of Rights*,

---

[74] Saro-Wiwa, *Genocide in Nigeria*, 14. See also, for example, Saro-Wiwa, *A Month and a Day*, 169.

[75] Interviewee 23 (MOSOP-USA leader), personal discussion with author, St. Louis, MO, March 14, 1998.

[76] Saro-Wiwa, *Genocide in Nigeria*, 82. See also, for example, Saro-Wiwa, *A Month and a Day*, 166, 170.

[77] Saro-Wiwa, *Genocide in Nigeria*, 8.

which called on the state to regulate oil company activities, MOSOP emphasized Shell's overweening power, its tight linkages to the Nigerian government, and its assumed ability to control the military dictators.[78] Stories about Shell's shipments of guns to Nigeria, its employment of private security services, and its summoning of notoriously violent Nigerian military forces to quell protests all cast Shell as a malignant force, not merely a negligent business. Of particular importance is that MOSOP sought to portray Shell as being responsible for Ogoni deaths and injuries in protests at oil facilities. Beginning in mid-1993, a sharp rise in state violence furnished an evidentiary basis for such charges. As an MOSOP principal stated in a public meeting on "Human Rights and Environmental Justice" in Nigeria, Shell was involved in "exploitation without responsibility, terrorism, and armed repression."[79]

With the abuses drawing greater media attention and with MOSOP loudly condemning Shell, environmental NGOs began to show interest in the conflict. Where previously the Niger Delta's problems had seemed complex, parochial, and distant to the NGOs, the new Ogoni frame made the issues appear more understandable and relevant. For one thing, framing the dispute around Shell created a connection between the Ogoni in the Delta and grassroots environmentalists in the developed world. Greenpeace, although still worried about some of the issues that had earlier kept it from supporting MOSOP, now backed the Ogoni. As one of its key contributions, the NGO began work on a report, *Shell-Shocked: The Environmental and Social Costs of Living with Shell in Nigeria*, ultimately issued in 1994. A consultant on the report described his close work with Saro-Wiwa as a "symbiotic relationship": MOSOP sent Greenpeace information on Shell's local operations and human rights violations, and Greenpeace publicized the Ogoni cause as part of its broader Oil Campaign.[80] In this exchange, Greenpeace also provided MOSOP with health and safety information on petroleum pollution to influence the Nigerian debate on Ogoni demands. Similarly, other environmental groups were attracted to the Ogoni not only because of the seriousness of the issues in the Niger Delta but also because of the group's usefulness as a symbol of wider conflicts with multinational corporations. As a Sierra Club manager acknowledged, "We wanted to hold

---

[78] Saro-Wiwa, *A Month and a Day*, 193.
[79] Interviewee 24 (MOSOP activist), personal discussion with author and public talk, St. Louis, MO, March 14, 1998.
[80] Interviewee 14 (Greenpeace International consultant), June 26, 1996 and July 24, 1996.

Shell out to dry so that others would learn a lesson."[81] Shell made an inviting target. Its consumer orientation, image-consciousness, and high-profile "green" advertising contrasted starkly with MOSOP's allegations of Shell's environmental devastation of its homeland. As state violence deepened on the Delta, Greenpeace, Friends of the Earth, and others also stressed Shell's close ties to the government.[82] This portrayal reached a climax after Saro-Wiwa's execution, with campaign literature by Greenpeace Netherlands on the theme "Shell has blood on its hands."[83] The media likewise took a growing interest in the Ogoni cause because of the environmental frame, in one reporter's words because of the "injustice of the situation – an enormously wealthy corporation contributing nothing to a community in which it was working."[84]

Not surprisingly, Royal Dutch/Shell did not sit idly by during these attacks. Instead, it began monitoring MOSOP's activities and the growing overseas campaign. Then it launched a public relations blitz, deploying its formidable resources. Denial and distancing played a key role, with the company arguing that its operations generally met local standards and that the parent company and its overseas subsidiaries should be distinguished from SPDC's operations in Nigeria. Shell also retaliated, accusing the Ogoni network of lying about Shell's environmental record and responsibility for repression. In addition, Shell in veiled terms, and the Nigerian government explicitly, suggested that MOSOP was a secessionist movement bent on the destruction of Nigeria. Using a familiar theme in battles against community-based organizations, Shell also questioned MOSOP's credentials as a representative of the Ogoni masses.[85] This rhetoric and action backfired badly, however. Notwithstanding the niceties of corporate structure with which Royal Dutch/Shell sought to shield itself, activists drew an obvious link between SPDC's pipelines twisting across the Ogoni landscape and Shell gas stations dotting the street corners of North America and Europe. Moreover, Shell's sensitivity to the charges convinced many in the environmental community that Shell had something to hide. As one

[81] Interviewee 28 (Sierra Club manager), telephone interview by author, April 27, 2001.
[82] Greenpeace International, *Shell-Shocked: The Environmental and Social Costs of Living with Shell in Nigeria* (London (?): Greenpeace International, 1994).
[83] Greenpeace Netherlands, "Ogoni Blood on Shell's Hands," Press release, October 31, 1995. See also Greenpeace USA, "Get the Shell Out."
[84] Interviewee 34 (*The Guardian* (London) reporter), telephone interview, July 24, 1996.
[85] Shell International, "Tensions in Nigeria," information sheet, n.d. [May 1993?], 2, Gumberg Library. Saro-Wiwa's response is in Saro-Wiwa, *A Month and a Day*, 166–70.

activist stated, "Shell was denying stuff all over the place. But Ken was sending out images, catching a multinational lying. This was very important in
attracting interest in the story."[86]

As this quotation suggests, another factor underpinning the environmental organizations' shift to support was the newfound Ogoni ability to
substantiate their case. Previously, environmental NGOs had openly questioned both MOSOP's grievances and its legitimacy. By the beginning of
1993, the movement had taken steps to remedy these deficiencies. As Saro-
Wiwa later affirmed, the prior rejections had given him a "much valued
education" not only about the issues that most concerned NGOs but also
about the mode in which they were presented.[87] Regarding the scope of
environmental damage, MOSOP used videotapes and photographs to substantiate its charges of Shell's misdeeds. Rising numbers of media reports
added further confirmation. For NGO principals, the visual and documentary evidence proved powerful. As one recalled: "I remember at the Vienna
Human Rights Conference seeing a photo display by the Ogoni – just
shocking – of oil wells and Shell's refineries flaring in their backyard, in their
communities. The photos were devastating; the stories remarkable.... I
came back from Vienna and nominated Ken for a Goldman [Prize] – which
he later won.... It seemed so overwhelming to me like a story with which
our members could identify."[88] Still, some of the Ogoni's more cautious
patrons pressed for further evidence – and sought to produce their own.
Greenpeace prepared its own report, The Body Shop commissioned a
British consulting firm to investigate the Niger Delta environment, and
other NGOs, including the World Council of Churches, sent representatives to make independent inquiries.

On the other issues that had earlier troubled environmental NGOs –
Ogoni identity and MOSOP's legitimacy as the group's representative –
few now had doubts. Saro-Wiwa wrote copiously on Ogoni culture and
history, aiming both to forge a more cohesive Ogoni "nation" and to build
international sympathy. As MOSOP gained recognition, Saro-Wiwa's documentation was accepted with fewer questions. The apparently solid basis
on which the world knows the Ogoni – and the Ogoni know themselves –
owes itself largely to Saro-Wiwa's busy pen during the early 1990s.[89] Most

---

[86] Interviewee 1 (Greenpeace International communications officer), July 24, 1996.
[87] Saro-Wiwa, *A Month and a Day*, 93.
[88] Interviewee 28 (Sierra Club manager), April 27, 2001.
[89] Wiwa, *Shadow of a Saint*, 68–69.

important in demonstrating grassroots backing for MOSOP, however, was the well-choreographed, publicized, and recorded Ogoni Day march. The march served important purposes at home, demonstrating Ogoni resolve and putting opponents on notice of the wide popularity of MOSOP's demands. But the march and later mobilizations, documented in video-tapes, photographs, and eyewitness testimony, also satisfied NGO staff that the organization was a genuine and unified mass movement.[90] MOSOP's umbrella-like organization and its fragile coalition of new and older elites help explain its ability to muster so many. In addition, the prospect and then reality of international aid excited Ogoni hopes and mobilized more people.[91]

In sum, by mid-1993 MOSOP had reversed the earlier rejections of key environmental gatekeepers by proving its organizational bona fides and framing the conflict around Shell. In turn, environmental NGOs and the media in the developed world amplified the changes. For them, the environmental and multinational corporate issues were more pertinent to key constituencies and audiences than the "political" issues that MOSOP had earlier highlighted. As a staffperson in Greenpeace's London office put it, Shell's "insidious presence" and alleged involvement in pollution and massacres gave the Ogoni story "legs," keeping it in the public eye in Europe, North America, and elsewhere.[92]

To what extent did MOSOP's anti-Shell frame reflect the reality on the ground? There is no doubt that the oil industry has negatively affected the Niger Delta environment. And Shell's operational practices, although they may have been standard in Nigeria, were well below those in the developed world. Oil spills, flaring, and blowouts contributed heavily to pollution, and even normal operations such as drilling and seismic surveys created significant problems for local communities. Efforts by the company to ameliorate these effects and contribute to community development had had meager results, although the Nigerian government was most culpable for the region's poverty and marginality. Shell's responsibility for human

---

[90] Interviewee 3 (UNPO staffperson), July 18, 1996; Interviewee 28 (Sierra Club manager), April 27, 2001.

[91] Interviewee 12 (MOSOP leader), personal interview by author, July 23, 1996; Interviewee 16 (MOSOP activist), personal discussion with author, July 21, 1996; Interviewee 18 (MOSOP leader), personal interview by author, July 21, 1996; Saro-Wiwa, *A Month and a Day*, 71–77, 130–32; Naanen, *Effective Nonviolent Struggle*, 14–15.

[92] Interviewee 1 (Greenpeace International communications officer), July 24, 1996.

rights violations remains unclear, although the company employed its own private security force in the area to protect its personnel and, on at least one occasion, paid field allowances to government forces protecting its facilities. There have also been allegations that Shell negotiated for the importation of arms for use by the Nigerian police and that Shell employees threatened local community members. In the case of the Umuechem massacre, Shell operatives facing peaceful protests called for help from Nigerian paramilitary forces infamous for their brutality.[93] Notwithstanding Shell's role in the Niger Delta's many conflicts, however, MOSOP's rhetoric of "warfare" and "genocide" was overstated.

Yet the Ogoni's dilemma was acute. For a weak challenger fighting powerful foes, external allies hold out hope. But this can only be fulfilled if sponsorship is won in the face of NGOs' competing priorities and limited resources. Incendiary words backed by broad proof can help break through. Ogoni leaders saw political advantage to be gained from emphasizing environmental issues. As Saro-Wiwa's son commented, when his father "insisted that the Ogoni had lived in harmony with their neighbours and the environment until the Europeans arrived, he knew it was a romantic notion, . . . a myth that was supposed to fire the individual imagination and collective quest for cultural identity and survival."[94] Domestically, long-standing Ogoni anger at Shell could be channeled into MOSOP's political agenda, which in any case involved the environment. Internationally, the Delta's real ecological problems could attract NGOs, where the political and economic marginality of a tiny Nigerian minority had not. Yet even as he began highlighting Shell's ruin of the environment, Saro-Wiwa made no secret of the group's political agenda. As he put it in 1993, "You cannot safeguard the environment if you do not have political power."[95] Nor did he conceal the Ogoni desire for oil drilling eventually to resume albeit "in a clean and safe way, under payment of adequate compensation."[96] For Greenpeace, Friends of the Earth, and others, however, the environmental aspects of

[93] Human Rights Watch, *The Price of Oil: Corporate Responsibility and Human Rights Violations in Nigeria's Oil Producing Communities* (New York: Human Rights Watch, 1999); Rivers State, *Judicial Commission of Inquiry*.

[94] Wiwa, *Shadow of a Saint*, 68–69.

[95] Karl Maier, "Oil Spillage Fuels Nigerian Rivalries," *Independent* (London), August 15, 1993, 10.

[96] Guido de Bruin, "Human Rights: Nigeria's Ogoni People Fight on against Oil Company," *Inter Press Service*, May 24, 1993, http://www.lexis-nexis.com/ (accessed August 2, 2004).

the Ogoni case were the primary concerns, providing the NGOs with their own opportunity "to have a go at Shell – attack them."[97] With this focus, however, the Ogoni's central issues – political power and oil revenues – took a secondary position. Indeed, many on the front lines of the network knew nothing of these demands. At times, Saro-Wiwa railed against this fact: "The West worries about elephants. They stop the export of rhino horns and things like that. And then they cannot worry about human beings dying."[98] But MOSOP also used the developed world's preferences to promote the movement. In sum, environmental issues were clearly important to MOSOP both at home and abroad. For most benefactors in the developed world, however, the Ogoni conflict appeared to be primarily environmental. By contrast, for MOSOP, political autonomy remained fundamental. The cleanup of ecological damage – without a change in political and economic relations between the Ogoni and the Nigerian state – would not "solve" the Ogoni problem.

State Violence and the Human Rights Frame

Whereas adoption by environmental NGOs hinged on MOSOP's strategic framing, human rights NGOs became involved in 1993 primarily because of changes in the conflict itself – the rise of abuses against the Ogoni. Previously, Amnesty International, Human Rights Watch/Africa, and others had criticized Babangida's authoritarianism and rights violations. But abuses had not occurred in Ogoni territory, and Amnesty had specifically refused to act on Saro-Wiwa's claims of "slow motion" cultural and environmental "genocide." In 1993, however, as Ogoni mobilization mounted, as external intervention grew, and as other Niger Delta minorities began imitating MOSOP's tactics, the Nigerian state responded harshly. MOSOP had been warned of repression from state officials and observers knowledgeable about the Nigerian dictatorship – and, of course, MOSOP leaders were fully aware of the dangers they ran. More cautious Ogoni opposed mass action and left the movement in June 1993. For those close to Saro-Wiwa, however, peaceful escalation appeared the best method of attracting external attention and pressuring the state. In this view, protest held clear risks but larger benefits for a group with few domestic allies and seemingly little

---

[97] Interviewee 14 (Greenpeace International consultant), June 26, 1996.
[98] Chris McGreal, "Plight of the Ogoni," *Newsweek*, September 20, 1993, 43.

to lose. As Saro-Wiwa wrote, the international community would be likely to act only if it was "sufficiently shocked" by the Ogoni plight.[99]

This shock occurred as the Nigerian military moved to squelch MOSOP's mounting mobilizations in mid-1993. Through MOSOP's established connections to NGOs, particularly UNPO, news of the Biara incident and Saro-Wiwa's detentions rapidly spread. In response, Amnesty International shifted its earlier stance, and Human Rights Watch/Africa entered the conflict, reporting on the detention, torture, and killing that soon enveloped the region. As the conflict intensified, the human rights organizations also stressed Ogoni grievances against Shell. This enlargement of the NGOs' usual interest in government-sponsored abuses resulted in part from the nature of the conflict. By mid-1993, there was evidence that Shell, Chevron, and other major oil companies had condoned and in some cases facilitated violations by security forces in the Niger Delta. The growing allusions to Shell also reflected broader changes in how the human rights NGOs viewed their missions. Increasingly during the early 1990s, NGO staff drew linkages between environmental problems and human rights violations. With the killing of Brazilian rainforest activist Chico Mendes and abuses against environmental activists elsewhere, human rights NGOs began recognizing that environmental issues and the activities of multinational corporations in the developing world frequently had human rights implications.[100] With MOSOP framing its struggle around Shell's impacts in the Niger Delta, the Ogoni cause fit naturally with the NGOs' expanding agendas. Finally, strategic factors played a role in the human rights organizations' highlighting of the Ogoni's environmental claims. As an Amnesty International staffperson explained: "Over the years, we've moved more and more to the environmental issue, talking a lot about Shell and the oil companies looting the area.... It was the best way to attract public attention. People, you know the general public, if they read about an oil company spoiling the life of simple people, it's good for the campaign. Better than talking about autonomy.... Environmental issues are big issues. You can't get people interested in autonomy issues.... [They are] too complex, people have a feeling there are more sides to the story, that it's a difficult issue.... [Environmental issues] are simple, straightforward: Shell

---

[99] Saro-Wiwa, *Genocide in Nigeria*, 9. See also Sam Olukoya, "We, Who're About to Die: In a Suicidal Defiance, Ogonis Do Battle with Soldiers to Prevent Laying of Oil Pipelines in Their Land," *Newswatch* (Lagos), May 17, 1993, n.p.

[100] Aaron Sachs, *Eco-Justice: Linking Human Rights and the Environment*, Worldwatch Paper no. 127 (Washington, DC: Worldwatch Institute, 1995).

is wrong, the Ogoni are good."[101] At Human Rights Watch, a researcher stated that the NGO increasingly focused its reports on oil multinationals operating in the Niger Delta because they represented an "easier target" than the Nigerian state due to their image-consciousness and sensitivity to consumer boycotts.[102]

Deepening Repression/Widening NGO Involvement: July 1993–December 1995

With Saro-Wiwa's detention in June 1993, a new dynamic arose, attracting larger numbers of environmental, human rights, and other NGOs. First, the arrest of a prominent delegate slated to attend a major international conference aroused keen interest among the thousands of NGO staff, journalists, and activists there. MOSOP members present at the Vienna World Conference on Human Rights meeting emphasized Saro-Wiwa's plight and read messages he smuggled out of jail. Although the Ogoni leader was released after a month and a day, the government's deepening repression in the summer and fall of 1993 raised strong concerns abroad. Nationally, the military regime annulled the June elections. In response, democracy advocates, labor unions, and the likely winner of the elections, Moshood Abiola, called a national strike, which the government met with detentions and repression. Widespread protest continued, however, and in August General Babangida resigned in favor of a hand-picked "interim" government that was overthrown in a November coup by General Sani Abacha.

Quickly, the new regime clamped down on dissent, beginning a five-year period of harsh repression throughout Nigeria. With regard to the Ogoni, Abacha halted negotiations and deployed paramilitary units, killing protesters, razing villages, jailing MOSOP leaders, and eventually sealing the region from outsiders. Ogoni settlements were also attacked by raiders from neighboring ethnic groups, including the Andoni in July 1993, the Okrika in December 1993, and the Ndoki in April 1994 – all with probable government foreknowledge or encouragement.[103] Despite the dangers, MOSOP organizing and sporadic protests continued through early 1994.

---

[101] Interviewee 20 (Amnesty International staffperson), personal interview by author, July 17, 1996.

[102] Interviewee 26 (Human Rights Watch staffperson), telephone interview by author, May 2, 2001.

[103] Human Rights Watch/Africa, "Ogoni Crisis," 12, 14; Civil Liberties Organisation, *Trials and Travails.*

But state repression also increased divisions within the Ogoni community that were already sharp after schisms over the election boycott. On May 21, 1994, four Ogoni leaders opposed to MOSOP were murdered by a mob of militant Ogoni, perhaps egged on by government provocateurs. In response, the Rivers State Internal Security Task Force arrested Saro-Wiwa and other MOSOP leaders, accusing them of incitement to the murders. In the wake of May 21, several hundred other Ogoni were also detained for weeks, many of them tortured while in custody. In the summer of 1994, the security forces raided Ogoni villages nightly, killing scores in extrajudicial executions, raping many others, and looting residences. By the end of 1994, most of the MOSOP leadership had been killed, jailed, or driven into exile, and public protest had dwindled.

With the worsening violence, MOSOP's ability to set the conflict's agenda diminished, as it found itself increasingly responding to military onslaughts. Nonetheless, it steadfastly maintained the environmental frame, underlining Shell's responsibility for and linkage to state actions. Working closely with UNPO, MOSOP continued to disseminate information about the rising turmoil. The broader NGO response was strong. In 1994, MOSOP won the Right Livelihood Award (the self-styled "Alternative Nobel Prize") for its nonviolent struggle for civil, economic, and environmental rights, and in 1995 Saro-Wiwa won the Goldman Prize as an international "environmental hero." Both awards brought substantial resources and publicity to the group. As Saro-Wiwa's trial progressed and repression in the Delta deepened, a host of social justice and rights organizations, including International PEN, Great Britain's Parliamentary Human Rights Group, and the World Council of Churches, also came to the Ogoni's aid.

This robust response reflected the growing humanitarian crisis in the region and in the country as a whole. In NGO eyes, the Ogoni were in desperate need of support. MOSOP's earlier lobbying also meant that Saro-Wiwa and the Ogoni were already known to key NGOs. Through 1995, MOSOP's excellent communications network, fed by local Ogoni leaders who, at great personal risk, continued to report on repression, continued to alert the world to events in Ogoniland. Moreover, the detentions, trial, and execution of Saro-Wiwa created tense and horrific spectacles. By the summer of 1995, the "David and Goliath" aspects of an indigenous people and their brave leader confronting a major corporation and pariah government attracted the media. Shell's public relations fumbles and the Nigerian government's brutality all made for dramatic press coverage. A first peak of attention and support occurred during Saro-Wiwa's jailing during

June–July 1993. As Saro-Wiwa reported to Ogoni leaders several months later: "Detention drew world attention to the plight of the Ogoni people. Newspapers and magazines in Europe devoted feature articles to the cause. Amnesty International, Greenpeace, International PEN and other worldwide organizations intervened and interceded with the Nigerian government on our behalf. Amnesty International even adopted three of us as 'prisoners of conscience.' "[104]

Primed by this incident, public interest in Saro-Wiwa's second detention was keen and became intense, particularly in the United Kingdom, Ireland, the Netherlands, and Germany, by the time of his trial in 1995. Galvanized by the Nigerian government's repression, key NGO patrons, especially UNPO and Greenpeace, did much of the work of promoting the campaign that Saro-Wiwa had done before but could no longer do from a prison cell in Port Harcourt. Throughout this period, the major focus remained Shell's role, the continuation of human rights violations, and Saro-Wiwa's kangaroo trial.

During peaks of attention to the Ogoni cause, a transnational bandwagon also arose, stemming partially from the Ogoni's dire needs and partially from the NGOs' organizational imperatives. For early MOSOP backers such as Greenpeace and Friends of the Earth, the costs of publicity and the risks of alliance had weighed heavily. But by 1995, as Saro-Wiwa's trial proceeded in the glare of media coverage, there were advantages for NGOs in attaching themselves to an already popular cause. Latecomers did not have to base their decisions on the stories of a single man from an unknown ethnic group. If UNPO, Greenpeace, Friends of the Earth, and especially Amnesty International and Human Rights Watch had put their credibility on the line for MOSOP, other NGOs could feel confident about joining the bandwagon without extensive investigation of their own. Moreover, rather than bearing the costs of publicizing an obscure cause, they associated themselves with a cause célèbre. Latecomers had principled and altruistic reasons for doing so: The human rights situation facing the Ogoni was perilous. Yet the foundations established by early supporters eased their decisions. As an Ijaw leader and member of Saro-Wiwa's legal defense team commented, "Campaigners tend to go toward the sexy and the romantic; the thing that is popular, a lot of people want to get involved. [They] don't

---

[104] Ken Saro-Wiwa, "Report to Ogoni Leaders Meeting at Bori, 3rd October, 1993," speech, 2, Gumberg Library.

want to be the people to start the dirty work of putting the bits and pieces together, putting the nails together, knocking one piece of wood on the other."[105]

In the case of Survival International, constituent pressure in 1993 and 1994 played a major role in the organization's reversal of its 1992 decision to reject MOSOP's appeals. According to Survival's head of Africa operations, as the campaign "gathered momentum" Survival received many questions from its members about the organization's stance toward the Ogoni. As a result, Survival managers came to believe that they had to take a public stand despite earlier misgivings about the Ogoni. In doing so, however, Survival sought to place its own imprint on support, "broaden[ing] the discussion" to show that the Ogoni "were not alone in suffering environmental damage and repression" in the Niger Delta.[106] Analogous grassroots enthusiasm pushed the Sierra Club into deeper involvement. According to the group's campaign coordinator: "Our members began to follow it – on listservs; emails. They were shooting out alerts about how they could help....It grew – much more than I expected....I didn't have to twist arms of Sierra Club Board Members....I thought I would have to pull them, but they pulled me on."[107]

Competition among NGOs also affected the campaign, particularly in the Netherlands, where Royal Dutch/Shell's role as villain loomed large. The Netherlands branches of Greenpeace and Friends of the Earth felt the pressure most intensely, at times leading to the two NGOs' adopting each other's tactics and duplicating each other's efforts. Ultimately, however, the competition had two effects. On the one hand, it pushed the NGOs to differentiate their activities: Greenpeace moved to a more confrontational approach, exemplified by its October 1995 "Ogoni Blood on Shell's Hands" press release, whereas Friends of the Earth sought to keep lines of communication open to Shell, at times leading NGO negotiations with the company. On the other hand, as NGO staff came to see the deleterious effects of competition, they organized an informal alliance of Dutch NGOs, the "Ogoni Platform," which sought to present a unitary position in discussions with Shell.

---

[105] Interviewee 29 (Ijaw Youth Council leader), personal interview by author, April 24, 2002.
[106] This and the subsequent quotation are from Interviewee 10 (Survival International staff-person), June 18, 1996. See, for example, Survival International, "Nigeria: Government Repression of the Peoples of the Oil Producing Areas, Rivers and Delta States," press release, November 1, 1995, Gumberg Library.
[107] Interviewee 28 (Sierra Club manager), April 27, 2001.

Structure of the Network

At its peak, the Ogoni network spanned scores of organizations and thousands of individuals across the world. These supporters came from advocacy NGOs, governmental and intergovernmental institutions, the media, foundations, and universities. Although the network was loosely organized and its membership shifting, four partially overlapping but nonetheless distinct sets of backers can be discerned based on identity with MOSOP goals, relationship to Ogoni leaders, level of activity, and functions. MOSOP leaders, galvanizers of the network, stood at its core, acting as critical intermediaries between the local and transnational levels. Initially, itinerant Nigeria-based Ogoni, particularly Saro-Wiwa, played this role. With his jailing and with heightened repression in Abacha's Nigeria, newly expatriated Ogoni activists, as well as a limited number of longer-term migrants, took over. Most of MOSOP's direct NGO contacts took place outside Nigeria, in North America and Europe, although in a few cases, larger organizations also sent representatives to Nigeria, where they contacted a wider set of Ogoni.

UNPO was MOSOP's oldest and most consistent benefactor. Although UNPO remained independent and had to balance its work for the Ogoni with commitments to other members, it formed a solidarity-like relationship, coming to share MOSOP's agenda to a greater degree than any other organization in the Ogoni network. UNPO devoted a major share of its personnel and resources to the Ogoni and played many roles. For one thing, it trained Ogoni leaders on such topics as nonviolent struggle, international law, diplomacy, and media relations. The training sessions provided MOSOP with opportunities to meet other UNPO members, some of whom publicized the Ogoni in their home countries. As one example, the UNPO member from Scania, a region of Sweden, successfully urged Swedish newspapers to write articles about the Ogoni. More importantly, UNPO served as a central clearinghouse for MOSOP information, particularly during the critical 1993–95 period when MOSOP built its network and faced its gravest threats. MOSOP faxed press releases to UNPO, which edited them for style and sometimes substance, then transmitted them to dozens of media outlets and NGOs around the world.[108] Independent verification was seldom possible from The Hague, but from early in its relationship, UNPO

---

[108] Interviewee 13 (UNPO manager), July 11, 1996; Interviewee 21 (UNPO staffperson), personal interview by author, July 11, 1996.

staff members instructed MOSOP on writing "reliable and believable press releases: on the need for names, ages, spouses."[109] They also suggested ways to improve MOSOP's photographs and videotapes for overseas audiences: "I used to tell Ken, 'This video you sent me, it's nice, but this is what you have to tell the cameraman: He has to get up on top of buildings, get a sense of how many people are in the crowd.' I discussed with Ken that the camera person is on the ground. 'You're telling me there are thousands of people on the ground; I can't see them. They need to be up on top of the buildings, looking down, to get a sense of all the heads, all the sea of people.'"[110] At moments of crisis in Nigeria, UNPO acted as a readily accessible and seemingly reliable source of information. Reporters searching for background on a breaking story in an inhospitable locale could gain documentation, videotapes, and names of well-coached Ogoni spokesmen resident in Europe. As Saro-Wiwa reported to his fellow Ogoni leaders in 1993, "Thanks to the efforts of the UNPO, the European press, BBC radio and television, CNN, Channel Four TV and Voice of America have given us good coverage. The American press, particularly the *New York Times* and *Newsweek*, have also covered our story."[111]

Finally, UNPO served as a matchmaker, providing MOSOP with strategic advice about likely NGO prospects and introducing Ogoni leaders to such groups as the World Council of Churches, the Dutch Foreign Ministry, and various European Union bodies. At the 1993 Vienna World Conference on Human Rights, UNPO introduced MOSOP leaders to principals from The Body Shop after its founder, Anita Roddick, had earlier informed UNPO's Secretary General that she was eager to adopt an indigenous group in conflict with a major multinational resource company.[112] UNPO personnel developed close ties to staff in other NGOs, particularly in the Netherlands, facilitating exchanges of information and increasing NGO trust in the reliability of UNPO's information. UNPO sometimes sought to model itself after Amnesty International, issuing "urgent action alerts" and portraying itself as an objective source of information. But UNPO made no secret that its membership included the Ogoni and that it shared its

---

[109] Interviewee 3 (UNPO staffperson), July 18, 1996.
[110] Ibid.
[111] Saro-Wiwa, "Report to Ogoni Leaders," 3 (italics added).
[112] Interviewee 13 (UNPO manager), July 11, 1996. At the same conference, The Body Shop adopted another UNPO referral, the independence movement on Papua New Guinea's Bougainville Island, which also had environmental grievances against the Australian mining firm RTZ. Ibid.

member's political goals. Some NGOs in the Ogoni network saw a conflict of interest and sought independent verification of UNPO claims and press releases; other organizations missed the conflict or believed it had been "solved" by UNPO's record of reliability. Many therefore came to rely on UNPO – and thus on MOSOP – as a primary source of information about the conflict.[113]

MOSOP's second ring of support comprised major NGOs that had extensive contacts with the Ogoni but did not share the Ogoni's broader political goals. These organizations – Greenpeace, Friends of the Earth, Amnesty International, and Human Rights Watch/Africa – publicized key events in Nigeria, issued lengthy reports, presented testimony to national governments, and urged media reporting. The environmental NGOs also developed anti-Shell strategies with the Ogoni, including a European "Boycott Shell" initiative. The most important role played by these organizations, however, was gatekeeping, certifying the Ogoni to a third tier of supporters with little independent capacity to investigate the issues or players. Certification was based in part on the gatekeeper NGOs' general credibility and clout but also on their extensive involvement with and promotion of the Ogoni.

For those in the third ring, such activism provided strong signals about the conflict's importance and MOSOP's bona fides. Of the groups in this third ring, some operated primarily at the international level, for instance prize committees such as the Goldman Prize and Right Livelihood Award organizations. Most, however, were national organizations, either semi-autonomous divisions of transnational NGOs or independent domestic organizations. They provided significant direct and indirect support to the Ogoni, although in many cases their contacts with MOSOP were limited and their knowledge of the conflict arose primarily from transnational gatekeepers. National chapters of Greenpeace and Friends of the Earth organized anti-Shell boycotts in Germany, the Netherlands, and the United Kingdom. The Sierra Club hosted Saro-Wiwa and other Ogoni leaders in visits to legislators, policymakers, and journalists in Washington, D.C. In the late 1990s, Essential Action distributed kits for college activists to inform students about the Ogoni and mobilize against Shell. Organizations in this third tier acted both as followers of second-level NGOs and as

---

[113] Interviewee 2 (Friends of the Earth International staffperson), July 17, 1996; Interviewee 15 (UNPO staffperson), personal interview by author, July 12, 1996; Interviewee 20 (Amnesty International staffperson), July 17, 1996.

smaller-scale gatekeepers in their own right. In the case of the prize committees, the awards validated the Ogoni to international audiences in addition to attracting short-lived publicity and providing large infusions of cash. For others in this third tier, the gatekeeping role was primarily domestic, informing and energizing a diffuse, fourth ring of support including local chapters of national organizations and independent activists. Among these latter groups, contacts with MOSOP leaders were isolated or nonexistent. Instead, information came primarily from national gatekeepers in the form of e-mail listservs, videotaped presentations, or written reports. Yet, in the late 1990s, it was primarily individuals in this fourth group who conducted sporadic actions against local Shell service stations (often to the bewilderment of customers and service station owners in places as far-flung as New Delhi, St. Louis, and Vancouver).

Execution and Exhaustion: The Decline of Support, 1995–2002

Saro-Wiwa's hanging and the ongoing repression against the Ogoni crippled the movement inside Nigeria. By 1996, most Ogoni leaders had been jailed, killed, exiled, or driven underground. With the region under army occupation, activism became risky, although some continued, especially on key dates such as Ogoni Day and the anniversary of the "Ogoni Nine's" execution. Internationally, MOSOP continued its activities through protests, conferences, publications, and Web sites organized by exiled leaders. And in the aftermath of the executions, the Ogoni's support briefly reached new heights. The British Commonwealth expelled Nigeria, and the United States and other nations imposed diplomatic sanctions (although more meaningful actions, such as a boycott of Nigerian oil exports, never occurred). Anger over the killings spurred protests at Nigerian embassies and Shell gas stations across Europe and the United States. On college campuses, the Ogoni became an issue, with calls to boycott Shell and save the Ogoni 20, another group of detained activists. And MOSOP's overseas offices received substantial new resources from The Body Shop and other sources. Moreover, as Saro-Wiwa's son acidly recalled, in the first years after Saro-Wiwa's hanging, NGOs that had "politely turned him away" previously "were now falling over themselves to write proposals and get funding for projects to ensure that 'Ken Saro-Wiwa's death was not in vain.'"[114] In the United States, relatives of Ogoni killed or injured in the conflict filed a

---

[114] Wiwa, *Shadow of a Saint*, 161.

class action lawsuit against Shell for complicity in human rights violations. With representation by the New York–based Center for Constitutional Rights, the suit has slowly wound itself through the courts. During this period, human rights and environmental issues again took top billing outside Nigeria. Lost in the anti-Shell and anti-Abacha rhetoric, however, were MOSOP's core ethnopolitical demands, as some of the Ogoni's indigenous rights allies complained.[115]

After Saro-Wiwa's execution, the Ogoni also became associated with the Nigerian democracy movement. By 1996, Saro-Wiwa was probably better known abroad than such imprisoned politicians as 1993's likely presidential election winner, Moshood Abiola, and the country's ex-President, General Olusegun Obasanjo. Saro-Wiwa's martyrdom was a potent symbol of Abacha's beastliness, and the transnational democracy movement used it as such. In doing so, however, many activists objected to MOSOP's boycott of the 1993 election. The depth of their engagement with the broader Ogoni autonomy movement was also questionable. In his 1997 anti-Abacha polemic *The Open Sore of a Continent*, for instance, exiled Nigerian author Wole Soyinka dwelled on Saro-Wiwa's killing even while repeatedly misidentifying MOSOP as the Movement for the *Salvation* of the Ogoni People.[116] As an Amnesty International campaigner stated in 1996: "There's a human rights disaster going on in Ogoniland, but there's also a human rights crisis in the whole of Nigeria. So we also tried always when we talked about the Ogoni and when I talked to the press about the Ogoni issue . . . to raise the issue that there's a human rights disaster in Nigeria: there's a [man who should be president] in prison, there's a former head of state in prison, trade union leaders, the death penalty. It's a disaster in Nigeria. And people know about it through the Ogoni issue, but it's more than that."[117]

For the Ogoni, association with the Nigerian democracy movement was also a mixed blessing. During the early 1990s, Saro-Wiwa had criticized the movement's tepid reaction to the *Ogoni Bill of Rights*, which he attributed to "ethnocentrism" among even progressive sectors of the dominant groups.[118] By the late 1990s, however, the removal of Abacha and the restoration of an elected government were clearly necessary for progress on any front in Nigeria. Moreover, the democracy movement, although

---

[115] Welch and Sills, "Martyrdom of Ken Saro-Wiwa," 14; Interviewee 13 (UNPO manager), July 11, 1996.

[116] Wole Soyinka, *The Open Sore of a Continent* (Oxford: Oxford University Press, 1997).

[117] Interviewee 20 (Amnesty International staffperson), July 17, 1996.

[118] Saro-Wiwa, *Genocide in Nigeria*, 101.

fractious, had strong ties to major human rights organizations, powerful African American politicians, and a small group of African-oriented NGOs, such as the Washington Office on Africa. On the other hand, the Ogoni agenda, with its call for Nigeria's fundamental restructuring, went well beyond that of the democracy movement. Lending MOSOP's name to the broader movement risked submerging these core issues, and many Ogoni therefore had reservations about doing so.

Since Abacha's death in 1998 and Nigeria's transition to a shaky but enduring democracy in 1999, MOSOP's overseas backing has slowly declined in breadth and depth. Although the Ogoni movement does not face the anonymity of the early 1990s, it has not regained the acclaim it reached immediately before and after the executions. In itself, this is scarcely surprising. The crisis surrounding the killings of Saro-Wiwa and his fellow activists was a singular event. More importantly, however, some of the Ogoni's key supporters have become less energetic. Although major human rights organizations have continued regular reporting about the Niger Delta, the Sierra Club and Friends of the Earth reduced their involvement and Greenpeace moved on to other issues. Even UNPO, although maintaining the Ogoni's membership, reduced its activism. Much of the dynamism of the continuing campaign shifted to several small, specialized NGOs. One was the Berkeley-based Project Underground, formed in part by environmental NGO veterans of the Ogoni campaign to help local populations around the world fight the international mining industry. Another was Washington's Essential Action, which maintained e-mail listservs and acted as a clearinghouse for information about the Ogoni movement (and many others) through the 1990s. A third is the Stakeholder Democracy Network, a European NGO that helps Third World communities affected by multinational corporations communicate and negotiate with company stakeholders elsewhere.

What explains the slow decline in support during this period? For one thing, Saro-Wiwa's killing robbed MOSOP of one of its biggest assets, its talented leader. Despite his canonization by the environmental movement, Saro-Wiwa's physical absence dealt a devastating blow to the movement. No Ogoni leader matched his energy, verve, and charisma – characteristics repeatedly mentioned by NGO staff familiar with the movement's leadership. A more pedestrian but nonetheless critical characteristic, Saro-Wiwa's ability to link the global and the local, also died with him.

A second factor is that, although the underlying problems facing the Ogoni remained the same, the primary "villains" softened. Most obviously, the notoriously repressive Abacha regime gave way in 1999 to a civilian government anointed by a flawed but internationally certified vote won by former General Olusegun Obasanjo. State-sponsored human rights violations have declined in the new Fourth Republic, with the army now out of Ogoni territory (although there have been several major abuses in other parts of the Delta). Recent policy changes have also raised the amount of oil revenues allocated to Niger Delta communities, albeit not to the levels that the minorities desire. Although the Obasanjo government has not accepted a "sovereign national convention" to reconfigure the Nigerian federation, as activists from the Ogoni and other minorities still demand, it is now difficult to paint the Nigerian government in the dark tones that made sense during the Abacha period. Shell likewise has changed. It has increased its development and community relations spending, endorsed basic human rights principles, and sought to negotiate a reopening of its Ogoni facilities. Even if Shell's actions represent only public relations ploys, they have made it harder to portray the company in the same emotion-laden terms as before.

Finally, the emergence of internal MOSOP strife after Saro-Wiwa's killing raised concerns for NGOs. Scattered across Europe, North America, and African refugee camps, newly expatriated Ogoni elites had difficulty maintaining a common strategy and united front. Conflicts over leadership and strategy have dogged the Ogoni since 1995. From Toronto, Ken Saro-Wiwa's brother Owens Wiwa kept the flame of activism alive among NGOs in Canada and the United States. Among other expatriated Ogoni in North America and Europe, however, he was not recognized as undisputed leader. Nor did these expatriates necessarily subscribe to the leadership of Saro-Wiwa's chosen lieutenant, Ledum Mitee, who after his acquittal by the military tribunal in 1995 primarily worked out of MOSOP-UK's London office before returning to Nigeria after Abacha's death.

At times, these conflicts appeared to be little more than personal, even family, feuds, incomprehensible to outsiders who saw them as trivial compared with the environmental and human rights issues in the campaign. One of the most public disputes surrounded plans for the exhumation and reinterment of the "Ogoni Nine," permitted by the new Nigerian government in 2000. A group led by Saro-Wiwa's relatives favored family burial, arranging for a Canadian pathologist to identify the remains. But another faction demanded a joint funeral as a new rallying point for the local movement. When the pathologist arrived, he "walked slap into the middle of a million different agendas" and could do nothing – as the press widely reported.[119]

As this incident suggests, worse than the disputes themselves was the fact that they occurred in the open. In MOSOP's first years and even after the June 1993 election boycott, conflicts between conservative and insurgent leaders had been invisible outside Nigeria. Saro-Wiwa and a few trusted associates from the latter faction were the Ogoni's primary links to the world, and most contacts took place outside Nigeria. For their part, NGO staff, inspired by videotapes of huge protests under Saro-Wiwa's command, suspected nothing of the tactical and ideological differences roiling the Ogoni elite. Only with the murders of the four Ogoni chiefs in April 1994 did factionalism become apparent. But by then MOSOP's most important connections had been solidified. And for these NGOs, MOSOP appeared to be the accepted representative of most Ogoni, with the dead chiefs merely Shell sellouts and government stooges. Given Saro-Wiwa's popularity, this view is probably valid, although a plebiscite was never held.

After Saro-Wiwa's execution, however, divisions among expatriate MOSOP members, who had long appeared unified behind a common platform and revered leader, played themselves out in the international spotlight. MOSOP's careless use of the Internet exacerbated the problem.[120] As one long-time Ogoni backer despaired in a 1999 e-mail message to the Essential Action Shell-Nigeria listserv: "The internal dispute in MOSOP is getting very silly indeed. I recall that more than a year ago the various Ogoni factions were asked politely – by a very long list of esteemed supporters – to stop using the list to pursue their various vendettas against one another. Why hasn't this happened? ... There is a problem when the list is being used as a soap box for the increasingly eccentric and paranoid views of a small minority of Ogoni activists. The main problem is it turns people off getting involved, or even reading mail from the list which is becoming a chore."[121]

---

[119] Jason Burke, "Battle Rages for Ken Saro-Wiwa's Bones: The Executed Nigerian Playwright's Planned Reburial Has Sparked Feuds," *Observer* (London), March 26, 2000, 4; Norimitsu Onishi, "Not for a Nigerian Hero the Peace of the Grave," *New York Times*, March 22, 2000, 3.

[120] Interviewee 37 (Stakeholder Democracy Network activist), telephone interview, May 10, 2002.

[121] Tim Concannon (director, Stakeholder Democracy Network), message to shell-nigeria-action@venice.essential.org listserv, December 9, 1999.

Importantly, these disputes had little impact on activism by human rights NGOs, whose interest in stemming rights abuses made MOSOP's internal politics largely irrelevant. Human Rights Watch, for instance, continued close monitoring of the Ogoni and issued several major reports on the Niger Delta. For NGOs closer to the solidarity mold, particularly environmental organizations, however, the internal MOSOP turmoil created uncertainty and disillusionment. For one thing, it was unclear which of the competing camps represented the Ogoni community. For another, there was no guarantee that assistance would bolster the Ogoni in their struggle against Shell and the Nigerian state rather than being squandered on internecine disputes. NGOs responded in two ways. Some sought to broaden their programs by highlighting the problems of the Niger Delta as a whole or by focusing on the shortcomings of Shell and other multinationals. Others, such as Greenpeace and the Sierra Club, simply reduced their involvement. As a Sierra Club leader stated: "The MOSOP splits made it more difficult because we were getting directions and pleas from two sides. We didn't want to take sides; we were in it to support the community as a whole. I'm not sure we'll ever know, and I don't know frankly what to believe. I know wrongs were committed and have not yet been rectified. They'll sort it out; these are family feuds. It is hard to know. That was one of the reasons we backed off a bit."[122]

The Other Niger Delta Minorities

During 1993–95, as the Ogoni mobilized and NGO activism expanded, other Niger Delta minorities facing similar political, economic, and environmental problems emulated MOSOP's strategies. Supplementing long-established minority organizations, discontented segments of the Ijaw, Ogbia, Ikwerre, Urhobo, and Nembe Creek communities formed organizations with names, structures, and goals resembling MOSOP's. Several issued manifestoes modeled after the *Ogoni Bill of Rights* and sought advice from Saro-Wiwa on how to mobilize domestically. Some of these newly formed organizations mounted short-lived protests against the government and oil companies in their home regions. Others exerted pressure on the government through institutional mechanisms. The Abacha regime's killing of Saro-Wiwa and its broader repression against the Ogoni, however,

[122] Interviewee 28 (Sierra Club manager), April 27, 2001. See also Interviewee 26 (Human Rights Watch staffperson), May 2, 2001.

discouraged activism and mass protest after 1995. With Abacha's death in 1998 and the transition to a flawed but real democratic system, there has been a surge of mobilization. In addition to a revival of party politics, dozens of new organizations established along ethnic, pan-ethnic, and non-ethnic lines have flourished under the more moderate Obasanjo government.[123] Many of the ethnically based groups have roots in the minorities' long-standing grievances about their political marginalization in Nigeria. New and sometimes radical youth associations also supplement more traditional communal organizations. Although organized independently and some-times fighting among themselves over land issues and scarce government resources, many of these ethnically based groups also share common goals: more jobs for indigenes, increased petroleum revenues, greater develop-ment, and environmental cleanup. Most also share several broader demands: "resource control" over the petroleum on which they sit and a "sovereign national convention" to renegotiate the foundations of the Nigerian fed-eration. The pan-ethnic groups, whose activism has generally been lower than that of the ethnic groups, seek similar goals but on a Niger Delta–wide basis. Meanwhile, new organizations focusing on human rights, civil liber-ties, and environmental protection have also arisen. In some cases, these are national-level Nigerian groups drawn to the Delta by the gravity of its problems; in other cases, they are home-grown organizations.

During 1993–95, when MOSOP enjoyed its greatest overseas suc-cess, the other Niger Delta minorities and activist groups remained little-known outside Nigeria. Even among those that lobbied abroad, lack of standing, contacts, and resources limited their promotional efforts. More-over, through 1998, the Abacha government hindered Nigerians' access to overseas NGOs, while the Niger Delta's special problems were sub-merged within the larger pro-democracy movement. Since the democratic transition, international activity in the Niger Delta has grown. Several development organizations, including the Netherlands-based NOVIB (Oxfam Netherlands) and the Swedish International Development Cooper-ation Agency (SIDA), have committed funds to the Delta. The U.S.-based John D. and Catherine T. MacArthur Foundation has also started a major initiative in the Niger Delta, providing grants to build the skills and capaci-ties of local organizations addressing issues of "environmental conservation,

---

[123] Augustine Ikelegbe, "Civil Society, Oil and Conflict in the Niger Delta Region of Nigeria: Ramifications of Civil Society for a Regional Resource Struggle," *Journal of Modern African Studies* 39, no. 3 (2001): 437–69.

political participation, community health, and local governance."[124] Nonetheless, only a few of the many activist organizations on the Delta have benefited directly. For the most part, these have been organizations espousing human rights and environmental programs rather than the openly ethnic organizations that often have the greatest appeal on the ground.

A major impediment to the other minority organizations has been their tactics, which differ significantly from MOSOP's. Throughout the Ogoni protests, MOSOP leaders emphasized nonviolence both to their domestic constituents and especially to supporters outside Nigeria. For a tiny minority fighting a brutal dictatorship that cared little about its international image, this tactic was partly simple prudence. Early NGO backers such as UNPO also stressed to Saro-Wiwa the importance of peaceful activism in building outside engagement. And Saro-Wiwa appears to have believed in nonviolence as a political tool, receiving training in the tactic as an UNPO member, steeping himself in the ideas of Gandhi and Martin Luther King, and consistently advocating peaceful protest in his writings. As cleavages within the Ogoni elite widened, however, Saro-Wiwa used incendiary language to attack his rivals, in early 1994 frequently denouncing them as "vultures" before excited Ogoni audiences. Moreover, the MOSOP leadership could never control all its grassroots constituents. During 1993–95, as military and paramilitary violence mounted and thousands were killed, abused, and displaced, discipline became impossible. Nonetheless, although some Ogoni used violence, these unusual events contravened MOSOP policy and were quickly condemned by the leadership.

By contrast, among other ethnic groups, there has been a rise in militant youth organizations such as the Egbesu Boys of Africa, the Bakassi Boys, the Odua People's Congress, and the Movement for the Actualization of the Sovereign State of Biafra. Occupation and sabotage of oil facilities, as well as kidnapping or murder of multinational personnel, have made headlines in an international press newly attentive to the Niger Delta. Meanwhile, peaceful and less dramatic tactics – nonviolent rallies, speechmaking, and manifestoes demanding minority rights – generally have not. One illuminating exception involved hundreds of Itsekiri women who occupied ChevronTexaco's Escravos oil terminal in December 2002. They attracted considerable if short-lived international media interest by threatening a

---

[124] John D. and Catherine T. MacArthur Foundation, "Program on Global Security and Sustainability," http://www.macfound.org/programs/gss/nigeria.htm (accessed June 30, 2004).

potent act of shaming in Nigerian society, publicly disrobing if their demands for more jobs and development projects were not met. After a lengthy standoff, they won negotiations and concessions from the company.[125] In addition, in parts of the Delta, Ijaws, Itsekiris, Urhobos, and other groups have repeatedly clashed in local power struggles. Nor have these minorities had internationally recognized spokesmen to distance the group as a whole from the actions of a few. As a result, the most prominent of the other minorities have come to appear more violent – and less appealing to key NGOs – than the Ogoni. A principal at the Sierra Club put it this way when asked why the Club had been reticent about supporting other Delta minorities: "Now you're going to get me in trouble. Let me just say this: What we liked about the Ogoni struggle was that it was democratic, non-violent. Two thousand Ogoni died in a nonviolent struggle. They had not taken up arms against Shell. They had protested when pushed, had written letters, had filed lawsuits for what it was worth at the time. We liked the way this community had represented itself, had handled itself. There are other communities on the Delta who frankly have been more violent. That scares us. That scared us away. That's not who we are, so we weren't as quick to jump to their defense."[126]

The other Niger Delta minorities have also suffered because of broader problems in their organizational cultures, problems that the Ogoni had avoided. In the eyes of many NGO staff members, MOSOP had taken a familiar and intelligible form surprisingly similar to their own groups'. In explaining aid for the Ogoni movement, for example, a manager at the Sierra Club said: "Here was a community a world away yet that shared so many similarities with our members in this country. They were organized democratically in their struggle for freedom from pollution, and our members really identified with their struggle. . . . There was this incredible person in the community fighting this multinational oil company and the alliance with Abacha. . . . What attracted us to MOSOP was because it was organized so similarly to the Sierra Club; I went to a MOSOP meeting [in the United States] and it really reminded me of a Sierra Club meeting. They could have been following Robert's Rules of Order, in fact they probably

---

[125] Norimitsu Onishi, "As Oil Riches Flow, Poor Village Cries Out," *New York Times*, December 22, 2002, A1.

[126] Interviewee 28 (Sierra Club manager), April 27, 2001. Notably, however, human rights NGOs have reported on these groups, particularly after government abuses such as the 1999 killing of hundreds of Ijaws in Odi. See, for example, Human Rights Watch, *Price of Oil*.

were."[127] Outside NGO purview, however, the reality may have been different. Saro-Wiwa exercised strong control over the insurgent youths who energized the movement and frequently overruled opposition from conservative Ogoni chiefs, especially as confrontation with the state mounted in mid-1993. Even according to close allies within MOSOP, his unwillingness to compromise and, in several cases, his undermining of key decisions previously taken by other leaders, fed disaffection. Important examples include Saro-Wiwa's intransigence about boycotting the June 1993 national elections and his public opposition to a peace agreement signed by other Ogoni leaders ending hostilities with a neighboring ethnic group.[128] Again, however, little news of this strife reached overseas supporters in the crucial months when ties with NGOs were being forged. Whatever its actual level of internal democracy, MOSOP appeared to epitomize characteristics attractive to NGOs.

By contrast, as the preceding quotations suggest, the violent youths of the other Niger Delta ethnic groups looked very different from afar, although their democratic credentials may be no less than MOSOP's. Moreover, their disadvantage relative to the Ogoni increased in the early 1990s as MOSOP's overseas contacts improved its understanding of how to attract international audiences. For instance, as UNPO members, Ogoni leaders took formal courses in media relations and activism within United Nations agencies. In conversations with NGO staff, Saro-Wiwa learned the reasons that key NGOs such as Amnesty International and Greenpeace initially repudiated him. Moreover, Ogoni leaders developed a personal rapport with activists that helped the movement. Most of the other Niger Delta minorities have had none of these advantages and have remained isolated.

One partial and illuminating exception involves the Ijaw people, Nigeria's fourth-largest minority group, whose political and economic grievances parallel the Ogoni's. In the early 1990s, Ijaw activists formed organizations loosely modeled after MOSOP but using more confrontational, occasionally violent tactics. One of the most militant organizations, the Ijaw Youth Council (IYC), formed in 1998 to advance the groups' interests in the newly democratizing country. On its foundation, the IYC issued the *Kaiama Declaration*, a document with clear debts to and goals similar to the *Ogoni Bill of Rights*. Since this declaration, the IYC has mounted nonviolent teach-ins and mass protests, some bloodily suppressed by the Nigerian

[127] Interviewee 28 (Sierra Club manager), April 27, 2001.
[128] Naanen, *Effective Non-Violent Struggle*, 33, 37, 44–45.

army, but Ijaw youths affiliated with the IYC have also been implicated in occupations, kidnappings, and other actions against oil company installations. Not surprisingly, the IYC itself has garnered little international backing. Several Ijaws with close ties to the IYC, however, are leaders of non-ethnic organizations, most importantly Environmental Rights Action (ERA), a Nigeria-wide environmental organization founded in 1993.[129] ERA is now an affiliate of Friends of the Earth International, has secured large grants from European foundations, and in 1998 won the $100,000 Norwegian Sophie Prize for "inspir[ing] people working towards a sustainable future."[130] The best-known ERA leader, Oronto Douglas, is also an IYC principal. He has traveled abroad extensively on environmental and human rights speaking tours and has coauthored a Sierra Club book, *Where Vultures Feast: Shell, Human Rights, and Oil in the Niger Delta*.

Several factors have been important to ERA's and Douglas's success. First, ERA piggybacked on the Ogoni movement.[131] MOSOP raised the profile of the entire Niger Delta, facilitating Douglas's contacts with environmental activists in England during the early 1990s. Douglas's role as an attorney on Saro-Wiwa's defense team in 1995 further enhanced his standing. As the Ogoni star faded with Saro-Wiwa's killing and MOSOP's infighting, ERA has to some extent filled the void. Second, Douglas is an articulate and powerful English speaker, capable of firing receptive audiences with his passionate rhetoric. Finally, Douglas has learned one lesson of the Ogoni case: The plight of the Ijaw qua Ijaw is not enough to interest most NGOs. Similarly, Delta-wide issues of resource control by minority communities, now the dominant theme among activists in Nigeria, do little to excite outsiders because of their parochialism and complexity. On the international stage, ERA leaders follow MOSOP in charging that human rights abuses arise as a result of "environmental atrocities."[132] In addition, ERA has turned to a new and popular theme among environmental and human rights activists, the pernicious effects of globalization. Douglas has become a regular at worldwide protests by the emerging "global justice"

---

[129] Interviewee 29 (Ijaw Youth Council leader), April 24, 2002.

[130] Sophie Foundation, "About the Sophie Prize," http://www.sophieprize.org/ (accessed June 28, 2004).

[131] Information in this paragraph is based on Interviewee 29 (Ijaw Youth Council leader), April 24, 2002.

[132] Nnimmo Bassey and Oronto Douglas, "Prize Ceremony – Speech by the Prize Winner, 1998 – Environmental Rights Action, Nigeria," June 15, 1998, http://www.sophieprize. org/ (accessed June 28, 2004).

movement, where, in rhetoric that resonates well with his audience, he highlights the developed world's centuries-old plunder of Nigeria and its current manifestation, exploitation by oil multinationals.

Conclusion

The experience of the Niger Delta minorities holds important lessons about transnational networking. For local movements, attracting NGOs is not simply a matter of tossing a "boomerang" soliciting aid. During the early 1990s, Saro-Wiwa, a man later noted for his remarkable charisma, did just that to seemingly receptive NGOs. For the most part, his repeated personal pleas met rejection from key gatekeepers in the environmental and human rights fields. Given limited resources and competing claims, the NGOs quite rationally declined MOSOP's appeals because of their failure to match key NGO attributes, interests, and requirements. In a limited sense, however, MOSOP succeeded: It made itself known to powerful transnational actors. By contrast, most of the Niger Delta's other suffering minorities had neither the knowledge nor the capacity to do so, remaining not only isolated but also anonymous to potential patrons. The Ogoni's superior resources, skills, and contacts – not any special need – explain the difference.

These factors also contributed to the Ogoni's gaining wide NGO backing after 1993. Learning from earlier mistakes, MOSOP framed itself around the preferences of its overseas audiences. Part of this involved the movement's reshaping of its rhetoric and action, playing the "Shell card," and mobilizing in the glare of video cameras. MOSOP's new image as a victim of Shell's environmental crimes deepened because the media and NGOs, pursuing their own agendas and interests, highlighted the frame, probably further than MOSOP had originally envisioned. Government repression also altered the Ogoni's international appearance, raising the group's profile and transforming it into a victim of recognizable and severe human rights violations. From these diverse sources, many rooted in the realities of the conflict, some deliberately planned, others opportunistically seized, and the remainder obtruding unasked for, MOSOP developed an overall "package" that galvanized major backing. This was not cynical deception, and NGO supporters were not naïve dupes. Rather, the Ogoni case illustrates the difficulties movements face and the strategies they must use in marketing themselves internationally.

From the standpoint of international relations theory, the Niger Delta cases suggest the need to rethink current views of network formation, structure, and effects. Notwithstanding claims to the openness and morality of NGOs, they, like any organization, wear blinders and have set ideas. Jealous of their credibility and resources, NGOs reject supplicant groups more than they adopt them, as the Ogoni found at first and as other Niger Delta movements still learn today. Nor is this simply a matter of good intentions gone awry. Sympathy and morality clearly play an important role in NGO decisions on supporting local movements. Yet NGOs must also concern themselves with their own maintenance. Their reasons for rebuffing the Ogoni early on, forming a bandwagon around them later, and continuing to reject many of the other minorities today relate to organizational concerns – NGO resources, identities, and self-interest – as much as to movement needs. For local insurgents, therefore, the "price" of support from the most powerful NGOs often is framing to meet NGO predilections. If there is a relatively equal power relationship between movement and NGO, as in the case of MOSOP and UNPO, such changes may be small, but in the more typical situation they may be considerable. Movements such as MOSOP that understand and exploit NGO preferences will enjoy greater success abroad.

What of the consequences of MOSOP's transnational networking? Three effects merit attention: on the movement itself; on its international champions; and on its opponents. As this chapter has repeatedly shown, the character and activity of the Ogoni movement shifted in response to international opportunities and demands. The dictates of the transnational support market coaxed MOSOP to downplay (although never omit) its fundamental political autonomy goal and to emphasize important but secondary environmental aims. Moreover, once NGO intervention began, it helped strengthen the Ogoni movement at home. In the early 1990s, Nigeria's press reported about MOSOP's presentation at the U.N. Working Group on Indigenous Populations, its showcasing on British television, its membership in UNPO, and its sponsorship by prominent NGOs.[133] Saro-Wiwa also trumpeted MOSOP's successes directly to the Ogoni masses.[134] Together these accounts helped demonstrate to his people that the Ogoni cause was legitimate in the eyes of the world, that the Ogoni were part of a wider struggle for indigenous rights, human rights, and environmental improvement,

---

[133] Tayo Lukula, "International Bodies React to Ogonis' Agitation," *Guardian* (Lagos), June 8, 1993; Kenneth Ezea, "Human Rights Group Protests Saro-Wiwa's Deportation," *Guardian on Sunday* (Lagos), April 18, 1993, B3.
[134] Saro-Wiwa, *A Month and a Day*, 71–77, 99, 130–32.

and that their demands attracted seemingly powerful allies.[135] In short, the international response suggested that MOSOP's campaign held promise. The effects were particularly evident in late 1992 and early 1993 when small but significant international interest helped energize a movement that had scored no successes at home and many of whose titular leaders had become inactive after signing the *Bill of Rights*. Saro-Wiwa believed that one of the most important results of his address to the U.N. Working Group in July 1992 was its publication in Nigerian newspapers. This, along with Nigerian press coverage of *The Heat of the Moment* and related environmental protests at Shell's London offices, energized Ogoni elites and contributed to the revival of domestic mobilization in late 1992.[136] NGO support also had spillover effects, invigorating and in some cases spawning movements among other Niger Delta minorities. Of course, minority mobilization long predated MOSOP and there were ample domestic bases for discontent. But in the wake of MOSOP's international successes in the early 1990s and in some cases under Saro-Wiwa's tutelage, a number of minority organizations adopted rhetoric and structures paralleling the Ogoni's.

The group's overseas achievements along with its successful protests enhanced Saro-Wiwa's authority within MOSOP in 1993. This may have emboldened him to challenge the conservative Ogoni leaders he had previously indulged. MOSOP fractured as a result, and continuing animosity contributed to the April 1994 killings of the conservative Ogoni chiefs. Although long-standing divisions within Ogoni society and meddling by the state played the major role, this tragic outcome indicates that NGO intervention is far from neutral even within client groups. Instead, even the best-intentioned aid affects internal power dynamics, augmenting the role of some, diminishing that of others, with unpredictable, sometimes destabilizing consequences, particularly among communities under strain.

For their part, NGO supporters were also changed by their interaction with MOSOP. Key NGOs, foundations, and development agencies gained knowledge of important but formerly obscure African issues. Although some of MOSOP's earliest patrons have moved on to other issues, other organizations have begun focusing on the Niger Delta. More broadly, the Ogoni campaign sensitized NGOs to linkages between environmental, human rights, and multinational corporate issues in the developing world.

---

[135] Naanen, *Effective Nonviolent Struggle*, 14–15; Interviewee 12 (MOSOP leader), July 23, 1996.

[136] Saro-Wiwa, *A Month and a Day*, 99.

This has had lasting effects in the form of new programs linking these diverse concerns. In the United States, for instance, the Ogoni campaign "set the stage" for a strategic alliance between the Sierra Club and Amnesty International, and, on a more permanent basis, the Sierra Club has developed a human rights component, while Amnesty International has launched an environmental program.[137] These groups have successfully campaigned for the release of jailed environmental activists around the world. MOSOP alone cannot be credited for these developments since a number of other conflicts elsewhere in the world raised similar concerns during the 1990s, but the Ogoni crisis contributed significantly.

The most important issue remains: What did the transnational Ogoni campaign achieve against its chief opponents? A definitive answer is not possible given the multitude of factors involved, but some tentative conclusions may be offered. First, MOSOP elevated the international profile of the Ogoni and the Niger Delta, a signal accomplishment against stiff odds. At a minimum, this has forced Shell and the new Nigerian democracy to devote more attention and care to the problems facing the Delta. The campaign also appears to have had more concrete effects. With respect to Shell, although the company at first denied its susceptibility to international pressure, its actions belie this claim. After counterattacking against MOSOP, Shell later took more positive steps. It agreed to sponsor the multimillion-dollar Niger Delta Environmental Survey to assess environmental issues in the region. Under intense NGO pressure in early November 1995, Shell's chairman also made a private plea to General Abacha to spare Saro-Wiwa's life. Subsequently, the company incorporated human rights and environmental concerns into its worldwide business principles and signed the United Nations Global Compact. In the Niger Delta, Shell's local subsidiary has augmented its community development programs to about 60 million dollars per year, increased its employment of local populations, and tried to improve its environmental performance. It has also sought ways to reduce violence in the Delta and acknowledged "feed[ing]" conflict through its contracting and compensation policies.[138] For the Ogoni, the region's other minorities, and NGO monitors, these actions are inadequate

---

[137] Folabi K. Olagbaju and Stephen Mills, "Defending Environmental Defenders," *Human Rights Dialogue* 2, no. 11 (2004): 32; Amnesty International USA, Amnesty International, "Just Earth!" http://www.amnestyusa.org/justearth/index.do (accessed June 28, 2004).

[138] Karl Maier, "Shell 'Feeds' Nigeria Conflict, May End Onshore Work (Update 6)," Bloomberg.com, June 10, 2004, http://quote.bloomberg.com/apps/news?pid=10000085 & sid=aC3m6AFYzJjM & refer=europe (accessed July 30, 2004).

and cosmetic.[139] As a result, oil production in Ogoni territory has not resumed, and relations between the company and the community remain frayed, as they do with many other Nigerian minorities. Given the Niger Delta's increasingly violent conflict, Shell's ability to continue operations in the region while staying true to its new business principles remains open to question.[140] Nonetheless, the very fact that Shell is paying attention to these issues and that they remain the object of tough NGO scrutiny owes much to MOSOP's transnational campaign and may be considered a significant Ogoni success against powerful foes.

With respect to the Nigerian government, the discrete impacts of the transnational campaign are even harder to assess since the state has long been under pressure not only from the Ogoni but also from other minorities. Several developments are worth mentioning, however. During 1994–95, the Abacha regime presided over the National Constitutional Conference (NCC), which was charged with recommending the formation of more new states across Nigeria. It received petitions for 45, including 2 to be created from the new Delta State and 6 from Rivers, one of the latter a proposed Ogoni/Rivers East State. In late 1996, however, General Abacha opted for only six new states nationwide, including another dominated by the Ijaw, Bayelsa, carved out of Rivers State. The dream of Ogoni autonomy remained unfulfilled, however, as it does today. In another important measure, the NCC passed a resolution calling for a major expansion in the funds distributed to states under the derivation principle from 1 percent to 13 percent of mineral revenues in the Federation Account. Although the Abacha regime did not implement this reform, it was incorporated as Section 162(2) of the Fourth Republic's 1999 constitution and came into operation in 2000. Because the 13 percent derivation revenue is paid to state governments, however, its impact on the many state minorities who, like the Ogoni, are directly affected by oil production is uncertain. As a way of addressing this issue, in 2000 the ineffective OMPADEC was replaced

---

[139] Christian Aid, *Behind the Mask: The Real Face of Corporate Social Responsibility* (London: Christian Aid, 2004), http://www.christian-aid.org.uk/indepth/0401csr/index.htm (accessed June 30, 2004); Christian Aid, *Shell in Nigeria: Oil and Gas Reserves and Political Risks: Shared Concerns for Investors and Producer-Communities* (Lewes, United Kingdom: Christian Aid, 2004).

[140] In December 2003, a Shell-funded report predicted that the company would have to withdraw after 2008 for this reason. See WAC Global Services, "Peace and Security in the Niger Delta: Conflict Expert Group Baseline Report," Working Paper for Shell Petroleum Development Corporation, December 2003, Gumberg Library. A company spokesperson later repudiated this view. See Maier, "Shell 'Feeds' Nigeria Conflict."

by the Niger Delta Development Commission (NDDC), with a mandate to aid the local areas. The NDDC's prospects are clouded as well, however, with significant questions about its representativeness, funding, and ability to meet local needs. The Niger Delta remains tense today, with continued poverty, rampant interethnic violence, and regular shutdowns in oil production.

In sum, although Nigerian policy toward the Delta has changed and the Ogoni campaign probably played some role in these shifts, the fundamental problem faced by the Ogoni and the other minorities – their political marginality in Nigeria – remains unsolved and little-known abroad. Saro-Wiwa and hundreds of others are dead. Most Ogoni still lead lives of squalor and hopelessness. And MOSOP has declined. These failures stem primarily from the harsh circumstances facing the Ogoni. They were a tiny, minority movement whose claims threatened the most fundamental aspects of Nigeria's political and economic systems. Given these unfavorable conditions, MOSOP's defeats are hardly surprising, whereas its accomplishments, particularly its international elevation of the issues, are noteworthy.

What role did NGOs play in this mixed outcome? An answer to this question can never be definitive because of the difficulty of disentangling international factors from domestic ones. Nonetheless, the escalation of Ogoni protests, the advent of similar mobilizations by other Delta minorities, and the intervention of major NGOs beginning in 1993 corresponded with the rise of Nigerian repression. The Treason and Treasonable Offenses Act, announced during the early stages of NGO action, underlined the regime's sensitivity to the Ogoni's "conspir[ing]" with groups outside Nigeria. Whereas earlier the military had ignored the *Ogoni Bill of Rights* and Saro-Wiwa's inflammatory writings, the state now began a bloody crackdown. During this event, MOSOP's many overseas friends could do little to stop the brutality. And in the gravest crisis that MOSOP faced, the trial of the Ogoni Nine, MOSOP's supporters could not avert disaster even though they roused some of the most powerful governments in the world. To be sure, the Abacha regime was an exceptionally arrogant and brutal dictatorship evincing little concern for its reputation overseas. Nonetheless, this outcome hints at both the costs and limits of NGO activism. Notwithstanding the many benefits it bestowed, NGO intervention came at the price of MOSOP's downplaying its core minority agenda. The association between repression and international activism also suggests the need for caution both by local movements and NGOs. The pursuit of foreign backing may drive a movement to actions and rhetoric that, although necessary to attract overseas allies, have provocative effects at home. Once gained, NGO assistance may promote unrealistic expectations both about an insurgency's prospects and its patrons' power to help achieve them. Of course, movements like MOSOP enter the transnational support market with open eyes, acting autonomously and with full recognition of the dangers they face. But they often do so believing that transnational civil society can have more potent effects in their conflicts than is in fact the case.

4

The Making of an Antiglobalization Icon

MEXICO'S ZAPATISTA UPRISING

On March 11, 2001, 24 leaders of Mexico's Zapatista Army of National Liberation (EZLN) trooped into the Zócalo, Mexico City's huge central square. Seven years after their armed uprising, the Zapatistas arrived with government blessing, the group's spokesman, Subcomandante Marcos, proclaiming "We are here" to an audience of more than 100,000. Days later, Comandanta Esther addressed the Mexican Congress, urging adoption of a law granting significant new rights to the country's indigenous population. Throughout the Zapatistas' multiweek stay in the capital and their triumphal bus journey from remote bases in the southern state of Chiapas, foreign supporters accompanied the rebels. Conspicuous among them, dressed in white overalls and acting incongruously as security guards, strode dozens of *monos blancos*, or white monkeys, Italian activists prominent at European antiglobalization protests. In the Zócalo to greet the Zapatistas stood a host of left-wing luminaries: France's ex-first lady Danielle Mitterand, film producer Oliver Stone, and McDonald's "dismantler" José Bové. Around the world, thousands of Zapatista followers monitored the March for Indigenous Dignity, the "Zapatour," on the Internet. To pay for the event, the Zapatistas solicited donations from national and transnational civil society and opened a bank account accessible to depositors around the world.

Yet, in the first days of the uprising, such support had been anything but certain. On January 1, 1994, some 2,500 lightly armed Zapatista soldiers swept out of Chiapas's Lacandón Forest to capture San Cristóbal de las Casas, a city of about 100,000, as well as nearby towns. Previously clandestine, the Zapatistas proclaimed themselves the product of a 500-year struggle by Mexico's poor and dispossessed. They declared war on the Mexican president and army even while vowing loyalty to the country's constitution. Citing a host of social, economic, and political grievances, they demanded "work, land, housing, food, health care, education, independence, liberty, democracy, justice, and peace."[1] Within days, as government counterattacks mounted, the Zapatistas retreated. Meanwhile, the rebellion drew major coverage from the Mexican and international media. During its first week, over 140 domestic and foreign NGOs rushed representatives to Chiapas – despite uncertainty about who the Zapatistas were and what they really wanted.[2] Some monitored the Mexican army's bloody reprisals, while others formed an NGO "caravan" trying to interpose itself between the rebels and the army. In Mexico City, popular support for the Zapatistas skyrocketed, with demonstrations growing to tens of thousands by January 12, 1994. Outside Mexico, new-found Zapatista adherents picketed Mexican consulates and spread the group's communiqués over the Internet.

The burst of domestic and international action exerted tremendous pressure on the Mexican government. By January 11, the army suspended its bombardment of the retreating Zapatistas, and on January 12 President Carlos Salinas de Gortari declared a unilateral cease-fire, allowing the insurgents to retain their arms and a territorial base in the Lacandón forest. Over the following months and years, the Zapatistas received moral, tactical, and material support from diverse sources around the world. They attracted transnational NGOs in the indigenous rights, human rights, social justice, and peace sectors. They became heroes of leftist intellectuals, academics, and activists, spurring many to visit Chiapas to aid the rebels. They galvanized one of the world's first Internet solidarity networks, including numerous listservs and Web sites carrying Zapatista communiqués. And their masked spokesman, Subcomandante Marcos, won celebrity, inspiring many in the emerging antiglobalization or global justice movement that made itself known later in the 1990s in Seattle, Genoa, and elsewhere. This multiform assistance, seemingly so unlikely at the start of the rebellion, has been crucial to the Zapatistas, repeatedly saving them from army attacks and helping them achieve significant gains. Early in the uprising, the government implemented political reforms and economic development

---

[1] Ejército Zapatista de Liberación Nacional (EZLN), "Declaración de la Selva Lacandona: Hoy decimos ¡basta!" December 31, 1993, in EZLN, *Documentos y comunicados*, vol. 1 (Mexico City: Ediciones Era, 1994), 35. Unless otherwise stated, all translations are my own.

[2] U.S. House of Representatives, House Committee on Foreign Affairs, Subcommittee on the Western Hemisphere, *Mexico: The Uprising in Chiapas and Democratization in Mexico*, 103rd Congress, 2nd session, February 2, 1994, 17, 73 (statement and testimony of John Shattuck).

projects in Chiapas. Since then, social discrimination toward Mexico's large Indian population has declined. Most importantly, indigenous rights have been placed squarely on the national agenda, although a crucial 1996 agreement on this issue remains unfulfilled even in the new, more liberal administration of President Vicente Fox. Although this tiny movement among a remote fragment of Mexico's poorest has failed to attain many of its sweeping initial goals, its achievements against powerful domestic opposition are nonetheless striking.

In broader context, the Zapatistas' success on the international stage is even more improbable, differing from the experience of similar Mexican challengers during the same period. Mexico's decades-old indigenous movement is a case in point. Despite nationwide organizing among Indian populations, the movement had little overseas recognition during the early 1990s beyond a small circle of indigenous rights NGOs overseas. Even major protests in San Cristóbal surrounding the 1992 Christopher Columbus Quincentenary garnered little interest outside Mexico, and the Indians' domestic clout remained small. The Zapatistas' international support also contrasts with the isolation faced by another Mexican insurgent movement, the Popular Revolutionary Army (EPR). This group, which had a significant popular following in the poor southern state of Guerrero, made its first appearance in June 1996 with a prominent but peaceful protest against government repression of peasant political activism. In August and September 1996, the group attacked government installations in a half dozen states across southern Mexico, even hitting Acapulco. Since then, despite harsh government repression, the EPR has remained active, organizing cells among peasant communities in southern Mexico, occasionally striking military targets, and forming a fringe political party, the Democratic Popular Revolutionary Party (PDPR). All the while, however, the EPR's efforts to attract outside support have fallen flat.

How did the Zapatistas gain such strong backing? Why did this movement succeed abroad when others failed? This chapter emphasizes the Zapatistas' dramatic entry onto the Mexican and international scenes during the first days of the rebellion. Seizing San Cristóbal demonstrated rebel power and created a unique if ephemeral platform from which to project the movement, attracting the media, advocacy NGOs, and solidarity supporters who had previously neglected the region. The lasting reverberations from these attacks mandate close study of the revolt's first days. But long-term Zapatista backing has hinged also on the group's willingness and ability to modulate its goals, tactics, and other features to appeal to distant audiences.

Finally, this chapter highlights two players overlooked in the literature on transnational networking, the media and domestic Mexican vouchers. Neglect of the press is particularly striking. If analysts consider it at all, they typically view the media as a target of network activity, not a crucial vehicle for activating NGOs in the first place. However, this book's marketing approach, with its emphasis on local movements' raising awareness and increasing their value to possible supporters, conceives of the media as a key mechanism for achieving these tasks. The part played by national civil society has similarly received little analysis. Yet, in the Zapatista case, its members played a critical role in certifying the movement to overseas supporters.

Before proceeding, it is useful to briefly compare the Zapatistas with Nigeria's Ogoni movement. The EZLN differs from MOSOP in important respects: distinct ideological roots; broader goals; more militaristic organization; and more transgressive actions. The NGOs attracted to Chiapas also included proportionally more solidarity and fewer advocacy organizations than did the Ogoni network – that is, the two movements galvanized different, though overlapping, sectors of the NGO spectrum. And superficially at least, the groups won assistance in different ways. Despite these contrasts, there are fundamental commonalities in the movements' strategies that derive from the transnational support market in which both found themselves. For the Zapatistas, as for the Ogoni, the first crucial task was making themselves known to potential backers far from the conflict zone. Whereas the Ogoni used targeted NGO lobbying over several years, the Zapatistas exemplify an alternative method, that of spectacle aimed at dramatically alerting the world to grievances primarily through the media. Second, the Zapatistas, like the Ogoni, framed their movement for distant audiences. Although the seizure of San Cristóbal gave them more power vis-à-vis potential patrons than the Ogoni initially had, even the Zapatistas had to modify key attributes, less to gain help in the first place than to maintain and expand it later. Nonetheless, the same processes and parallel strategies recur in Nigeria and Mexico.

Roots of Rebellion in Southern Mexico

Southern Mexico has long been one of the country's most backward regions economically, socially, and politically.[3] Outside major cities, large portions

---

[3] The information for this brief background section is based on Jan Rus, Shannan L. Mattiace, and Rosalva Aída Hernández Castillo, "Introduction," in *Mayan Lives, Mayan Utopias: The*

of the population suffer poverty, illiteracy, and disease. Opportunities have been few and development minimal. Underlying these problems is uneven land distribution, a legacy of Mexico's colonial past. Historically, a small number of wealthy landowners has dominated a large population of landless and small-holding peasants. Conflict between these groups fueled the Mexican Revolution in 1910, and the country's 1917 constitution included provisions to remedy the situation. Under Article 27, agricultural land was to be redistributed to the rural poor and held permanently as communal *ejidos* by local villages. But after the presidency of Lázaro Cárdenas in the 1930s, reform efforts flagged. Periodically during the rest of the twentieth century, the government instituted redistribution schemes, but particularly in the southern states with weak central control, sharp inequalities persisted and most of the agrarian population remained destitute.

Among those in the deepest poverty, Indians have accounted for a disproportionate share. Across Mexico, those identifying themselves as indigenous today comprise about 30 percent of the country's 105 million people.[4] In southern Mexico, the proportion is larger, with dozens of cultural groups among which a significant portion of the population speaks only indigenous languages. For generations, there has been conflict in Chiapas, sometimes between different Indian communities over scarce resources but more commonly between impoverished Indian communities and *ladino* elites, large landholders of primarily European descent. Prejudice and racism have marked *ladino* relations with Indian populations, mirroring attitudes in Mexico as a whole. Compounding the deprivation and discrimination, local elites have used fraud, intimidation, and repression to maintain power over Indian and peasant communities that sought to vindicate Article 27.

Indigenous Peoples of Chiapas and the Zapatista Rebellion, Jan Rus, Shannan L. Mattiace, and Rosalva Aída Hernández Castillo, eds. (Lanham, MD: Rowman & Littlefield, 2003), 1–26; Lynn Stephen, *¡Zapata Lives! Histories and Cultural Politics in Southern Mexico* (Berkeley: University of California Press, 2002); June C. Nash, *Mayan Visions: The Quest for Autonomy in an Age of Globalization* (New York: Routledge, 2001); John Womack, *Rebellion in Chiapas: An Historical Reader* (New York: New Press, 1999), 1–59; Neil Harvey, *The Chiapas Rebellion: The Struggle for Land and Democracy* (Durham, NC: Duke University Press, 1998); Adolfo Gilly, *Chiapas: La Razon Ardiente: Ensayo sobre la rebelión del mundo encantado* (Mexico City: Ediciones Era, 1997); June Nash, "The Reassertion of Indigenous Identity: Mayan Responses to State Intervention in Chiapas," *Latin American Research Review* 30, no. 3 (1995): 7–41; George A. Collier, "Roots of the Rebellion in Chiapas," *Cultural Survival Quarterly* 18, no. 1 (1994): 14–18.

[4] Central Intelligence Agency (CIA), *The World Factbook* (Washington, DC: 2003), http://www.odci.gov/cia/publications/factbook/geos/mx.html (accessed June 1, 2004).

Map 4.1 Chiapas.

By the late 1980s, events at the national level helped turn the region's simmering frustrations into despair and anger. The ruling Institutional Revolutionary Party (Partido Revolucionario Institucional, or PRI), which decades earlier had legitimated itself by promising to uplift the poor, was now closely tied to the country's elite. After 70 years, the party remained in power through vote-rigging, co-optation, and coercion. In 1988, in an election marked by major fraud, PRI nominee Carlos Salinas de Gortari became president over the candidate of the leftist opposition Party of the Democratic Revolution (Partido de la Revolución Democrática, or PRD). Similarly, at the state level in southern Mexico, the PRI, dominated by a landholding oligarchy, used deceit and violence to maintain control. In 1989, economic conditions deteriorated when the national government lifted price protections on coffee, a major cash crop among southern Mexico's already desperate agrarian population. In 1992, Article 27 of the Mexican Constitution was amended, weakening the decades-old *ejido* system in favor of greater private ownership and further embittering the rural poor. In addition, the North American Free Trade Agreement (NAFTA), negotiated during the early 1990s and permitting imports of cheap North American corn and other products, threatened peasants' meager livings.

Individuals and communities responded to these dire economic, social, and political conditions in various ways. In the 1970s and 1980s, thousands of landless people moved to remote areas such as the Lacandón Forest, where they hoped to establish small homesteads. There and elsewhere, local communities organized to seek improvements and to protect themselves from abusive landowners. Some joined independent rural workers' unions that had long agitated for land reform and development assistance. Beginning in the 1960s, the Catholic Church, under the San Cristóbal diocese's new bishop, Samuel Ruiz, took a more political stance, too. Imbued by the tenets of liberation theology, Ruiz began a major program to help the region's poor and indigenous, in the process alienating landholding elites. With Ruiz's encouragement, the state's Indian population, diverse remnants of the Mayan empire, mobilized during the 1980s, reflecting a resurgence across Mexico and Latin America.

Conditions in Chiapas also offered fertile ground for radical politics. The EZLN began operations in the 1970s as the armed wing of the Forces of National Liberation (Fuerzas de Liberación Nacional, or FLN), a clandestine movement formed in 1969 and inspired by Mao Tse Tung, Ernesto "Che" Guevara, and Fidel Castro. Seeking violent overthrow of the capitalist system, the FLN's primary activity during the 1970s and 1980s involved secret organizing in various Mexican states.[5] Beginning in 1983, a handful of EZLN commanders moved to the Lacandón Forest. Finding their class-based worldview unsuited to the isolated Indian populations there, they spent years learning about local needs, indigenous culture, and ethnically based discrimination. With the collapse of Europe's communist regimes, the group had further reason to seek new ideas. By the early 1990s, the EZLN had developed a loose ideology that mixed its socialist roots with community concerns and customs. These shifts, which led the EZLN to break from the FLN in late 1993, also manifested themselves in organizational changes. Most notably, leaders of the diverse Indian groups that had entered the Zapatista fold, among them the Chol, Tzotzil, Tzetzal, and Tojolabal communities, formed the Clandestine Revolutionary Indian Committee-General Command (CCRI-CG), the EZLN's top decision-making organ. Subcomandante Marcos, the Zapatistas' primary spokesperson and military strategist, claims to take orders from this shadowy command. With Chiapas's charged atmosphere and acute poverty, EZLN numbers slowly grew, its advocacy of force both to protect constituents from landowners and to bring social change attracting thousands in the Lacandón. On the eve of its attacks, the EZLN remained a local group, but it was well organized and its desperate membership committed to act.

In Guerrero as well, radical groups had long operated. During the 1970s, the National Revolutionary Civic Association (ACNR) and the Party of the Poor (PDLP), both small and secretive exponents of revolutionary Marxism, waged guerrilla warfare against the government.[6] After the 1974 death of the PDLP's leader, the war ended, being replaced in the 1980s by persistent but largely nonviolent conflict between independent peasant organizations and government-controlled unions. Conflict between the PRI and the leftist opposition PRD was also fierce, particularly after Salinas de Gortari's 1988 presidential victory, when protests against the election's fraudulence were met with bullets, leaving dozens dead over the following two years. In the wake of the Zapatista rebellion, the PRI-led state government cracked down on legal peasant organizations, most notoriously on

---

[5] Womack, *Rebellion in Chiapas*, 35–36.

[6] Maribel Gutiérrez, *Violencia en Guerrero* (Mexico City: La Jornada Ediciones, 1998); Alejandro Martínez Carvajal, *Ejército Popular Revolucionario (Guerrero)* (Acapulco: Editorial Sagitario, 1998).

June 28, 1995, when state security units killed 17 members of one group near Aguas Blancas. The precise timing of the EPR's formation and entry into Guerrero is uncertain, but the group secretly recruited both within the state and elsewhere across southern Mexico during the mid-1990s, eventually attracting hundreds of members and winning support from thousands more, particularly in the hardscrabble communities of rural Guerrero. Although there are large Indian and mixed populations in the state, EPR ideology and rhetoric are rooted in class-based critiques of the Mexican system.

In the following sections, I examine factors that have helped and hurt each group in gaining outside support. To facilitate analysis, I offer a brief chronology of the Zapatista conflict, focusing on events of national significance (while omitting much about the ongoing, sometimes bloody turmoil at the local level). As mentioned previously, army attacks against the retreating Zapatistas ended on January 11, 1994, leaving 145 confirmed dead, hundreds more wounded, and 20,000–35,000 people displaced.[7] The ceasefire left the Zapatistas with their arms and their freedom. The government also agreed to talks in February 1994, pledging reforms to Mexico's electoral process, increases in social spending, and changes in Indian rights. Meanwhile, peasants elsewhere in southern Mexico seized the opportunity created by the revolt to invade large landholdings. In Chiapas alone, organizations belonging to the State Council of Indian and Peasant Organizations (CEOIC), a nongovernmental umbrella group, took over 100,000 hectares from 342 estates by mid-April 1994.[8]

From February 16 to March 2, the Zapatistas negotiated with a top PRI official on diverse social, economic, and political issues. Daily bargaining sessions and news conferences were broadcast on national television from San Cristóbal's central cathedral, transfixing Mexican audiences. On March 2, the parties reached a tentative agreement, but after three months of secret consultations with its base communities, the EZLN reported its overwhelming rejection. By this time, with a national election looming, the Zapatistas' prominence had diminished. To counter the decline, the movement issued the Second Declaration of the Lacandón Forest on June 10, 1994, proclaiming civil society's "sovereignty" to democratize Mexican politics and the Zapatistas' willingness to participate. To begin this process, the

---

[7] Physicians for Human Rights and Human Rights Watch/Americas, *Mexico: Waiting for Justice in Chiapas* (Boston: Physicians for Human Rights, 1994), 28, note 39.

[8] Ibid., 20, note 23.

Zapatistas invited thousands of NGOs and individuals representing civil society to the National Democratic Convention aimed at formulating a new "national project."[9] But in the August election, generally considered one of Mexico's cleanest except in Chiapas, the Convention had little impact and the PRI retained control of the country's powerful presidency. In late 1994, conflict worsened in the state as the Zapatistas rejected the PRI's new governor, mounting protests for his electoral opponent and declaring several "autonomous multi-ethnic" districts. In a peaceful mobilization in mid-December 1994, the Zapatistas established new positions in dozens of Chiapas communities and, days later, issued the Third Declaration of the Lacandón Forest, calling for indigenous autonomy nationwide. Meanwhile, other Indian groups established their own small autonomous zones elsewhere in Chiapas.[10]

In February 1995, the newly installed federal government of President Ernesto Zedillo issued arrest warrants for Zapatista leaders, publicly identified Marcos as Rafael Guillén, a former university professor, and opened a military offensive. In response, hundreds of thousands took to Mexico's streets, and transnational networks rolled into action to demand an end to the sweep. Within days and without capturing top leaders, the government was forced to halt its attacks and open new talks, which began in April in San Andrés Larrainzar. After months of procedural wrangling, the negotiators settled on "Indigenous Rights and Culture" as the first of several subjects. In February 1996, government and Zapatista representatives signed the San Andrés Accords, granting the country's indigenous people the right to "free determination," including autonomous political, social, and economic organization. However, months later, Zedillo repudiated a revised version of the Accords, prompting the Zapatistas to reject further peace talks while strengthening their own social, educational, and economic institutions in communities they controlled. Meanwhile, tensions in the region intensified, with the army tightening its grip around Zapatista areas. On December 22, 1997, paramilitary units affiliated with local landlords killed 45 unarmed civilians in the pro-Zapatista town of Acteal.

---

[9] EZLN, "Segunda Declaración de la Selva Lacandona," June 10, 1994, *¡Ya Basta!*, http://www.ezln.org/documentos/1994/19940610.es.htm (accessed July 15, 2004).

[10] Araceli Burguete Cal y Mayor, "The de Facto Autonomous Process: New Jurisdictions and Parallel Governments in Rebellion," Carlos Pérez, trans., in Rus, Hernández Castillo, and Mattiace, eds., *Mayan Lives*, 191–218.

Under these circumstances, direct dialogue with the government did not resume until the end of the PRI presidency in November 2000. Early on, Mexico's new leader, Vicente Fox, declared he could resolve the Zapatista conflict quickly, and within months he had met three Zapatista conditions for negotiation, most importantly removing army garrisons near rebel communities. He also proposed constitutional reforms that implemented many of the provisions originally proposed in the San Andrés Accords. The February 2001 Zapatour aimed to pressure a recalcitrant Mexican Congress to adopt these measures, but only a diluted version, banning discrimination against Indians but not permitting autonomy, passed both houses. Although immediately rejected by the EZLN and allied indigenous organizations, the measure nonetheless came into effect in August 2001. As of 2004, the conflict in Chiapas remains unresolved, with dozens of "autonomous" Zapatista communities continuing to exist outside state administrative control, subsisting on their own resources and transnational support.

"Making Ourselves Heard"

To return to the pre-uprising period, by 1993 the Zapatistas had expanded their membership significantly. With growing desperation in Mexico, few state institutions to help the rural poor, and the recent example of regime change in Eastern Europe, the Zapatistas came to believe that the time was ripe for revolt both domestically and internationally.[11] Yet they also realized that forcing radical economic and political reform in Mexico, let alone overthrowing the president, was well beyond their capabilities acting alone. In the view of Zapatista leaders, the group could succeed only by convincing powerful third parties to join them. Thus, from the beginning, the rebels sought to activate receptive audiences in Mexico and abroad. Critical to doing so was a means of alerting the outside world to the Zapatistas' existence, grievances, and demands. The New Year's Day attacks were that means. A communiqué dated January 6, 1994, expressly acknowledged that the "primary objective" of these "political-military actions" was to "inform the Mexican people and the rest of the world about the miserable conditions in which millions of Mexicans, especially us, the indigenous people,

---

[11] *L'Unitá* (Rome), "El Comandante Marcos, al Periodico L'Unitá: 'Mejor morir combatiendo que morir de disenteria,'" interview with Subcomandante Marcos, January 1, 1994, reprinted in *Proceso* (Mexico City), January 10, 1994, 8.

live and die."[12] As Marcos stated, "January 1 was our way of making ourselves heard."[13]

In this, the Zapatista strategy succeeded brilliantly, catapulting the rebels from anonymity to celebrity in a matter of hours. The attacks early on January 1, 1994, shook Mexico. By dawn, the group controlled Ocosingo, Altamirano, Las Margaritas, and most importantly San Cristóbal, where they made the most of their new platform, distributing written statements, granting lengthy interviews, and posing for photographs by the city's gathered media. Although the government first sought to portray the uprising as a trivial local matter, by January 3 it began attacking the Zapatistas with a large military contingent backed by heavy weaponry and air power. Faced with this onslaught, the rebels retreated to the jungles, their voice temporarily stilled. Yet their cause continued to be projected vicariously, with a flood of reporting in the domestic and foreign media, much of it quickly reposted on Internet listservs.

Central to their meteoric ascension was the Zapatistas' ability to gain press coverage. This in turn rested on their sudden leap to international stature and their access to the media. Although rumors about guerrilla attacks had swirled in San Cristóbal during the fall of 1993, the rebels were known to few Mexicans and even fewer outsiders before January 1, 1994. Certainly, no one thought of them as a significant force. But by declaring war on the Mexican state and, crucially, by making good on that declaration with the seizure of a large city and substantial territory, the Zapatistas transformed themselves from an unknown insurgency to a key player in the politics of a major country. This was one of the specific intentions of the New Year's Day actions. As Marcos explained in 1995, the Zapatistas delayed their attacks for over a year to build their forces and lay their plans: "To provoke a political effect, ... we would need a spectacular action, ... taking cities and raising flags with large armies, thousands, ... seizing county seats with many troops."[14] Over the ten days following their attacks, their standing

---

[12] EZLN, communiqué, January 6, 1994, *Documentos y comunicados*, 72–73.

[13] Blanche Petrich and Elio Henríquez, interview with Subcomandante Marcos, February 7, 1994, reprinted in EZLN, *Los hombres sin rostro: Dossier sobre Chiapas*, vol. 1 (Mexico City: CEE-SIPRO, 1994), 163.

[14] Carmen Castillo and Tessa Brisac, "Apéndice: Historia de Marcos y de los hombres de la noche," interview with Subcomandante Marcos, October 24, 1994, in Adolfo Gilly, Subcomandante Marcos, and Carlo Ginzburg, *Discusión sobre la historia* (Mexico City: Taurus, 1995), 141. For similar statements, see Petrich and Henríquez, interview with Marcos, February 4, 1994, 147.

only mounted as the tremendous sympathy they generated in Mexico and abroad pressured the government to offer an unconditional cease-fire and negotiations. Making the attacks still more newsworthy was their dissonance.[15] For years before final U.S. passage of NAFTA in November 1993, the Mexican government had heralded its arrival as a powerful "First World" country in a wide-ranging public relations campaign. Nothing could shatter that image more effectively than a guerrilla insurgency able to seize a major city on the very day of NAFTA's implementation. As an article title in the *Economist* boomed, "The Shock Waves Spread," shock waves caused by the real and symbolic impact of the Zapatista attacks.[16]

A second factor facilitated media reporting: easy access to the movement during the first days of the uprising. In part, this stemmed from Zapatista control over San Cristóbal, an important city that had long been a destination for international tourists interested in indigenous cultures and one having excellent transportation and communication linkages. If only for a single day, the Zapatistas secured a prime urban base, where they began cultivating expectant journalists and framing the conflict in their own terms. From San Cristóbal, it was simple for reporters to interview the impoverished Mayan Indians who made up the bulk of Zapatista constituents. Government action inadvertently smoothed media access. During the first week of the uprising, the Mexican state made few efforts to prevent reporters from covering the fighting. This "policy" probably resulted from unpreparedness, although the government unconvincingly trumpeted its transparency. By January 7, as military attacks intensified and bad press grew, the army banned journalists. By this time, however, several critical issues were in the open: chronic poverty and repression in Chiapas; the Zapatista retreat and willingness to negotiate; and disproportionate government reprisals against the EZLN and nearby civilian populations. Even after the army limited press access, reports of bombings and atrocities continued from areas outside the combat zone. And with the cease-fire on January 12, the media and NGOs again enjoyed broad access.

In all of this, the importance of the Zapatistas' audacious New Year's Day attacks can hardly be overestimated. Although the Zapatistas could not have predicted the full impact of seizing San Cristóbal and the other municipalities, their strategic instincts were correct. Had they not taken the towns but simply condemned government neglect and abuse, they would

---

[15] I thank Jonathan Fox for emphasizing this point.
[16] January 15, 1994, 39.

have received as little attention as numerous groups who had made similar statements during the 1993 NAFTA debate. Nonviolent protest would also have had less effect even if it had been sudden and dramatic. In March 1992, for instance, hundreds of Mexico's poor and indigenous participated in the 700 mile Xi'Nich (Ant) March from Chiapas to Mexico City, calling for the reinstatement of Article 27 and broader agrarian reform. Yet the actions won little media attention or public interest outside Mexico. Similarly, many of Mexico's indigenous groups participated in the hemisphere-wide events surrounding the Columbus Quincentenary. These well-planned and heavily promoted events conducted on "anti-Columbus day," October 12, 1992, included a protest in San Cristóbal by 10,000 Indians, many of whom would later participate in the Zapatista rebellion. Again, however, domestic and overseas notice was minuscule compared with that surrounding the uprising.

One can also draw a telling contrast with the EPR. In some ways, its first public appearance paralleled the Zapatistas': the group was unknown to most Mexicans and the world; its actions were a surprise; it chose a meaningful date and location, the June 1996 march commemorating the Aguas Blancas massacre; and it used flowery rhetoric to make its political points. In so doing, the EPR guaranteed itself press coverage in Mexico, though it won little outside the country. Only with the group's guerrilla assaults in late August 1996 did the international media show interest. But the dispersed nature of EPR actions and the group's failure to capture a territorial base limited its standing and made access far more difficult and less sharply focused than in the Zapatista case. Only months after its attacks, in February 1997, did the EPR succeed in granting its first interviews to the foreign press, and overall the group has been far less successful in attracting journalistic interest than the Zapatistas.[17] As one indicator, in the two weeks following each group's initial attacks, there were 337 stories on the Zapatistas and 120 on the EPR in major English-speaking international newspapers; in the ten weeks following the initial attacks, there were 743 stories on the Zapatistas and 201 on the EPR.[18]

---

[17] Julia Preston, "Mexican Rebels Vow a Long, Hard Battle," *New York Times*, February 6, 1997, A10; Sam Dillon, "Mexico Builds a Picture of a Fanatic Rebel Group," *New York Times*, September 5, 1996, A3.

[18] Lexis/Nexis Academic, General News, Major Papers file, http://web.lexis-nexis.com. This comparison was done using the search terms "EZLN or Zapatista" and "EPR or Popular Revolutionary Army." The two-week and ten-week comparison periods started on

Although their initial recourse to force gave them enduring stature, the Zapatistas have used two other mechanisms to maintain overseas awareness since 1994: distribution of written documents through the media and Internet; and personal contacts with individuals and groups drawn to Chiapas by the Zapatistas' needs and allure. Days after the cease-fire, packets of Zapatista communiqués began to reach receptive Mexican journalists, transported by hand to San Cristóbal. Mostly the product of Subcomandante Marcos's prolific, pointed, and playful pen, these writings spanned hard-hitting communiqués and manifestoes, tendentious fables (told by a beetle), a fanciful children's story, and at times inexplicable, almost hallucinatory ravings. First a dribble, then a stream, sometimes a torrent, the size of Marcos's output is impressive, particularly in the context of an ongoing political conflict and arduous lifestyle. Some have criticized Marcos as badly needing an editor; others count him as a literary giant. Both views miss an important point about his writings: Their very extent maintained interest in the Zapatistas. Even if all his messages were read by only a few, and even if their meaning was sometimes opaque, the outpouring kept the Zapatistas in supporters' minds and often in the public eye. Thus, Marcos has acknowledged that one of the Zapatistas' biggest errors in the conflict was breaking the flow of communications, most notably from January 1997 to July 1998, after President Zedillo's veto of the revised San Andrés Accords on indigenous rights. Although the Zapatistas claim that silence is a traditional Mayan response to perfidy (and that they used the period to invigorate their base communities), this cultural practice was not understood by overseas backers. As Marcos has admitted, the 1997–98 period led to "important losses" among distant audiences whose primary connection to Chiapas was through the Zapatista word.[19]

For the most part, however, the Zapatistas followed the adage that "our word is our weapon" – and built their rhetorical arsenal in the months and years after the cease-fire.[20] Significantly, many of their key documents were

January 1, 1994 and August 28, 1996, respectively. In the two weeks following the EPR's first public protests on June 28, 1996, there were only 26 stories.

[19] Elena Gallegos, "A Zedillo no le importa el tránsito a la democracia, asegura Marcos," interview with Subcomandante Marcos, *La Jornada*, November 16, 1998, http://www.jornada.unam.mx/1998/nov98/981117/al.html.

[20] Subcomandante Marcos, *Our Word Is Our Weapon: Selected Writings*, Juana Ponce de León, ed. (New York: Seven Stories Press, 2001).

explicitly addressed to the "peoples and governments of the world" and to the "national and international press," not just to the Mexican people.[21] Attracting supporters abroad by explaining and justifying their actions was clearly a central Zapatista strategy. Of course, these words would have been futile without wide circulation. In this, the Zapatistas again depended on intermediaries, both in the press and among a circle of early backers. Most of the Zapatista communiqués have been printed in full in Mexico's popular, left-leaning national daily *La Jornada*. Beginning in February 1995, the newspaper published them on its Web site. As early as January 1994, they were also translated and reprinted on e-mail listservs run by overseas supporters. From the rebellion's first days, news from Chiapas, communiqués from the Zapatistas, and bulletins about solidarity activities were distributed through an electronic list established in 1993 by academics and activists concerned about the impacts of Article 27's abrogation.[22] Run by the Applied Anthropology Computer Network and housed at Michigan's Oakland University, the ANTHAP listserv provided a critical early forum for information exchange by scholars and activists. Another important source of information, the Chiapas95 site at the University of Texas at Austin, was established by economics professor Harry Cleaver in the fall of 1994. From early in the uprising, Cleaver had circulated information he found on the Internet to members of his Austin-based solidarity group, Acción Zapatista. When this e-mail list became too large, he created an electronic list that provided information by and about the Zapatistas to hundreds of people, primarily in the United States.[23] Other supporters constructed Web sites in numerous languages that featured Zapatista documents and provided information on solidarity activities.[24] One of the earliest and most consequential of these was ¡Ya Basta!, formed in the spring of 1994 as the "mouthpiece for the Zapatistas in cyberspace" and managed by Justin Paulson, a computer

---

[21] See, for example, EZLN, communiqué, January 6, 1994, *Documentos y comunicados*, 72–73; EZLN, "Pliego de demandas," March 1, 1994, in ibid., 178–85; EZLN, "Tercera declaración de la selva Lacandona," *¡Ya Basta!*, http://www.ezln.org/documentos/1995/199501xx.es.htm (accessed July 15, 2004).

[22] Applied Anthropology Computer Network, Oakland University, ftp://vela.acs.oakland.edu/pub/anthap/Chiapas_News_Archive/ (accessed January 26, 1997; site now discontinued).

[23] Harry Cleaver, "Background on Chiapas95," http://www.eco.utexas.edu/faculty/Cleaver/bkgdch95.html (accessed July 15, 2004).

[24] Links to many of these are collected at Cleaver's Web site "Zapatistas in Cyberspace: A Guide to Analysis and Resources," http://www.eco.utexas.edu/faculty/Cleaver/zapsincyber.html (accessed July 15, 2004).

systems administrator at Swarthmore College.[25] Originally ¡Ya Basta! featured translations of Zapatista documents, primarily in English but also in Portuguese, French, and German; by 1995 Spanish became its dominant language. Often believed to be the Zapatistas' own Web site, it was independent and unofficial, although the Zapatista leadership approved the use of ezln.org as its domain name. As early as mid-1994, books of Zapatista communiqués and other writings were also published. There are now volumes in Spanish, English, French, German, Italian, and other languages. As a result, the profusion of Zapatista writings was easily accessible to interested audiences.

Although the Zapatistas' printed and electronic materials reached a wider audience than any other method – the ¡Ya Basta! Web site claimed four million visits by 2003 – face-to-face contact also played an important role. At first this was primarily with journalists. In the early months of the uprising, major national and international media scrambled to interview Zapatista leaders and report on the movement. Writers affiliated with left-leaning periodicals were particularly eager to report on the rebels and interview Zapatista comandantes. Backers from solidarity and advocacy groups took longer to arrive, although they trickled in from early on. Some had close contact with the rebels at the San Cristóbal negotiations in February 1994, affording the Zapatistas a critical opportunity to learn their newfound supporters' views.[26] By 1995, a thriving "revolutionary tourism" trade had developed, offering the faithful and the curious a chance to mingle with the rebels and visit Zapatista communities. In addition, Zapatista leaders occasionally journeyed outside the Lacandón to San Cristóbal, Mexico City, and abroad, where they proselytized for the movement and energized existing networks.

In mid-1994, the Zapatistas institutionalized their presence in the United States, appointing an official representative, the El Paso–based National Committee for Democracy in Mexico (NCDM), led by a Mexican American activist who had met with the rebels in June. The NCDM lobbied American legislators to pass resolutions supportive of the Zapatistas, campaigned to keep the media spotlight on Chiapas, and published a monthly newspaper on the conflict, *Libertad*. The Zapatistas have also "exported" their movement in less formal ways. At the rebels' urging, dedicated

---

[25] *¡Ya Basta!*, http://www.ezln.org/acerca.en.html (accessed July 15, 2004).
[26] Yvon Le Bot with the collaboration of Maurice Najman, *El sueño Zapatista*, interview with Subcomandante Marcos, August 1996 (Barcelona: Editorial Anagrama, 1997), 216–18.

solidarity activists have implemented Zapatista practices within their own societies, and many identify closely with the rebels. For instance, when asked when and how his organization was formed, the leader of the Italian *monos blancos*, which have modeled their protest tactics on the Zapatistas', stated, "We have a dream in which we were born on January 1, 1994, alongside the Zapatistas. The dream is good and not a total fantasy, but the reality is different."[27] The group was in fact formed in 1997. No matter; the actions of this and other groups, on issues ranging from local to global justice, play an important role in projecting Zapatista ideas abroad. Through all of these means, the Zapatistas raised awareness among new audiences and deepened commitment among those already knowledgeable.

Notably, the EPR had far less success in projecting its views. Like the Zapatistas, the EPR has produced a body of revolutionary writings justifying their actions and discussing their goals. But there are huge differences. In sheer bulk, Marcos's output dwarfs the EPR's. More importantly, distribution of EPR materials is limited, although the EPR also now has a Web site, apparently administered in Italy, featuring key documents and its magazine, *El Insurgente*.[28] Whereas numerous books collecting Zapatista writings have been produced, there are only a few collecting the work of the EPR. And, given its illicit status in Mexico, the EPR's personal contacts with its few foreign supporters have probably been rare. Certainly, it has never held large public gatherings or had to accommodate hordes of revolutionary tourists.

What explains the differences? The Zapatistas' successes in projecting the movement – and the EPR's failures – have hinged on the groups' respective standing, accessibility, and public relations skills. The prominence that the EZLN earned during the revolt's first days, their prolonged ability to hold the government at bay, and the resonant framing of their tactics, goals, and identity have convinced individuals and organizations on the international Left to carry Zapatista words on Web sites and listservs. After the February 1994 San Cristóbal negotiations, however, broader press interest waned as the Zapatistas' novelty wore off. Although *La Jornada* maintained

---

[27] Luís Hernández Navarro, "Entrevista con Luca Casarini, vocero de los monos blancos," *La Jornada*, July 15, 2001, http://www.jornada.unam.mx/2001/jul01/01075/mas-monos.html (accessed July 20, 2004).

[28] Partido Democrático Popular Revolucionario/Ejército Popular Revolucionario (PDPR/EPR), "Mexico: Partido Democrático Popular Revolucionario/Ejército Popular Revolucionario," http://www.pengo.it/PDPR-EPR/ (accessed July 15, 2004).

regular and substantial coverage, other national and international media reduced their reporting. In the mid-1990s, what the Zapatistas termed the army's "low intensity war," encirclement and monitoring of rebel territory, aroused slight journalistic attention because, for the most part, the government acted gradually and with little overt violence. To again expand public awareness, the Zapatistas adopted several strategies. In 1996, the NCDM launched its "Giving Voice to Silence Fund," a national campaign involving a speakers' tour, organizing, and fund-raising specifically aimed at keeping the conflict visible in the United States.[29] More importantly, the Zapatistas have sought to create and exploit political spectacle at home. On a small scale, the Zapatistas use the occasional visit by foreign notables to attract media coverage. They have also executed major events in Chiapas and elsewhere in Mexico, including the National Democratic Convention in August 1994, the Continental Encounter for Humanity and against Neoliberalism in April 1996, the First Intercontinental Encounter for Humanity and against Neoliberalism in July 1996, and the March for Indigenous Dignity in early 2001. These serve other functions within the movement, but generating journalistic interest and thereby spreading word of the Zapatistas is an important consideration. Although the events' star-studded, leftist coterie sometimes overshadows the complex political issues in the conflict, even fleeting and flippant coverage helps the rebels, as Marcos explained during one of the encounters in 1996: "All's fair in love and war. [The media] risk turning [us] into an attraction . . . but the indigenous will gain security. That is the main point. . . . So we say, welcome to the celebrities."[30]

The EZLN's relatively easy access to the outside world also played a major role in its ability to project the movement. Through most of the conflict, the Zapatistas have had little difficulty dispatching their deluge of revolutionary documents from the Lacandón forest to the world. And with Mexican government toleration, they exerted dominion over substantial

[29] National Commission for Democracy in Mexico, "Contribute $10 Towards National Press Campaign! Help Break the Media Blockade on the Low-Intensity War in Chiapas," fundraising flyer, n.d. [1996?], Special Collections, Gumberg Library, Duquesne University, Pittsburgh [hereafter cited as Gumberg Library].

[30] Régis Debray, "Si Desaparemos, sólo quedará la violencia, una Yugoslavia en el sureste Mexicano," interview with Subcomandante Marcos, April 1996, reprinted in *EZLN: La utopía armada: Una visión plural del movimiento Zapatista*, Marcelo Quezada and Maya Lorena Pérez-Ruiz, eds. (La Paz, Bolivia: Plural Editores/CID, 1998), 292.

territory, permitting entry by journalists and activists – sometimes thousands at a time – for the encounters. Indeed, for a time, the government went so far as to have the Catholic Diocese's Fray Bartolomé Human Rights Center stamp visas of those entering Zapatista-controlled zones. Why did the government permit both easy entry and exit to the Zapatistas? Initially, the Zapatistas' stunning success in Mexican civil society – and the government's commensurate hobbling – played a major role. Public opinion polls in Mexico showed a 61 percent approval rating for the Zapatistas on January 7, 1994, and a 75 percent rating on February 18 of that year.[31] The army's most vigorous attempt to capture the rebel leadership, in February 1995, had to be suspended before it reached its goal, as protests rapidly mounted at home and abroad. Similarly, had popular pressure not prevented it, the authorities could have limited if not halted Marcos's spate of media interviews. Stanching the flow of Zapatista communiqués would have been more difficult, but the government could have slowed it but for the rebels' popularity. Instead, most likely because it believed such overt hindrances would only strengthen sympathy for the rebels, the state has for the most part permitted the Zapatistas to communicate to the world with relative freedom.

One revealing exception involved a government policy of impeding entry by sympathetic foreigners beginning in 1998. Stoking nationalistic sentiments against interference in domestic affairs, Mexico implemented a special visa rather than an ordinary tourist visa covering those engaged in political work. This reduced the flow of supporters to Chiapas and allowed the government to track them more closely. Beginning in early 1998, Mexico also ousted scores of international human rights observers and solidarity activists for violating their visa terms, with some permanently banned from Mexico. For their part, the Zapatistas, fearing that these actions would undermine local power and overseas enthusiasm, used the deportations to excite further overseas interest in Chiapas. Expelled activists lobbied U.S. and European policymakers and met with the press.[32] Under the Fox government, heavy-handed actions have eased, although the new visas remain.

---

[31] Tim Golden, "Rebels Battle for Hearts of Mexicans," *New York Times*, February 26, 1994, 5.

[32] Global Exchange, "Foreigners of Conscience: The Mexican Government's Campaign against International Human Rights Observers in Chiapas," http://www.globalexchange.org/countries/mexico/observers/report/ (accessed July 20, 2004).

Beyond access, Zapatista skills at media relations also contributed strongly to their maintaining outside interest. The movement's leadership carefully planned a media strategy, viewing the press as critical to publicizing the cause. As one aspect of this, the Zapatistas have accentuated good relations with the "honest press." In one of the earliest EZLN communiqués, for example, the Zapatistas apologized profusely for their soldiers' detention of several reporters and returned money stolen from them.[33] Marcos devoted another early communiqué to a lengthy explanation of the "reasons and non-reasons" that certain media outlets were chosen to receive Zapatista communiqués.[34] For local audiences, the Zapatistas chose *Tiempo*, a San Cristóbal daily long sympathetic to and popular with the Indian and peasant populations. In addition, for rural populations elsewhere, the Zapatistas placed great emphasis on radio. Finally, for national and urban audiences, the Zapatistas chose three periodicals, the left-leaning daily *La Jornada* and weekly *Proceso*, as well as the mainstream *El Financiero* – each, in Zapatista estimation, objective, open-minded, and influential both at home and abroad. Conversely, two major Mexican television networks, accused of bias by the Zapatistas, were specifically precluded from covering the San Cristóbal negotiations. The Zapatistas engaged in similar strategic thinking with regard to the foreign press, as indicated by early interviews granted to major periodicals such as the *New York Times* and invitations to cover the San Cristóbal negotiations sent to the *Washington Post*, *Los Angeles Times*, *Houston Chronicle*, *Le Monde*, CNN, AP, UPI, AFP, and Reuters.[35]

The Zapatistas' use of the Internet is often noted as further evidence of their savvy. Indeed, from the early days of the uprising, the "electronic fabric of struggle" was an important means of spreading the Zapatista word.[36] Yet this virtual connection has in fact been largely the work of third parties, not the Zapatistas themselves. The Zapatistas did not have their own Web site until 2001, only establishing one for the March for Indigenous Dignity. Especially in the early days of the revolt, their communiqués made their way onto the Internet sluggishly, most after hand delivery to and initial publication in *La Jornada*. Thus, as an initial matter, the electronic aspects

---

[33] EZLN, communiqué, January 5, 1994, *Documentos y comunicados*, 69–71.
[34] Marcos, communiqué, February 11, 1994, EZLN, *Documentos y comunicados*, 137–44.
[35] EZLN, communiqué, January 29, 1994, *Documentos y comunicados*, 110–12.
[36] Cleaver, "Zapatistas in Cyberspace."

of the Zapatistas' "netwar" were a consequence, not a cause, of their gaining critical support from technologically adept third parties.[37] Nonetheless, there can be little doubt that the many pro-Zapatista Web sites also elevated the group's profile among receptive audiences around the world.

In the EPR's case, the same factors go far in explaining its *failure* to make itself heard. Most importantly, with no territory under its control, secretive yet probably significant local support in Guerrero, and government recognition only as a terrorist faction, the EPR never came close to attaining the Zapatistas' standing in Mexico. For these reasons as well, access to the group has been limited and problematic. The international press's relatively few interviews with the EPR were possible only with great difficulty and after elaborate security precautions.[38] To attract attention and demonstrate its weight, the EPR therefore resorted to violence.[39] In this it was none too successful, however, since even though it was active in several states, its hit-and-run attacks paled by comparison with the Zapatistas' capture of major towns and substantial territory. To gain more resources, the EPR turned to armed robbery rather than donated supplies. This in turn alienated many of the same sectors of Mexican society that rallied to the Zapatistas, depriving the EPR of a domestic constituency that might have given it greater standing or pressured the government to loosen access. Eventually, the EPR learned a lesson from the Zapatistas and developed a media campaign,[40] Their efforts to cultivate the international press were often amateurish, however, and, under constant threat from government forces, the group had little chance to improve them.

This comparison underlines that to gain major support local movements must raise international awareness about themselves. The Zapatistas did so using multiple methods undergirded by the standing and access they attained. The EPR has had much more difficulty. Thus, the linkage between visibility and support is more than a truism. For many insurgent groups,

---

[37] See David Ronfeldt, John Arquilla, Graham E. Fuller, and Melissa Fuller, *The Zapatista Social Netwar in Mexico* (Santa Monica, CA: RAND, 1998); John Arquilla and David Ronfeldt, *Networks and Netwars* (Santa Monica, CA: RAND, 2001).

[38] Preston, "Mexican Rebels Vow," A10.

[39] Salvador Corro, "En una sangriente noche de terror, las fuerzas del EPR destruyeron el mito de la pantomima," [In a bloody night of terror, EPR forces destroy the myth of the pantomime], *Proceso*, September 1, 1996, 13.

[40] Dianne Solis, "Mexico's 'Guerrilla Cavemen' Try a Little PR," *Wall Street Journal*, February 7, 1997, A14.

attracting attention without estranging potential backers presents a complex strategic dilemma.

Arousing Civil Society

Despite their importance, Zapatista consciousness-raising strategies cannot by themselves explain the group's wide support at home and abroad. This was most obvious in the early days of the rebellion. The Zapatistas had attacked without warning, precipitating combat that by January 12 had cost hundreds of lives, displaced thousands of civilians, and caused major damage. Although suddenly on the front pages, they had no record against which to compare their bold pronouncements. And many of their claims were muddied by harsh government rhetoric condemning the group as terrorists. Why then did so many third parties leap to their aid? Even in the uncertain early days of the rebellion, ethical, substantive, and organizational matches provide an explanation. After January 12, 1994, the movement began improvising in response to the unexpected results of its attacks. It had not been wiped out by the Mexican army but neither had it been joined by the Mexican masses in a march on the capital. Rather, it had excited both national and transnational civil society to demand an end to hostilities and a start to negotiations. For the Zapatistas, this ambiguous result spurred changes in tactics and ideology aimed at cementing and augmenting third-party commitment. As in the Ogoni case, this sometimes involved significant modifications in key features of the insurgency. Other shifts represent subtle changes in emphasis among the movement's wide variety of original issues. Finally, in several instances, the Mexican government inadvertently enhanced the rebels' appeal.

From "Military Wonder" to Societal Catalyst

The first and most obvious change in the Zapatistas involved tactics – a shift from war to what might best be described as "armed nonviolence." The Zapatistas had long seen military action as crucial to achieving their goals. For years prior to January 1, 1994, they had readied for battle, training their troops, building mock-ups of towns they planned to assault, and engaging in brief firefights with government troops that menaced their camps. When they began the uprising, the Zapatistas declared themselves a belligerent force under the Geneva Conventions. Although their January 1 attacks, with the public burning of government files and rapid recourse to media interviews, were larded with symbolism, the Zapatistas used real (not just wooden) guns, bullets, and even land mines. Unlikely as it now seems, the Zapatistas believed their attacks would not only draw attention but also spur a nationwide uprising, allowing them to "conquer" the Mexican army, "advance to the capital," and initiate "summary judgments."[41] While scrupulously demanding that their forces follow the laws of war and avoid civilian casualties, the Zapatistas saw themselves not as a social movement but as an *army* of national liberation in the tradition of Mexico's revolutionary past. Even after the cease-fire, the Zapatistas remained bellicose. Indeed, Marcos and other Zapatista commanders frequently extolled armed struggle: "[The January 1 offensive] was a military wonder, and nobody seems to want to admit that.... It seems clear to me that there is consensus among the government, all of you [the press], and civil society that the world has to be shown that military alternatives are not a viable option.... I don't know why. The January offensive demonstrated that it is possible to carry out sizable military operations if a series of conditions are present.... We don't give arms a value they don't have. We don't worship arms, but we understand what they represent at one political moment or another."[42]

Nonetheless, since the first days of January 1994, the Zapatistas, although retaining their guns, have not used them offensively and have done so defensively only in isolated instances. Instead, they have made words their chief weapons. This shift stemmed partly from necessity: The strength of the Mexican military made a frontal assault on the Mexican state futile. If the Zapatistas had broken the cease-fire, they would have handed the army an easy excuse for a crackdown. In this circumstance, however, the Zapatistas could have transformed themselves into a guerrilla force, as the EPR and many rebel groups in Latin America's past have done. Instead, they chose armed nonviolence – in large part because their initial supporters demanded it. As the previous quotation indicates, from early in the revolt, the Zapatistas felt a powerful "consensus" urging them to put down their arms. Although remonstrating against this view, the rebels rapidly acquiesced in it. As Marcos stated in a 1996 interview: "Once there was a cease fire, we began to have greater access to what was happening

---

[41] EZLN, "Declaración de la Selva Lacandona," 1993, 34–35.
[42] Petrich and Henríquez, interview with Marcos, February 6–7, 1994, 155, 156, 163.

outside.... Then we became aware that the whole plan we'd developed was no longer possible. We encountered this other force that had appeared – the people, not the government – that was asking us to talk.... This completely broke our plans and ended by defining Zapatismo, neo-Zapatismo."[43]

As this passage indicates, this tactical shift was strongly informed by the Zapatistas' straits. Outside aid was crucial to the Zapatistas' achieving their goals – indeed to their very survival. Accordingly, the movement adapted. As another Zapatista leader commented on the period after the ceasefire: "We follow a path, but see that it is not what is needed now. [So] we take another path. It is not because we are diverted, but because the necessity of change is imposed on us.... We are obeying civil society, as much national as international. We really have to show them this choice and obedience..., accommodating to that which is necessary.... This is how we are creating Zapatismo."[44] Comparison with the EPR underlines that this "accommodation" was in fact a tacit exchange. Civil society would also have preferred the EPR to abandon its weapons. But in the Zapatista case, these demands came with the promise of support, opening the possibility of achieving their goals if they laid down their arms. For the EPR, nothing of the sort was on offer. Thus, the Zapatistas had a real incentive to maintain a cease-fire. The EPR had little – and moved in the opposite direction, from peaceful protest to violent attacks.

For similar reasons, the Zapatistas pioneered a related tactical innovation, championing a broadly defined "civil society" as the vessel of democratic reform in Mexico. From the beginning of the uprising, the Zapatistas had explicitly appealed to NGOs and public opinion both in Mexico and abroad. Early on, however, the rebels saw civil society as an instrument for achieving a set of predetermined goals. Although the Zapatistas never considered themselves a Leninist vanguard – indeed from the beginning they claimed not to seek power for themselves – their earliest public pronouncements mandated a central role for their ideas and themselves in changing Mexico.[45] Thus, in the Revolutionary Laws, they decreed a panoply of new economic and social principles, bedrock tenets for an egalitarian and democratic new Mexico. And in the February 1994 San Cristóbal dialogue, the Zapatista leadership negotiated issues affecting many Mexicans

---

[43] Le Bot, interview with Marcos, August 1996, 209–10.
[44] Le Bot, interview with Tacho, August 1996, 200–202.
[45] *L'Unità*, interview with Marcos, January 1, 1994, 8.

beyond their own constituents. Third parties, both domestic and foreign, would help them achieve these ends and protect them from government repression, but civil society's role in transforming Mexico initially appeared secondary.

Within months, however, Zapatista attitudes had evolved. Energizing a more vibrant civil society became an end in itself, one that would lead to a democratic but otherwise unspecified new Mexico. The Zapatistas no longer claimed a central role for themselves. Nor did they seek to impose a radical program on Mexico, the Revolutionary Laws notwithstanding. Instead, civil society was increasingly conceived as a creative "space" marked by open speech, debate, and deliberation from which a new politics would emerge. As Marcos stated on May 11, 1994, the Zapatista "revolution" would "only be a first step, an antechamber[,] . . . an equilibrium between the different political forces, in order that each position has the same opportunity to influence the political direction of this country. . . . If there is a neoliberal proposal for the country, we shouldn't try to eliminate it, but confront it. . . . We are talking about a democratic space where the political parties, or groups that aren't parties, can air and discuss their social proposals."[46] In this view, the Zapatistas would "lead by obeying" (*mandar obedeciendo*), following the democratically determined preferences of civil society and its "vanguard," the NGOs.[47]

Signaling this shift, June 1994's Second Declaration of the Lacandón Forest called on "all honest Mexicans of good faith" to attend a nonpartisan National Democratic Convention.[48] The Convention would plan a transitional government and propose a new constitution before August 21's national election, whose expected fraudulence the Zapatistas believed would lead to the collapse of the Mexican government. Significantly, the Second Declaration envisioned reform without formal participation by Mexico's political parties, even the leftist opposition PRD. Meeting in a jungle site specially built by the Zapatistas and symbolically christened Aguascalientes, over 6,000 mostly Mexican delegates, 600 journalists, and 300 observers

---

[46] Eugenio Aguilera, Ana Laura Hernández, Gustavo Rodríguez, and Pablo Salazar Devereaux, interview with Subcomandante Marcos, May 11, 1994, reprinted in EZLN, *¡Zapatistas! Documents of the New Mexican Revolution (December 31, 1993–June 12, 1994)*, Autonomedia, ed. and trans. (New York: Autonomedia, 1994), 298.

[47] EZLN, communiqué, February 26, 1994, *Documentos y comunicados*, 175–77; EZLN, communiqué, June 10, 1994, ibid., 259.

[48] EZLN, "Segunda declaración de la Selva Lacandona," *¡Ya Basta!*, http://www.ezln.org/documentos/1994/19940610.es.htm.

debated the form of a future democratic Mexico.[49] (With the PRI victory in the August 1994 elections, however, the Convention's proposals had little impact.)

Since 1994, the Zapatistas have extended this civil society approach, holding several ambitious assemblies in Chiapas, most importantly the First Intercontinental Encounter for Humanity and against Neoliberalism in July 1996. Similar encounters have been held in Europe, South America, and Australia, their stated purpose being the development of alternatives to the contemporary "neoliberal" world order. Attracting an ideologically diverse throng of thousands, the First Encounter involved open give and take among its numerous delegates. In effect, it implemented the Zapatistas' new view of civil society. In many sessions, Zapatista delegates simply listened or summarized the ideas of participants. The result was lengthy debate and deliberation, culminating in a vague agenda for future action. Most concretely, the Encounter led to a related tactical innovation, the establishment in the delegates' home societies of small-scale social justice and protest movements whose form and content, the Zapatistas insisted, should hinge primarily on their own local circumstances. As Thomas Olesen has characterized it, this has created a network of "mutual solidarity" across national borders:[50] Distant organizations loosely affiliated with the Zapatistas but whose main focus is reforming their own societies monitor the conflict and periodically take actions aiding the Zapatistas. In return, the Zapatistas offer inspiration and moral support in these other struggles.

As a final example of the new role assigned to civil society, the Zapatistas have orchestrated national and international polls on key issues. One important instance occurred in June 1995 when the Zapatistas called for a referendum asking among other things whether "the people" still agreed with their original demands and whether the EZLN should form its own independent political wing or unite with existing civil society organizations. Although the wording of these planks was ambiguous, the poll, administered by the country's national organization of election observers, the Alianza Cívica, attracted 1.3 million voters from every Mexican state and

---

[49] Aguascalientes was also the name of the town where, in 1914, Mexico's victorious revolutionary leaders met to plan their new society.

[50] Thomas Olesen, *International Zapatismo: The Construction of Solidarity in the Age of Globalization* (London: Zed Books, 2005).

another 55,000 electronic ballots, mostly from sympathizers abroad.[51] On the question of goals, the voters overwhelmingly affirmed the Zapatistas' democracy and social justice agenda. On tactics, the poll results prompted the movement in June 1996 to form a political wing, the Mexico City–based Zapatista Front of National Liberation (FZLN).

Why did the Zapatistas adopt this civil society approach? Necessity, opportunism, and conviction all played a role. As in their eschewing military action after the New Year's Day attacks, the Zapatistas were moved in part by the need for aid from third parties unwilling to hand a little-known social movement a blank check for radical restructuring. When they found that they could no longer hope to impose their Revolutionary Laws on Mexican society, the Zapatistas switched to using their newfound stature to jawbone for change. Making a virtue out of necessity, they have repeatedly invited ideas and input from their constituents and supporters, modeling on a small scale the role they came to envision for civil society writ large. Yet the movement's evident familiarity and comfort with these practices shows that they correspond to real elements in Zapatista ideology and routines. From early in the uprising, the Zapatistas have stated that the group operates democratically, a claim demonstrated for instance by the leadership's frequent consultations with its base communities and the latter's votes on such key issues as the government's February 1994 peace proposal.

Whatever the precise mix of motives, the EZLN's rapid turn to armed nonviolence and civil society has both deepened and broadened outside backing. First, in several important instances, the sharp contrast between Zapatista peacefulness and government or paramilitary violence has spurred receptive audiences at home and abroad to more vigorous involvement. On February 9, 1995, for instance, when the new Zedillo government opened an offensive to retake rebel territory and arrest the leadership, the Zapatistas did not respond militarily but fled to the Lacandón Forest. Within days, Zapatista supporters mounted massive protests in Mexico City as well as major cities in Europe and the Americas. Under tremendous pressure, the government called a halt to its operations, with top Zapatista leaders still at large and the group's popularity raised to a new peak. More strikingly, the same dynamic operated during the opening days of the rebellion, when little was known about the rebels. Despite their instigation of the fighting,

---

[51] In 1999, the Zapatistas used a similar tactic in an attempt to pressure the Mexican government to implement the San Andrés Accords, attracting three million voters in Mexico and 58,000 abroad.

the Zapatistas quickly came to be perceived as less violent than the government. The EZLN offensive lasted only a few days, many Zapatista fighters were poorly armed, the rebels were careful to target only military and government installations, and they nonviolently retreated to the countryside. Thus, when brutal army counterattacks began, the rebels and their civilian constituency quickly came to appear as the likely victims of a vengeful government. For individuals and organizations familiar with Mexico's repressive human rights record, this threat alone spurred action, even without certainty about who the Zapatistas were or how the government would in fact react. On January 2, 1994, for instance, Jorge Mancillas, an expatriate Mexican professor working in California and having personal connections to well-known American politicians and activists, decided to form a high-profile human rights observer delegation. He did so despite ignorance of what the Zapatistas really stood for – in his words, despite uncertainty about whether the Zapatistas would turn out to be "one of those awful brutal aberrations like the *Sendero Luminoso* (Shining Path) or the Khmer Rouge." Fearing a bloody government over-reaction more, Mancillas believed immediate action was necessary.[52]

Similarly, changes in the relative violence of the Zapatistas and the army spurred other third parties into action. During the first days of the uprising, key editorial voices in the domestic and international press had condemned Zapatista actions and praised government moderation – even while criticizing long-term Mexican neglect.[53] On January 4, however, when the military offensive intensified and army human rights violations surfaced, the retreating Zapatistas and nearby civilians appeared poised for slaughter. News coverage rapidly reflected these changes. As one example, the *New York Times* described a stark contrast: on the one hand, trained government forces deploying air power and heavy weapons; on the other, "an army of innocents" bearing "pistols, ancient carbines and even toy wooden rifles."[54]

---

[52] Jorge Mancillas, "The Twilight of the Revolutionaries," in *The Zapatista Reader*, Tom Hayden, ed. (New York: Thunder's Mouth Press/Nation Books, 2002), 157.

[53] "No a los violentos" [No to the Violent], editorial, *La Jornada*, January 2, 1994, 1; "Privilegiar el dialogo" (To Promote Dialogue), editorial, *La Jornada*, January 3, 1994, 3; "The Other Mexico," editorial, *New York Times*, January 4, 1994, A14. See generally Raúl Trejo Delabre, *Chiapas: la comunicación enmascarada; los medios y el pasamontañas* (Mexico City: Diana, 1994).

[54] Tim Golden, "Mexican Rebels are Retreating; Issues are Not," *New York Times*, January 4, 1994, A1. See also Dudley Althaus, "Retreating Rebels Strafed by Mexican Planes," *Houston Chronicle*, January 5, 1994, 1(A); Juanita Darling, "Aircraft Strafe, Bomb Fleeing Mexican Rebels," *Los Angeles Times*, January 5, 1994, A1.

Among NGOs, action also intensified as the conflict's character shifted. During the first days of the rebellion, Human Rights Watch/Americas had merely monitored the situation from the United States. After the government turned from stunned defense to heavy-handed offense, however, the NGO deepened its involvement significantly, sending its own observers to the conflict zone. The group's director, Juan Méndez, explained the shift this way: "At the beginning we were pleased by the measured form in which the Mexican federal government appeared to be responding, but now we are worried because this moderation appears to have disappeared."[55] Numerous other human rights organizations, including Amnesty International, Physicians for Human Rights, and the International Commission of Jurists, also issued warnings or dispatched fact-finding missions to Chiapas as army attacks sharpened.

As the Zapatistas' annihilation apparently loomed, dismay over disproportionate government responses rose. Although the Zapatistas had initiated the fighting, they came to be perceived as victims (albeit highly proactive victims) not only of long-term societal oppression but, more importantly, of excessive government reprisals. This lightning transformation created a simple but urgent humanitarian imperative for action. Did this change result from a considered Zapatista strategy? Although the evidence on this is mixed – the Zapatistas' retreat had much to do with their being outgunned – the movement leadership has claimed such a strategy. In February 1994, Marcos asked rhetorically, "Why is it necessary to kill and die, to get you [the country], and through you, the world, to listen to [us] ... say a few small, true words without seeing them lost in the void?"[56] In an interview two years later, Marcos was more explicit: "[T]he war was planned with this in mind: the indigenous communities were prepared for retreat and resistance, and counted on the fact that a successful military action was initially going to require that the government fire its machines of death, though not with impunity. We would have to raise the cost of indigenous blood ... saying that this country was assassinating the indigenous, including indigenous blood in the market of values.... The communities would have to prepare themselves and resist for the time necessary for public opinion worldwide and nationally to begin to bubble up and pressure

[55] Juan Méndez, quoted in Jim Cason and David Brooks, "La televisión de Estados Unidos destaca las presuntas ejecuciones y el bombardeo aéreo," *La Jornada*, January 6, 1994, 17.
[56] Subcomandante Marcos, press conference, February 22, 1994, in EZLN, *¡Zapatistas! Documents*, 214.

the government."[57] Whether or not these are post hoc rationalizations, the Zapatistas quickly profited from this dynamic. If the Zapatistas had initiated further fighting or even defended themselves militarily, their support would likely have fallen. As the U.S. spokesperson for the Zapatistas, NCDM leader Cecilia Rodriguez, stated in 1996, "The first party to fire a shot loses politically" (although not necessarily on the ground – the February 1995 army onslaught and smaller-scale government incursions in the years following slowly narrowed the Zapatistas' territorial control).[58]

By contrast, the EPR appears not to have considered such a strategy. Although their initial public foray in June 1996 was peaceful, the EPR attacked government installations months later. When this provocation elicited army retaliation that threatened civilian populations, the EPR could have held its fire. Despite the Zapatista precedent, however, the EPR continued sporadic assaults for years. More strikingly, the group advertised linkages to Mexico's notoriously violent guerrilla movements of the 1970s. As a result, even in the face of major government onslaughts against rebel territories and numerous casualties, including many civilians, the EPR won little sympathy at home or abroad. Notwithstanding human rights reports castigating the government for these attacks, the EPR has not enjoyed the victim status that benefited the EZLN, the government's tarring of the group as "terrorists" has stuck, and few have taken to the streets in defense of Mexico's "violent rebels."

In addition to deepening support, the Zapatistas' tactical framing also broadened it. On the one hand, among the radical left in Latin America, Europe, and the United States, the Zapatistas' previous use and continued flaunting of weapons tapped romantic revolutionary notions. Many of these militants, formerly active in solidarity networks backing armed insurgencies in Guatemala, Nicaragua, and El Salvador, found the Zapatistas attractive as well. Although some in this camp rejected the Zapatistas as too moderate, many others heard echoes of Che Guevara. As one Denver-based activist has stated: "A lot of people come to the Zapatista struggle because they are enamored with this idea of armed indigenous resistance, they want to go down and volunteer, they want to go down and join, they want to pick up a gun.... [A] lot of people go to the Zapatistas because of this glamour, and

---

[57] Le Bot, interview with Marcos, August 1996, 185.

[58] Cecilia Rodriguez, "Chiapas Update: The Zapatistas and United States Intervention in Mexico" (speech, Center for International Studies, Massachusetts Institute of Technology, Cambridge, MA, November 20, 1996) (answer to author's query).

they will say, is there any way I can join the Zapatistas, I want to run around the mountains with a mask and a gun."[59] For these enthusiasts, the prosaic realities of the Zapatista struggle since January 12, 1994 – organizing village by village, negotiating point by point, bearing arms only as symbols – may come as a shock. But hundreds have nonetheless taken up the Zapatista call.

Simultaneously, the Zapatistas' exaltation of civil society also appealed to less militant activists and NGOs. The 1990s was in many ways the decade of civil society – at least if judged by the ink spilled in discussion of this vague concept. Particularly for those with little clout in the institutional politics of their own countries, the idea of an alternative realm ostensibly free of self-interest and power-mongering proved appealing. The Zapatistas were one of the most prominent exponents of civil society's "sovereignty" in the 1990s, and unlike many others they sought to implement their ideas locally, nationally, and internationally. For some on the radical Left, the Zapatistas' refusal to espouse an orthodoxy proved disconcerting; seeking an ideology, a message, or at least a hero, they came to the Zapatistas desperate for leadership – only to find the Zapatistas trying to lead by obeying.[60] For many, however, the Zapatistas' unwillingness to act as a revolutionary vanguard – their apparent rejection of power for themselves – represented a novel and inspiring affirmation of democracy that seemed likely to avoid the arrogance, errors, and repression of state socialism. Supporters could help and observe Zapatista communities in the hills of Chiapas, join international encounters, or participate in mutual solidarity networks overseas. All offered experience in the actual workings of "civil society," helping to foster such grand experiments as the World Social Forums late in the decade.

Since early in the uprising, the Zapatistas' nonviolence has also proved attractive to more moderate peace, social justice, and development NGOs. At the negotiations in San Cristóbal's central cathedral in February 1994, the Zapatistas called for civil society organizations to protect them from possible attacks. Thousands from national and transnational NGOs as well as the local population heard the call, forming a "peace cordon" that protected the Zapatistas from assassination or capture. Meanwhile, social justice and development NGOs set up operations in Chiapas. Those with explicitly nonviolent mandates avoided contact with the Zapatista army itself but, with an end to the fighting, began major new initiatives for the

---

[59] Olesen, *International Zapatismo*, interview with Kerry Appel, October 24, 2000, 172.

[60] Midnight Notes Collective, eds., *Auroras of the Zapatistas: Local and Global Struggles of the Fourth World War* (Brooklyn, NY: Autonomedia, 2001), 57, 95, 98.

impoverished communities in whose name the Zapatistas had rebelled. One of many examples was the Unitarian Universalist Service Committee (UUSC), which prior to the uprising had done no work in Chiapas. Shortly after the end of the fighting, the UUSC entered Chiapas and embraced the Zapatistas' call for "fulfillment of the promises of democracy" for Mexico's poor and indigenous.[61] Because nonviolence is a central tenet of the group's social change mission, however, the UUSC supported the Coordination of NGOs for Peace (Coordinadora de Organizaciones No Gubermentales por la Paz, or CONPAZ), a newly formed Chiapas-based coalition of human rights, social justice, and indigenous rights NGOs pursuing key Zapatista goals through peaceful means. In so doing, the UUSC could simultaneously maintain its core ethical tenets while backing the Zapatistas' "low intensity revolution."[62] Like the UUSC, another NGO, the Interreligious Foundation for Community Organization (IFCO), assists local communities supportive of the Zapatistas through well-publicized humanitarian aid caravans led by its IFCO/Pastors for Peace ministry. Others such as the Mennonite Central Committee, maintain strict neutrality, helping all communities, both pro- and anti-Zapatista, in the conflict zone.

To summarize, the Zapatistas' tactical shifts opened the group to assistance from a wide variety of third parties at home and abroad. The contrast with the EPR's tactical evolution is strong. Although mouthing democratic verities in their early writings, the EPR failed to put these into action until late in their history with the founding of their fringe political party. But this occurred after national and international perceptions of the group had already hardened. In fact, the EPR's more recent statements leave little doubt that it still cherishes a different path to worldly delivery: class struggle ending in their own seizure of state power as a revolutionary vanguard.[63] Because of this tactical choice, domestic and transnational NGOs have kept their distance from the EPR. Moreover, Guerrero has not attracted the number of development and social justice NGOs that descended on Chiapas in the Zapatistas' wake. To their credit, some NGOs, such as Global Exchange and the Mexico Solidarity Network, have started

---

[61] Richard S. Scobie, "Report from Mexico," pamphlet, Unitarian Universalist Service Committee (UUSC), Cambridge, MA, December 1995, 1; Interviewee 44 (UUSC staffperson), personal interview by author, April 13, 1996.

[62] Scobie, "Report from Mexico" (quoting Samuel Ruiz), 2.

[63] See, for example PDPR/EPR, "La lucha de clases en el campo" [Class struggle in the countryside], *El Insurgente*, February 2003, http://www.pengo.it/PDPR-EPR/El_insurgente/el_insurgente51/texto /insurgente51.htm (accessed July 28, 2004).

campaigns in Mexico's "forgotten step-child."[64] But Guerrero remains far less known than Chiapas, and modest recent interest in the state among international environmental NGOs has had nothing to do with the EPR.[65]

Embracing Indigenousness/Reviling Neoliberalism

In addition to changing tactics, the Zapatistas have reconfigured their goals to attract outside backing. Years before the uprising, Zapatista leaders had demonstrated their pliancy by downplaying their original Maoist ideology in the quest for a grassroots constituency in the Lacandón. The amalgam they created in the EZLN combined their early emphasis on class warfare with identity-based indigenous concerns. Since the uprising, the Zapatistas have shown further facility at these adaptive arts in a changing national and international context.

The Zapatistas revealed their initial vision for a Mexico freed from its "class enemies" in the December 1993 Revolutionary Laws, secretly published in Mexico City for distribution after the capital's liberation.[66] Although not outlining everything about the new society, the ten Laws offer insight into key aspects. In many ways, the Laws resembled the plans of socialist-inspired revolutionary movements from Latin America's past; in others, they suggested something different. The Revolutionary Agrarian Law, for example, permitted communities and cooperatives to have unlimited land but called for expropriation of private holdings greater than 50 hectares of good land or 100 hectares of poor land, which would have made it one of the strictest land laws in Latin American history.[67] Agribusiness holdings were to be redistributed as collective property to landless peasants and farm workers. In turn, the latter would have been required to produce foodstuffs satisfying the needs of the people and creating "collective consciousness of work and benefits." All debts owed by the rural poor to the government, foreigners, or capitalists were to be forgiven. "Just and fair domestic trade" would have been permitted, but only between regions not self-sufficient in a product; exports would have been allowed

---

[64] Global Exchange, "Current Campaigns: Guerrero," http://www.globalexchange.org/countries/mexico/campaigns.html (accessed July 20, 2004).

[65] Sierra Club, "International Campaigns: Mexico," http://www.sierra-club.org/human-rights/Mexico/ (accessed July 20, 2004).

[66] EZLN, *Documentos y comunicados*, 37–48.

[67] Ibid., 43–45; Womack, *Rebellion in Chiapas*, 251.

only for "excess production."[68] The Urban Reform Law, which abolished real estate taxes and suspended or slashed rents, permitted groups of families to occupy improved lots, vacant public buildings, and large private residences. Under the Work Law, local commissions would have regulated wages and prices, although without power to reduce salaries. Foreign companies would have been required to pay their workers home country wages, and "nonproductive businesses" were to be nationalized.[69]

Notably, the Zapatistas also promulgated laws covering the rights and obligations of their armed forces and the "peoples in struggle" against the "oppressor government and the large national and foreign exploiters." These granted the undefined "peoples in struggle" the right to choose their own leaders and required the EZLN both to respect the civil authorities so elected and to observe their rules, customs, and agreements.[70] In addition, within the Revolutionary Laws' limits, the "peoples in struggle" could demand that the EZLN not intervene in matters of civil order or the disposition of newly liberated agricultural, commercial, financial, or industrial capital. Finally, those not deemed "enemies of the revolution" were permitted to bear arms to defend themselves and their property. Under the same law, however, the "peoples in struggle" would have been required to act as EZLN guides, porters, and nurses, while local authorities were obligated to provide food, lodging, and means to accomplish military missions.[71] The War Tax law established a sliding scale ranging from no taxes for "the civilian population that lives by its own resources, without exploiting any labor whatsoever and without gaining any advantage from the people," to 7 percent for small commercial business and property holders and 20 percent for large capitalists.[72] Significantly, the Revolutionary Laws also covered women's rights.

Although the Revolutionary Laws give the clearest, if still incomplete, indication of Zapatista plans, their declaration of war, the far vaguer, briefer, and more moderate Declaration of the Lacandón Forest, gained greater prominence, giving the rebellion its distinctive character early on. In retrospect, Marcos has described the Declaration as a "cocktail" of diverse tendencies, a text of minimal agreement among the EZLN's many elements.[73]

---

[68] EZLN, *Documentos y comunicados*, 44.
[69] Ibid., 46–47.
[70] Ibid., 40.
[71] Ibid., 40–41.
[72] Ibid., 38–39.
[73] Le Bot, interview with Marcos, August 1996, 175.

The same could be said for Zapatista media statements on the first day of the uprising. In these written and oral statements, Zapatista grievances spanned local, national, and international issues, everything from poverty to political repression to foreign domination. To achieve their goals, they declared war – but only on the president and the army – calling on the legislative and judicial branches to restore the nation's "legality and stability" and openly embracing all forms of support, whether armed or unarmed. Even Zapatista identity was fuzzy: Their army, composed of poor and indigenous fighters, many illiterate and non–Spanish-speaking, was fronted by educated *mestizos* who justified the revolt by invoking the Mexican constitution and one of the country's heroes, Emiliano Zapata, a man nominally venerated by the state itself.

According to Marcos, when the Zapatistas revolted on January 1, they had only a vague ideology that reflected continuing disagreements rooted in contradictions between their socialist origins and indigenous base. But this very nebulousness permitted a diversity of third parties to find or impute overlapping interests. Thereafter, expansive grievances, goals, and identity became a means of attracting third parties. The Zapatista slogan, "for us nothing, for everyone everything," has therefore found surprising resonance despite its vacuity – or perhaps because of it. Indeed, when the Zapatistas have defined their ideology more specifically, they have sometimes lost support. As Marcos stated in 1996: "Zapatismo must be very clear on this: It can't pretend to create a universal doctrine, to lead a new International or something like that. It is especially this generality, this indefinition of Zapatismo, that is important. It is important to maintain this, not to define ourselves, because contact with international Zapatismo means . . . the possibility of resisting and having a shield more effective than the EZLN, than civil organizations, than national Zapatismo."[74] Further expressing these considerations, the Zapatistas have frequently characterized themselves as a "mirror" in which oppressed groups everywhere can see themselves. And in criticizing the homogenizing effects of globalization, they have repeatedly called for the creation of "a world in which many worlds fit."[75]

Nonetheless, responding to audience interest, government recalcitrance, and ongoing political change, the Zapatistas have defined their goals and

[74] Ibid., 226.
[75] EZLN, "Cuarta declaración de la selva Lacandona," *¡Ya Basta!*, http://www.ezln.org/documentos/1996/19960101.es.htm (accessed August 1, 2004).

identity in certain ways. Almost immediately, they rejected standard socialist dogma. Although top leaders had radical backgrounds, their Revolutionary Laws promoted collectivism, and on January 1 some commanders publicly called for an end to capitalism in Mexico, the Zapatistas' more authoritative public declarations since then have consistently eschewed socialism. Within Mexico, their calls for moderate democratization – overthrow of the president (but not the other branches of government) in the name of the constitution and Mexican patriots – initially resonated with a public fed up with the rampant corruption that had brought Carlos Salinas de Gortari to power in 1988. But by 1995, their impact on broader Mexican politics had declined and they began to identify themselves in new ways, as Indians with two key struggles: for indigenous rights and against "neoliberal globalization."

One striking omission in the Revolutionary Laws concerned indigenous peoples. Despite detailed attention to economic and agrarian topics, as well as emphasis on the rights of women, the Laws were silent about Indians or indigenous issues. The Declaration of the Lacandón, while claiming that the rebels were the product of "500 years of struggle," also emphasized their nationalist goals. There was no mention of Indians or of indigenous rights, cultural preservation, or racial equality, issues central to Mexico's existing Indian organizations. According to Zapatista leaders, this early framing was a deliberate (if hotly debated) strategic choice aimed at appealing to diverse audiences within and outside Mexico. To explain why the Zapatistas initially omitted indigenous concerns, Marcos has stated the following: "The danger that the comrades saw was that we would be perceived as an indigenous war, when . . . it had to be resolved at the national level. . . . They said, 'If you go too much toward the indigenous, it would isolate us. You have to open us up. If you grasp the indigenous, grasp the universal too. Include everyone.'"[76] Thus, if we credit Marcos's statements, the Zapatistas' initial public presentation (and perhaps their own self-conception) was as champions of all Mexico's powerless and poor, not specifically Mexico's Indians.

By the second week of the uprising, however, an indigenous frame had become salient. Of particular importance was Marcos's remark on the first day that NAFTA was a "death sentence . . . an international massacre" for the Indians.[77] Notably, Marcos gave no special prominence to this statement

---

[76] Le Bot, interview with Marcos, August 1996, 176–77.
[77] *L'Unitá*, interview with Marcos, January 1, 1994, 8.

among the dozens he made to the press that day. Yet his provocative words fit perfectly with the national and international setting for the rebellion and were highlighted in press accounts. In response, the government worked to impugn the rebels as "foreigners" and "professionals of violence" who had "manipulated" the region's Indians.[78] Rebutting these charges, within days the Zapatistas repudiated any connection to earlier Mexican terrorist groups such as the Party of the Poor or the Revolutionary Workers Clandestine People's Union Party (PROCUP) and stressed their Indian constituency and leadership.[79] With vouching by third parties such as Samuel Ruiz and with media reports creating "critical distrust" of the government's charges, the Zapatistas quickly won this important battle over identity.[80] In the February 1994 San Cristóbal negotiations, they promoted their indige-nousness and sought reforms that benefited Mexico's Indians. Until late summer 1994, however, broader goals continued to dominate, as indicated by the Zapatistas' sponsorship of the National Democratic Convention, in which indigenous rights remained off the agenda.

After the August 1994 election, however, with their ability to influence national politics eroded, the Zapatistas moved to the more promising in-digenous issues. Thus, in late 1994, the Zapatistas began pressing goals long dear to the country's established Indian movements, most importantly in October, when they called for constitutional reform that would establish "multi-ethnic autonomous zones." By the beginning of 1995, in the Third Declaration of the Lacandón Forest, the Zapatistas' indigenous identity took the fore. Since then, it has remained central, with many Zapatista communiqués adopting a sometimes enigmatic indigenous form and with frequent allusions to Indian ways of thought and decision making. More concretely, the Zapatistas agreed that "Indigenous Rights and Culture" would become the first (and thus far only) subject of the San Andrés nego-tiations. With the government balking at the Accords' implementation dur-ing both PRI rule and the administration of Vicente Fox, indigenous issues have remained the Zapatistas' primary focus. In sum, Zapatista adoption of an indigenous frame had both instrumental and noninstrumental sources.

---

[78] Salvador Guerrero Chiprés, "Mesa de atención especial para Chiapas, anuncia gobernación: Hay manipulación de indigenas," *La Jornada*, January 4, 1994, 13; Elena Gallegos and Emilio Lomas, "Seguimos dispuestos al diálogo: CSG," *La Jornada*, January 7, 1994, 1.

[79] EZLN, communiqué, January 6, 1994, *Documentos y comunicados*, 72–78; EZLN, commu-niqué, June 3, 1994, *Documentos y comunicados*, 254–55.

[80] Vincente Leñero, "El Subcomandante se abre," interview with Subcomandante Marcos, February 17, 1994, *Proceso*, February 21, 1994, 15.

On the one hand, it reflected a core aspect of rebel identity – however, one that was strategically submerged early in the rebellion. Later, the Zapatistas highlighted their Indianness as the identity's resonance became clear and as the movement's ability to affect broader Mexican politics diminished.

From the beginning, this frame unleashed support both from indigenous organizations inside and outside Mexico and from nonindigenous organizations sympathetic to a group so long neglected and abused. For some non-Indians, the Zapatistas' identity struck a mystical chord. Tom Hayden, 1960s radical and latter-day U.S. politician, wrote that his voyage to Chiapas represented "a personal Holy Grail," helping him reclaim the "collective indigenous roots" (Irish in his case) that lay "mangled beneath the architecture of our modern selves."[81] Recognizing his own romanticism – "I felt slightly like another in the long line of crazy gringos seeking rebirth in Mexico" – Hayden was nonetheless moved in part by these sentiments.[82]

Among indigenous organizations at home and abroad, the response was equally strong but more complex. Early on, the North American Indian media provided extensive coverage of the uprising. Many indigenous groups quickly lent assistance, believing themselves to share common identity and grievances with the Zapatistas. Canada's Assembly of First Nations, for example, which conceptualized the rebellion as "another Native land rights battle," mobilized its constituency by analogizing Mexico's revision of Article 27 to the Canadian government's sale of tribal reservations without Indian consent.[83] Imprisoned American Indian leader Leonard Peltier offered the Zapatistas solidarity: "Your blood is our blood. Your fight is our fight. Your victory is our victory."[84] But especially during the rebellion's first year, there were also questions about the movement's socialist origins, non-Indian leaders, and initial avoidance of indigenous issues. For some international supporters, these questions led to strained attempts to package the Zapatistas as heroes in a hallowed history of indigenous resistance.[85] For others, there was suspicion rooted in the history of "mestizo socialists"

---

[81] Tom Hayden, "In Chiapas," in *The Zapatista Reader*, 78, 83.

[82] Ibid., 78.

[83] Jose Barreiro, "Native Response to Chiapas," *Akwe:kon: A Journal of Indigenous Issues* 11, no. 2 (1994): 78.

[84] Leonard Peltier, "Statement of Support," in *First World, Ha Ha Ha! The Zapatista Challenge*, Elaine Katzenberger, ed. (San Francisco: City Lights Books, 1995), 139–40.

[85] Ward Churchill, "A North American Indigenist View," in *First World, Ha Ha Ha!*, Katzenberger, ed., 149–51, 154.

who used Indians as "ideological capital" and "military cannon fodder" in the pursuit of nonindigenous goals.[86]

Mexico's Indians could not be so squeamish. Indigenous movements had for years prior to the rebellion sought to draw national and international attention but with limited success. The rebellion suddenly spotlighted their issues. Many quickly backed the Zapatistas, although not their armed attacks. In response, the Zapatistas began highlighting their indigenous identity and promoting proposals for indigenous rights.[87] Early on, the Zapatistas' relationship with Mexican indigenous organizations was rocky, with Indian organizations objecting to the August 1994 National Democratic Convention's neglect of their issues. But by 1995, with indigenous rights the focus at the San Andrés talks, the bond was close. During the negotiations, the Zapatistas adopted the recommendations of the National Multi-Indigenous Assembly on indigenous rights; they let non-Zapatista indigenous advocates play a major role; and prior to signing the final agreement, they suspended the talks to consult with hundreds of delegates from 27 indigenous peoples across Mexico. Even if fronted by a nonindigenous leader, the EZLN offered a powerful vehicle for articulating Indian grievances, catalyzing formation of a new National Indigenous Congress, and keeping Indian demands squarely on the national agenda.

The EPR stands in stark contrast with this pattern. Although there are numerous reasons for its failures, the group's rhetoric differs from the Zapatistas' in neglecting the indigenous people and their demands.[88] Originally, its goals, like the Zapatistas', were expansive, calling for an armed "short-cut" to democracy, civil rights, and "just international relations."[89] Bowing to the realities of the post–Cold War era, the EPR avoided open calls for a communist revolution, although it railed against capitalism and exploitation. Unlike the Zapatistas' equally vague rhetoric, however, the

---

[86] "Self-Determination and Maya Rebellion in Chiapas: Commentary," *Fourth World Bulletin* 3, no. 2 (1994): 5.

[87] EZLN, "Pliego de demandas," March 1, 1994, *Documentos y comunicados*, 178–85. See Donna Lee Van Cott, *Defiant Again: Indigenous Peoples and Latin American Security* (Washington, DC: Institute for National Strategic Studies, National Defense University, 1996).

[88] This paragraph is based in part on Kathleen Bruhn's detailed content analysis comparing early Zapatista and EPR documents, "Antonio Gramsci and the *Palabra Verdadera*: The Political Discourse of Mexico's Guerrilla Forces," *Journal of Interamerican Studies and World Affairs* 41, no. 2 (1999), 29–55.

[89] Ejército Popular Revolucionario (EPR), "Manifiesto de Aguas Blancas," June 28, 1996, http://www.pengo.it/PDPR-EPR/doctos_basicos/manifiest_aguas.htm (accessed July 20, 2004).

EPR's words sparked little enthusiasm because they were accompanied neither by bold deeds nor by a large local constituency committed to act. More recently, with its efforts to excite support proving fruitless, the EPR has taken off the wraps: Its Web site and official organ, *El Insurgente*, now include pictures of Marx and calls to proletarian revolution.[90] Not surprisingly, this class-based vision continues to omit indigenous issues – and has remained unpopular at home and abroad.

Zapatista framing against NAFTA and, later, "neoliberal globalization" created another strong bond with backers, particularly overseas. The strength of this tie has made these issues appear more important to the Zapatistas than they in fact were – at least before their transnational resonance became clear. Indeed, at first, the Zapatistas gave NAFTA no greater prominence than other grievances. Although understanding the attention-grabbing potential of revolting on NAFTA's implementation date, military considerations – the element of surprise and the Zapatistas' need to train their troops – predominated in the choice of dates. (Had free trade been their central grievance, the Zapatistas could have revolted several months earlier at a strategic moment *before* NAFTA's approval by the Mexican or U.S. governments, perhaps preventing, delaying, or altering the agreement.) As in the case of indigenousness, there were no references to NAFTA or neoliberalism in the Revolutionary Laws or the Declaration of War. More importantly, the history of Zapatista activism in Chiapas, extending back to the early 1980s, well before NAFTA became a major issue, also shows that concern over the trade agreement came late to the movement. Discrimination, marginalization, and repression extending generations into the past and having primarily domestic sources provided the fertile soil on which the revolt grew. Of course, in the years immediately preceding the uprising, liberal economic policies, from the reduction in coffee price protection to the gutting of Article 27 and the prospect of NAFTA, fueled discontent in the Lacandón. Yet, as Zapatista supporter Noam Chomsky acknowledged: "The NAFTA connection is partly symbolic; the problems are far deeper."[91]

In a context primed for NAFTA's implementation, however, the Zapatista attacks on January 1 and Marcos's passing response to a reporter's question, that the treaty was a "death sentence" for the indigenous,

[90] PDPR/EPR, "Mexico: Partido Democrático Popular Revolucionario/Ejército Popular Revolucionario," http://www.pengo.it/PDPR-EPR/ (accessed July 20, 2004).

[91] Noam Chomsky, "Time Bombs," in *First World, Ha, Ha, Ha!*, Katzenberger, ed., 176.

immediately resonated.[92] Key media reports focused on the condemnation of NAFTA. In the United States, the Clinton administration addressed the issue in press conferences (if only to deny any connection between the uprising and the trade agreement), and U.S. congressional hearings in early February 1994 explored possible cross-border impacts of the revolt. Within days, the labor, environmental, and human rights NGOs active in the transnational anti-NAFTA network – groups such as the San Francisco–based Fair Trade Campaign – issued press releases declaring that the Free Trade Agreement had already sparked violence. Little of this was foreseen by the Zapatistas. As Marcos has admitted, the rebels were "lucky that [our] demands coincided, reflected, or mirrored demands in other parts of the country and the world."[93] In response, however, the Zapatistas nimbly adjusted their rhetoric. At the February 1994 San Cristóbal negotiations, one of the Zapatistas' major written demands had now become renegotiation of NAFTA. In numerous press interviews, the Zapatistas also highlighted the deadly impacts of neoliberal economic policies. And since their 1996 encounter "for Humanity and against Neoliberalism," the Zapatistas have come to serve as key inspirations and symbols for the global justice movement.[94]

Why did NAFTA and neoliberalism have such resonance overseas? Part of the reason was clearly overlap between Zapatista goals and those of the NGO coalition that had recently worked to oppose NAFTA's passage. The uprising appeared to vindicate the coalition's criticisms of NAFTA, fueling charges that the U.S. and Mexican governments had withheld vital information about an issue that might have thwarted NAFTA's passage. As a staffperson for then U.S. Congressman Robert Torricelli reportedly stated before February 1994 hearings on the uprising, "What had the White House known about Chiapas and when had they known it?"[95] More importantly, the Zapatistas' attacks on neoliberal policies also meshed with

[92] *L'Unitá*, interview with Marcos, January 1, 1994, 8.

[93] Vázquez Montalbán, interview with Marcos, February 21, 1999, 1 (Revista Domingo), http://web.lexis-nexis.com (accessed July 10, 2004).

[94] Luis Hernández Navarro, "Entrevista con Luca Casarini, vocero de los monos blancos," *La Jornada*, July 15, 2001, http://www.jornada.unam.mx/2001/jul01/01075/mas-monos.html; Midnight Notes, *Auroras of the Zapatistas*; William F. Fisher and Thomas Ponniah, eds., *Another World Is Possible: Popular Alternatives to Globalization at the World Social Forum* (New York: Palgrave MacMillan, 2003); John Holloway, *Change the World without Taking Power: The Meaning of Revolution Today* (London: Pluto Press, 2002).

[95] John Ross, *Rebellion from the Roots: Indian Uprising in Chiapas* (Monroe, ME: Common Courage Press, 1995), 135.

and contributed to an important new theme for the post–Cold War Left – opposition to globalization. In this view, the revolt was a battle for recognition and dignity, for the right to be "different" in an age of global homogenization, and for the idea of local, democratic resistance to dark forces embodied in NAFTA, the World Trade Organization, and the International Monetary Fund. The Zapatistas' idea that their conflict is part of a Fourth World War against globalization (the Cold War being the Third) reinforces the view that insurgents and distant backers fight a common foe.[96]

But the resonance of NAFTA and globalization involves more than coincidence of goals. These frames transformed what might have appeared to be a localized land dispute (as the government unsuccessfully tried to portray it), or at most a national political upheaval, into a conflict directly relevant to the lives of distant audiences. As one activist wrote, "Of course, conditions are very different in the Lacandona Jungle than in the metropolitan European jungle. But there also exist common elements since neoliberalism, that is to say capitalism, penetrates our lives and determines them."[97] More pointedly, these frames linked the plight of indigenous people to the policies and interests of foreign countries, whether accurately or not, making the conflict understandable to distant audiences. As one example, NAFTA could symbolize the threat to indigenous people in a way that Mexico's revision of Article 27 of its constitution could never do. In effect, the NAFTA and globalization frames internationalized responsibility for Chiapas's local issues while at the same time suggesting relatively accessible targets (at home rather than in Mexico) for protest. Not surprisingly, the Mexican government vociferously challenged the frames, arguing that NAFTA had nothing to do with the rebellion. Although this view had some validity as a narrow matter of the EZLN's origins, a variety of neoliberal policies had indeed hurt the Indians, and NAFTA threatened worse. Again then, although Zapatista framing around the trade agreement and neo-liberalism have important strategic purposes, they are not mere ploys. Instead, they correspond to real aspects of the conflict, even if these were downplayed in the Zapatistas' early self-representations. But when these elements found resonance among a variety of alienated, left-leaning audiences – something that the Zapatistas only understood well after the revolt[98] – global justice

---

[96] Subcomandante Marcos, "Chiapas: la guerra," November 20, 1999, *¡Ya Basta!*, http://www.ezln.org/documentos/1999/19991120a.es.htm (accessed July 18, 2004).

[97] Ana Esther Ceceña, "Zapata in Europe," interview with Friederike Habermann, in *Auroras of the Zapatistas*, Midnight Notes Collective, eds., 83.

[98] Vázquez Montalbán, interview with Marcos, February 21, 1999.

and the defense of "difference" became increasingly central to their rhetoric and action.

These points also explain other issues that the Zapatistas have raised. Early in the uprising, the Zapatistas appealed to American self-interest by warning of overwhelming migration flows if Mexico's problems were not solved. This issue, however, never caught on, most likely because the Zapatistas' potential backers on the Left were unmoved by such a threat, whereas audiences fearful of migrants saw neo-liberal rather than radical reform of Mexican society as the best preventative. More successfully, throughout the rebellion, the Zapatistas have sought to link foreign military hardware to violence against them. In the United States, the NCDM's presentation of the issues stressed American involvement, particularly the Mexican army's use of U.S.-supplied drug interdiction helicopters against the Zapatistas. Similarly, allegations that the army used Swiss Pilatus PC-7 aircraft to bomb Zapatista targets early in the rebellion provoked outrage in Switzerland. As a final example of this dynamic, the Zapatistas made much of a 1995 internal memorandum by a consultant to Chase Manhattan Bank, a major investor in Mexico, recommending that the government eliminate the Zapatistas to build confidence in the country's ailing economy. Hailed as the "first hard evidence directly link[ing] Wall Street" to the conflict, the memorandum produced a storm of press and activist criticism – and led to the consultant's firing.[99]

Although the foregoing examples demonstrate the Zapatistas' adaptability and opportunism, it should be noted that they have been unwilling to frame themselves in other ways – losing potentially important support as a result. The Zapatistas' relationship with foreign environmentalists is a case in point. Elsewhere in the world, many indigenous groups have worked closely with environmentalists to protect native lands. And in the first days of the uprising, some American and European environmentalists saw the rebellion as vindicating their opposition to NAFTA. Expecting to find a ready client, Greenpeace sent a mission to Chiapas, and the Sierra Club expressed interest in the Zapatistas as well.[100] In doing so, the environmental organizations projected their own interests onto a celebrated

[99] Pascal Beltrán del Río, "Hay que eliminar a los Zapatistas: Recomendación del Chase Manhattan Bank al Gobierno Mexicano, *Proceso*, February 13, 1995, n.p.; Ken Silverstein and Alexander Cockburn, "Chase Memo Tumult: Come Blow Our Horn," *Counterpunch*, February 15, 1995, 3.

[100] Steve Kretzmann, "Realidad Check," *In These Times*, April 17, 1995, 31; John Ross, "Unintended Enemies: Save a Rainforest, Start a Revolution," *Sierra*, July/August 1994, 45.

foreign movement despite little evidence of overlapping goals. What these organizations quickly found, however, was a conflict between environmental and Zapatista goals so severe that they quickly withdrew their nascent support. Although the Zapatista uprising had many causes, an important underlying factor is Chiapas's highly unequal distribution of land – a problem exacerbated by Mexican government policies rationalized on environmental grounds. These policies, a 1972 decree granting 645,000 hectares of the Lacandón Forest to 66 families designated original owners of the land and a 1978 decree creating the 380,000 hectare, UNESCO-sponsored Montes Azules International Biosphere and Ecological Reserve, called for eviction of much of the Lacandón's population of poor, mostly Indian settlers. The result in the 1970s and 1980s was severe, sometimes bloody conflict as settlers, backed by the Catholic Church and leftist groups, resisted the government's repeated attempts to remove them.[101] As a result, in 1994, when environmental groups considered involvement in the Zapatista uprising, they found difficult historical impediments. As one Zapatista exclaimed: "Ecologists? Why do we need them here? Here, we need work and land."[102] Such sentiments have continued to boil, with one Zapatista community invading an ecotourism ranch owned by an American couple in 2003 while denouncing ecotourists as "fools trying to change our lives so that we will cease being what we are: indigenous peasants with our own ideas and culture."[103]

Inventing an Icon

Beyond their evolving tactics, goals, and identity, the Zapatistas have shown facility in tapping international cultural currents. Most significantly, Marcos's language, attitudes, and image entranced key audiences around the world, from radical students to mainstream journalists.[104] His countless interviews and inventive writing alluded to everything from radical politics to classic literature to popular entertainment. Joking with the press

---

[101] James D. Nations, "The Ecology of the Zapatista Revolt," *Cultural Survival Quarterly*, Spring 1994, 31–33.

[102] Ross, "Unintended Enemies," 47. See also Juanita Darling, "Under Pressure to Solve Crisis, Mexico Turns to the Land," *Los Angeles Times*, February 23, 1994, A4.

[103] Tim Weiner, "Mexican Rebels Confront Tourism in Chiapas," *New York Times*, March 9, 2003, Section 5, page 3.

[104] Julia Preston and Samuel Dillon, *Opening Mexico: The Making of a Democracy* (New York: Farrar, Straus and Giroux, 2004), 442.

even on the first day of the uprising, Marcos became an international icon of revolt, complete with trademark pipe, mask, and bandoliers. In contrast with the resolute seriousness of most revolutionary politics, Marcos made the Zapatistas unpredictable, even fun. In a period of retrenchment on the Left, his refreshing willingness to admit uncertainty about the Zapatista struggle and laugh at himself only added to his magnetism. More alluring still, Marcos refused to identify himself and rejected pecuniary benefit from his status. In his own words, Marcos became a "mito genial," an inspired act of myth-making.[105] As a result, the government's well-publicized 1995 identification of him as ex-professor Rafael Guillén failed to dent his popularity. For his part, Marcos refuses to confirm this identity, declares that he is but an ordinary man caught up in extraordinary times, and claims to be a proxy for all oppressed minorities. The EZLN has repeatedly warned against a personality cult, claims to wear masks to prevent it, and credits the media for elevating Marcos, chiefly because of his fluency in Spanish.

At a minimum, however, Marcos and the Zapatistas have opportunistically responded to and skillfully exploited the explosive worldwide interest in him. As Marcos has stated, "I don't gain anything personally. It is the movement that benefits, because this way more people pay attention to the issue."[106] (In 1996, Marcos had it both ways, posing as man on horseback for favorite movie director Oliver Stone.) Marcos acts as an interpreter, bridging the huge linguistic, cultural, and social gaps between impoverished indigenous communities and distant audiences. Without his ability to translate both worlds to one another, the Zapatistas would not have attained the domestic or foreign support they won. No other Zapatista leader has Marcos's verve, command of Spanish (and English), or mastery of the international zeitgeist. Thus, if Marcos had been killed on the first day of the uprising, the group's ability to promote its other resonant features would undoubtedly have suffered.

That said, Marcos's personal qualities – sometimes seen as the sole source of the Zapatistas' success – need to be put in perspective. What if Marcos had spouted the Maoist rhetoric of Abimael Guzmán, leader of Peru's Shining Path? Or the Zapatistas had adopted similarly murderous ways rather than halting the use of force after a day? Without the Zapatistas' appealing goals

---

[105] Ann Louise Bardach, "Mexico's Poet Rebel," interview with Subcomandante Marcos, March 25, 1994, *Vanity Fair*, July 1994, 68.

[106] Medea Benjamin, "Interview: Subcomandante Marcos," n.d. [March 25, 1994?], in *First World, Ha Ha Ha!*, Katzenberger, ed., 69.

and tactics, a charismatic but fanatic Marcos would have attracted far less overseas enthusiasm. Most importantly, if the Zapatistas had not taken San Cristóbal and had not forced the government to the bargaining table a month later, failing thereby to attain signal international standing, Marcos's flurry of words would doubtless have gone little noticed. His "charisma," his remarkable capacity to move the media and intrigue millions, therefore feeds off the actions of the EZLN itself. His fans' reactions have also contributed mightily to his persona, early on by their breathless interest in his identity and later by their investing him with the mystique of a latter-day Che Guevara. Marcos's own analysis of his appeal is accurate: The Marcos "image" fulfills his audience's needs – their "romantic, idealistic expectations, namely the white man in the indigenous world, akin to references in the collective unconscious, Robin Hood."[107]

Not surprisingly, the EPR has thrown up no one approaching Marcos's stature. Indeed, failing to understand the power of rhetoric and symbol, the EPR has condemned the Zapatistas as mere "poets." But the anonymity of the EPR leadership hinges on more than inarticulateness. Although the EPR's rhetorical output pales in comparison with the Zapatistas', they have displayed some flourishes. "We arise from the sorrow of orphans and widows, from the absence of disappeared loved ones, from the pain of the tortured," they declaimed in their first manifesto.[108] The greater problem is twofold: not securing a territorial soapbox from which to promote themselves, and purveying an outdated Marxist product. As a result, the dialectic of celebrity, the push and pull between audience and actor that apotheosized Marcos, never began for the EPR.

Beyond the Marcos phenomenon, the prominent role of Zapatista women has also resonated with the cultural predilections of key audiences. The Revolutionary Laws, despite numerous omissions, prominently included a Women's Law guaranteeing equal rights to work, education, voting, and military and political office holding – as well as the right to decide on a marriage partner and number of children.[109] These were radical propositions in the culturally conservative context of rural, Catholic indigenous Mexico, reflecting both the urban origins of the EZLN and the influence of female leaders. The Zapatistas have also made much of their

---

[107] Julio Scherer García, "La entrevista insólita," interview with Subcomandante Marcos, March 10, 2001, *Proceso*, March 11, 2001, http://www.ezln.org/entrevistas/20010309. es.htm (accessed July 19, 2004).

[108] EPR, "Manifiesto de Aguas Blancas," June 28, 1996.

[109] EZLN, *Documentos y comunicados*, 45–46.

"first revolution," when, several years before the uprising, women gained equal rights within the movement (against strong male opposition). And, on several occasions, male leaders have publicly apologized for remarks offensive to women. This deployment of the feminine is clearly not tokenism; women hold positions of real authority in the EZLN. But the Zapatistas are also keenly aware of its advantages on the international stage. For audiences in urban Mexico and abroad, issues of gender and sexuality have proved fascinating. Zapatista women have been profiled in major women's magazines, with reporting sometimes bordering on the hagiographic. One journalistic interview provides a lengthy discussion of EZLN policies on sexual relations (both heterosexual and homosexual) among a fighting force striving to maintain military discipline.[110] Others focused on the 1995 rape of the American leader of the NCDM during a solidarity visit to Chiapas.[111] Meanwhile, sympathetic scholars and activists have highlighted Zapatista progressiveness on gender issues.[112]

Nothing Succeeds Like Success

For many third parties, a final reason for supporting the Zapatistas concerned costs and benefits. This book's marketing approach assumes that even "principled" transnational actors have internal needs paralleling those of other organizations. I examine these needs by separately analyzing the costs and benefits of an advocacy or solidarity group's backing a particular insurgency. The costs include most obviously the expense of providing support and the risk to NGO reputations of doing so. The latter risks, deriving primarily from information deficits concerning clients physically and culturally removed from the insurgency, take two basic forms, backing an insurgent organization that is either unrepresentative of its asserted constituency or whose grievances are unfounded. To minimize these risks, an NGO must incur transaction costs in obtaining information about a movement. On the other hand, there are potential advantages to support. If an NGO associates itself with a prominent insurgency, it will often benefit, for instance through an increase in membership, funding, or both. How

---

[110] Aguilera, interview with Subcomandante Marcos, May 11, 1994, EZLN, ¡Zapatistas! Documents, 302–309.

[111] Jennifer Bingham Hull, "Cecilia Rodriguez; Zapatista, Feminista," Ms., November/December 1996, 28.

[112] Karen Kampwirth, Women and Guerrilla Movements: Nicaragua, El Salvador, Chiapas, Cuba (University Park: Pennsylvania State University Press, 2002); Stephen, !Zapata Lives!, 176–97.

potential backers balance the costs and benefits will vary, but one important consideration is the timing of a movement's appeal. In the Ogoni case, where MOSOP sought NGO assistance *before* raising overseas awareness, cost considerations dominated. Because the Ogoni were virtually unknown when Saro-Wiwa began lobbying, NGO staff worried about the risks of support, demanded proof of MOSOP's claims and constituency, saw few benefits to patronage, and initially rejected Ogoni appeals. By contrast, the Zapatistas sought help *after* they had rocketed to international prominence, giving them significant value and therefore relative power vis-à-vis potential backers. As a result, there was a different dynamic, with the benefits of assistance outweighing its costs.

With regard to costs, there is no doubt that many who ventured into the conflict zone as human rights observers or nonviolent protective accompanists faced mortal dangers. Whether brave or foolhardy, these individuals took real risks and in some cases paid high costs. Compared with the risks of backing other insurgent groups, however, the risks of supporting the Zapatistas were lower. For one thing, the movement's early and continuing success in attracting the media made information about it easy to find, reducing transaction costs such as the need for an NGO to do its own research about the group's legitimacy. More importantly, this information dispelled qualms about Zapatista grievances and, to a lesser extent, their representativeness in Mexico and rural Chiapas. In their initial statements, the Zapatistas claimed to be rebelling on behalf of all Mexicans against centuries of impoverishment, repression, and "undeclared genocidal war."[113] Alone, such rhetoric would surely have been dismissed as self-serving propaganda. Certainly the government worked hard to portray Zapatista statements in this light, blasting the rebels' violence and impugning their representativeness. With the retreating Zapatistas unable to respond, such accusations might have been expected to prevail. But, critically, powerful third parties rapidly vouched for the Zapatistas.

For one thing, initial media reports substantiated that the EZLN had several thousand mostly indigenous followers organized and committed enough to join in concerted attacks. The press also corroborated Chiapas's long history of poverty and political repression as well as apparent sympathy for the rebels among the region's poor. More authoritative validation of grievances came from reports by major human rights organizations. Amnesty International, Human Rights Watch, and Minnesota Advocates

---

[113] EZLN, "Declaración de la Selva Lacandona." *Documentos y comunicados*, 35.

for Human Rights had all chronicled extensive rights violations in rural Mexico in reports published to little notice in the years preceding the revolt.[114] On January 7, 1994, the *New York Times'* op-ed page excerpted one of these reports on abuses against Mexico's indigenous people.[115] And in the days after the revolt, the human rights organizations issued urgent warnings of impending massacres based in part on their experience in the region.

More importantly, the Zapatistas quickly won endorsement from domestic sources. Demanding a cease-fire within days after the revolt, throngs of demonstrators on Mexico City's streets legitimated the rebellion. Mexican journalist Blanche Petrich captured the Mexican public's "unstoppable surge of sympathy and understanding for the uprising of the Native people. 'Why wouldn't they rebel!' people were saying. 'This country has been extremely unfair to them.'"[116] In addition, two internationally respected "local" authorities, the 1992 Nobel Peace Prize winner, Rigoberta Menchú from nearby Guatemala, and most importantly the Catholic Bishop of San Cristóbal, Samuel Ruiz, confirmed the gravity of Chiapas's problems. In late 1993, Ruiz, a liberation theologist and tireless advocate for the region's indigenous people, had won the Letelier-Moffitt Human Rights Award, an annual prize from the Washington, D.C.-based Robert F. Kennedy Memorial, for his decades of service to Chiapas's poor. Even before that, he was well known to key gatekeepers among human rights NGOs and to members of the international press based in Mexico. Although his sympathies for Chiapas's Indians were manifest, his integrity and knowledge were highly

---

[114] Minnesota Advocates for Human Rights, *Civilians at Risk: Military and Police Abuses in the Mexican Countryside* (New York: North America Project, World Policy Institute, August 1993), excerpts reprinted in "Human Rights, Chiapas, Spring 1993," *New York Times,* January 7, 1994, A31; Minnesota Advocates for Human Rights, *Conquest Continued: Disregard for Human and Indigenous Rights in the Mexican State of Chiapas* (New York: North America Project, World Policy Institute, October 1992); Americas Watch, *Unceasing Abuses: Human Rights in Mexico One Year After the Introduction of Reform* (New York: Human Rights Watch, 1991); Human Rights Watch, *Human Rights Watch World Report: Events of 1992* (New York: Human Rights Watch, 1993), 127–33; Lawyers Committee on Human Rights, *Critique: Review of the Department of State's Country Reports on Human Rights Practices for 1992* (New York: Lawyers Committee on Human Rights, 1993), 250–57.

[115] *New York Times,* "Human Rights, Chiapas, Spring 1993," January 7, 1994, A31, excerpting Minnesota Advocates for Human Rights, *Civilians at Risk.*

[116] Blanche Petrich, "Voices from the Masks," in *First World, Ha Ha Ha!,* Katzenberger, ed., 46. Other contemporaneous commentaries agreed that the Zapatistas "stirred the guilt of a nation that glorifies its pre-Hispanic past and ignores the suffering of its indigenous groups today." See Alan Riding, "Letter from Mexico: How Peasants Lit the Fires of Democracy," *New York Times,* February 27, 1994, Section 4, page 5. See also Gilly, *Chiapas: la razón ardiente,* 17–42.

respected. And the hostility he faced from local landlords only enhanced his reputation. When within days of the revolt Ruiz, along with Menchú, vouched for the Zapatistas' grievances and legitimacy, even if not their tactics, their assessments were accorded great weight, particularly among human rights and indigenous advocacy networks. The results in the first weeks of the revolt were media, NGO, and foreign government statements that, while decrying the Zapatistas' use of force, portrayed it as an understandable result of gross government neglect and abuse over many decades.[117]

A comparison with the EPR is instructive. With regard to its constituency, although the EPR enjoyed considerable sympathy among Guerrero's rural poor, it could not muster more than several hundred to nonviolent action in June 1996. Even fewer have participated in its armed attacks. By contrast, the Zapatistas had thousands of dedicated members willing to take risky action for the cause. With regard to EPR grievances, no one with the stature of Ruiz or Menchú stepped forward to legitimate these rebels – despite the fact that conditions facing Guerrero's indigenous and peasant groups are as bad as those in Chiapas. Indeed, potential vouchers quickly distanced themselves from the EPR. One important critic, the leader of the left-wing opposition PRD, implied that EPR members were agents provocateurs after they disrupted the June 1996 Aguas Blancas memorial march he presided over. Even more striking, after the EPR's August 1996 attacks, Subcomandante Marcos quickly repudiated any linkage between the movements (which the EPR had earlier sought to establish) and condemned the group's actions.[118] As a result, in Mexican society, the EPR came to arouse more fear than support, with none of the favorable demonstrations that the Zapatistas elicited in other parts of Mexico. As another contrast, the EPR has had major difficulties with factionalism, splitting in 1998. Although the EZLN also underwent ideological and personal conflict, most occurred out of public sight and well before the January 1994 uprising. Since the rebellion, the EZLN has remained remarkably unified despite its ambiguities, contradictions, and adaptations – meaning that backers need not fear their aid being squandered in internecine disputes.

Beyond the relatively low costs of supporting the Zapatistas, their lasting prominence in Mexico and abroad proved highly attractive to certain

---

[117] See, for example, Jorge Castañeda, "The Other Mexico Reveals Itself," *Los Angeles Times*, January 5, 1994, B7; *Economist*, "Mexico's Second Class Citizens Say Enough is Enough," January 8, 1994, 41–42.

[118] Marcos, communiqué, August 29, 1996, *¡Ya Basta!*, http://www.ezln.org/documentos/1996/19960829b.es.htm (accessed July 18, 2004).

audiences. In the early days of the uprising, third parties could benefit from association with a movement that had already captured public attention, a cause generally portrayed as just, and one in which important local notables actively encouraged outside oversight to prevent further bloodshed. In the weeks before the San Cristóbal negotiations, the Zapatistas enhanced their appeal by granting lengthy interviews to key journalists. They also released a flurry of pointed and irreverent communiqués addressed to Mexican and foreign publics, communiqués immediately distributed by the Mexican press, the Zapatistas' electronic network, and to a lesser extent the international media. Under these circumstances, there were strong organizational benefits for transnational NGOs to get involved with the Zapatistas. One could do well for one's own organization – one's own cause – by doing good for the Zapatistas. Of course, these groups had altruistic as well as interested reasons for intervening. Most believed their sending aid, protesting, or bearing witness would protect the indigenous people from government attack, the Zapatistas themselves repeatedly stated this, and government expulsions of foreign observers bear out this view. Similarly, the many religious, social justice, and development NGOs that dispatched personnel and resources to Chiapas sincerely believed that economic assistance would help improve local conditions and discourage further bloodshed. Nonetheless, organizational benefits also encouraged NGOs to help the Zapatistas.

In the first months of 1994, the Zapatistas disrupted Mexican society. Like a political black hole, they sucked in support from like-minded organizations and individuals, captivated broader Mexican society, won the attention of the opposition PRD party, and shook the foundations of Mexican politics – all while core Zapatista goals remained obscure. In the heady days of February 1994, as the Zapatistas' public approval ratings soared and they appeared poised to reform Mexico's political structure, many Mexican politicians and NGOs backed the Zapatistas or sought concessions from a weakened state. On the international plane, NGOs in a variety of sectors rapidly fell into orbit. For development and social justice NGOs, Chiapas suddenly became an important place to send aid, a conflict in the media spotlight. Their sometimes duplicative, disjointed, and inappropriate efforts have irritated the Zapatistas, with Marcos citing an aid package including a "pink stiletto heel, size six-1/2" to criticize overeager and uninformed backers. More seriously, the Zapatistas complain about "charity" foisted on local communities without consultation: "Imagine the desperation of a community that needs drinkable water and they're saddled with a library; the one that requires a school for the children, and they give them a course on herbs."[119] Such problems, recognized by the NGOs themselves, led to creation of local clearinghouses for aid such as the NGO Coordination for Peace (CONPAZ) and later Enlace Civil. These have helped ease inefficiencies resulting from the sometimes overwhelming NGO urge to *do something* in Chiapas.

For indigenous rights organizations there was a similar logic. The Zapatistas claimed to represent an Indian constituency, they were fighting for goals overlapping those sought by indigenous organizations worldwide, and in 1994 they had scored a stunning if uncertain victory over the oppressors of "500 years." Under these circumstances, upholding the Zapatistas could only benefit organizations involved in parallel struggles. Canada's Assembly of First Nations, for instance, cited the Zapatista revolt as proof of the need for a commission to monitor NAFTA's impacts on indigenous populations, human rights, and development throughout North America. More ambitiously, some Indian activists touted the Zapatistas as a model for achieving revolutionary change in their circumstances.[120]

For solidarity groups, the benefits of association with the Zapatistas led to a similar organizational dynamic. The EZLN's rebellion appeared to contrast with a string of leftist retreats and compromises since the end of the Cold War.[121] The fact that the Zapatistas' success on the ground was itself limited and that they also began negotiations soon after their revolt was overlooked in jubilation over a movement that captured a city, had wide popular appeal, and continued to win rhetorical battles with a powerful government. The group's vigor, its continuing demand for indigenous autonomy, its embrace of civil society, and its call to fight neoliberal globalization all heartened left-leaning audiences worldwide. Association with the Zapatistas conferred important psychic benefits even as it offered the possibility of learning novel and effective strategies for social change. As Italian activists gushed, the Zapatistas represented "a new symbol of hope, possible rebellion, a beacon that need not be turned off."[122] Many came to the Zapatistas in search of "some magic thing" that would "fan the flames

---

[119] Marcos, "Chiapas, 13th Stele: Part 2, a Death," Irlandesa, trans., August 1, 2003, http://www.sf.indymedia.org/news/2003/08/1631948.php (accessed July 18, 2004).

[120] Churchill, "North American Indigenist View," 149–51, 154.

[121] James Petras and Steve Vieux, "Myths and Realities of the Chiapas Uprising," *Economic and Political Weekly*, November 23, 1996, 3054.

[122] Ceceña, "Zapata in Europe," interview with Colletivo Internazionalista de Torino, 1997, 84.

of revolt" in their own countries.[123] In Noam Chomsky's words, the Zapatistas provided an "inspiring example" of "popular resistance on a global scale," a movement "that merits committed support and that should be studied carefully for the lessons it teaches."[124] For his part, Marcos described the Zapatistas' relationship with transnational backers as an "accord" in which the communities secure protection while supporters "obtain what they need: a reminder, a springboard to re-launch themselves" to fight injustice not only in Chiapas but also in their home countries.[125] Some adherents noted more personal benefits. Explaining her abrupt decision to attend the 2001 Zapatour after hearing it would be the Mexican equivalent of Martin Luther King, Jr.'s 1963 march on Washington, Canadian antiglobalization activist Naomi Klein enthused: "Having grown up after history ended, it never occurred to me that I might see a capital-H history moment to match it. . . . Next thing I knew, I was on the phone talking to airlines, canceling engagements, making crazy excuses, mumbling about Zapatistas and Martin Luther King. . . . [In Marcos,] the world now has a new kind of hero."[126]

The weighty benefits of joining the Zapatista bandwagon also led to bizarre but telling incidents. In the commercial realm, Zapatista acclaim and third-party opportunism combined to spark a small-scale industry selling everything from T-shirts to condoms, most emblazoned with a bootleg image of a ski-masked Zapatista. As one comandante complained: "People of our own blood, our own death, are selling us like merchandise. They are selling the heroic blood of our martyrs right here, in the streets of San Cristóbal."[127] On a grander scale, Italian clothing manufacturer United Colors of Benetton offered the Zapatistas an advertising contract, "another way of making your lives and your history known," publicist Oliviero Toscani affirmed.[128] The Zapatistas rejected him. Anxious to protect their "brand," the Zapatistas have decried Mexican political organizations such as

---

[123] Andrew Flood, "The Story of How We Learnt to Dream at Reality: A Report on the First Intercontinental Gathering for Humanity and against Neoliberalism," n.d. [1997?], http://flag.blackened.net/revolt/andrew/encounter1_report.html (accessed August 4, 2004).

[124] Noam Chomsky, in EZLN, ¡Zapatistas! Documents, back cover.

[125] Le Bot, interview with Subcomandante Marcos, August 1996, 226.

[126] Naomi Klein, "The Unknown Icon," Guardian (London), March 3, 2001, http://www.guardian.co.uk/print/0%2C3858%2C4145255-103390%2c00.html (accessed June 5, 2004).

[127] Subcomandante Juan, quoted in Ross, Rebellion from the Roots, 238.

[128] Harper's Magazine, "The Glorious Struggle for Market Share," April 1996, 30.

the EPR that initially sought to draw false ties to them. On the other hand, recognizing the advantages of mutual exploitation, Subcomandante Marcos quickly approved multiple reissues of Zapatista communiqués and letters.[129] In this case, the advantages of disseminating the Zapatista word outweighed questions about whether some portion of a book's price would in fact return to indigenous communities in southern Mexico. Similarly, the Zapatistas approved the "political tourism" that brought thousands to Chiapas.

Structure of the Network

The size, diversity, and duration of the Zapatista network make describing its structure harder than in the case of the Ogoni network. Even more so than in the latter case, Zapatista backers serve multiple functions and cross simple lines of categorization. Because of the relative ease with which organizations and individuals have entered Mexico, neat divisions based on levels of contact with the Zapatistas are also harder to draw. Nonetheless, several observations can be made. First, there are several overlapping strands within the broad Zapatista network, encompassing advocacy, social justice/development, and solidarity NGOs. The advocacy strand is composed primarily of human rights groups. At the local level, providing continuous monitoring of the conflict zone is the Fray Bartolomé de las Casas Human Rights Center. An arm of the Catholic diocese of San Cristóbal, the Center has long been noted for its sympathy and assistance to the Indian populations of Chiapas. Although its mission extends well beyond oversight of the conflict, the Center has been the source of crucial background information and verification of the Zapatistas' charges against their opponents. Throughout the conflict, however, the Center has maintained independence from the Zapatistas, has continuously denounced violence, and has at times been accorded status as a neutral party to the conflict by the Zapatistas and the government (though not by local elites). At times during the conflict, Bishop Ruiz also served as an intermediary between the EZLN and the government.

---

[129] Marcos, communiqué, June 30, 1994, in EZLN, *Shadows of Tender Fury: The Letters and Communiqués of Subcomandante Marcos and the Zapatista Army of National Liberation*, trans. Frank Bardacke, Leslie López, and the Watsonville, California Human Rights Committee (New York: Monthly Review Press, 1995), 21.

Outside Mexico, major human rights organizations such as Human Rights Watch, Amnesty International, and the International Commission of Jurists comprise the main components of this first strand of the Zapatista network. Most of their work involves issuing reports on major developments in the conflict, particularly abuses by the government and paramilitary groups. Although the NGOs often assign great weight to analyses by the Fray Bartolomé Center and to a lesser extent other Mexican human rights organizations, they generally conduct their own investigations. The advocacy groups, whose focus is upholding international human rights standards, have no direct links to the Zapatistas and do not coordinate strategies with them. In the first weeks of the rebellion, for instance, reports by these advocacy NGOs included information critical of Zapatista actions. Since then, however, such reports have focused on the source of nearly all human rights violations, the military and paramilitary forces. As such, they have helped convince European and North American governments to issue periodic declarations condemning Mexican policies in Chiapas.

A second strand of the Zapatista network comprises dozens of development, social justice, and peace NGOs. As among the advocacy NGOs, local organizations in Chiapas have played an important role. In the first months after the rebellion, when the region saw an influx of international NGOs, there was duplication, inefficiency, and uncertainty in aid provision. To help coordinate aid efforts, ten local groups long active on health, development, education, and women's issues formed CONPAZ in 1994 to organize nonviolent actions aimed at ameliorating repression, poverty, and displacement. Until CONPAZ ceased operations in 1997, it helped plan aid operations, matching foreign NGOs to hundreds of peasant organizations, indigenous groups, and local communities. Among the many transnational NGOs in this strand of the network, some had worked in Mexico or elsewhere in Central America before the uprising, whereas many others were drawn to Chiapas by the spotlight the rebellion shone on poverty and underdevelopment in the region. Unlike the advocacy groups, this second strand of organizations acts directly in Chiapas (although some groups also issue reports on rights and justice issues that are disseminated in their home countries). Among other things, they have started long-term development and conflict-resolution programs, funded local NGOs, participated in nonviolent accompaniment activities, or sent aid shipments. Depending on their mission and ideology, these organizations have worked with all poor communities or primarily with ones sympathetic to the Zapatistas. Importantly, however, NGOs in this strand of the network do not identify with the Zapatistas themselves, even though they may applaud justice and social change. Representative of these organizations is International Service for Peace (SIPAZ), a transnational coalition comprising dozens of small, religiously based NGOs, primarily from North America but also including groups from South America and Europe. United by a commitment to nonviolence, SIPAZ and its members maintain neutrality between the parties in conflict. With funding from its members, SIPAZ maintains a continuous presence in Chiapas. Although some of its member groups have also established permanent outposts in the region, others have more ephemeral contacts and rely primarily on SIPAZ to funnel them information.[130]

Solidarity organizations constitute the third strand of the Zapatista network. Many conduct activities similar to those undertaken by the previous groups. They issue reports, deliver aid, accompany local notables, and work in indigenous communities. Unlike the other organizations, however, solidarity groups take the Zapatista side in the conflict. In addition, solidarity NGOs are notable for their actions abroad, including protests against Mexican government policies, lobbying of home governments, and consciousness-raising. The latter includes such activities as sponsorship of Mayan Indians during overseas lobbying trips and organization of foreign observer or peace camp delegations for visits to Chiapas. Within Mexico, most solidarity activity is coordinated by a local NGO, Enlace Civil. Formed in 1996 at the initiative of local Indian communities, Enlace Civil is staffed by professionals with long experience in Mexican civil society organizations. As its main function, the group links Zapatista communities and allied Indian groups to national and transnational solidarity organizations. As such, Enlace Civil channels solidarity in directions approved by and helpful to the Indian communities. Although its particular projects are wideranging, Enlace Civil's overall goals mirror key aspects of the Zapatistas': constructing an alternative to the existing economic and political systems that in their view neglect and destroy Indian populations.[131] Solidarity organizations from North America, Europe, and elsewhere typically contact Enlace Civil before undertaking activities in Chiapas and remain in close contact during their visits. The latter serve a dual function, not only aiding and protecting the communities but also affording believers hands-on experience in building a new social system.

---

[130] SIPAZ, "What is SIPAZ?," http://www.sipaz.org/fini_eng.htm (accessed July 19, 2004).
[131] Enlace Civil, "Enlace Civil," http://www.enlacecivil.org.mx/lm_enlace.html (accessed July 19, 2004).

Transnational solidarity activists comprise a diverse set of organizations and individuals with varying levels of involvement in the conflict. Professionalized, national-level organizations have been prominent in the United States both in undertaking missions to Chiapas and in operations in their home countries. San Francisco–based Global Exchange, active since the start of the uprising, organizes protests against the Mexican government, lobbies U.S. government officials, and seeks to educate the American populace to events in Chiapas (as well as in other countries around the world). It has established a local office in Chiapas to continuously monitor the conflict and has brought hundreds of American activists to the region on so-called "reality tours."[132] Since 1998, the México Solidarity Network (MSN) has also sought to provide loose coordination to a diverse set of pro-Zapatista supporters in the United States. Its primary aims are to increase activism at the grassroots level and to link that activism to politicians, particularly in the U.S. Congress (although MSN's overall mission is broader: democracy, economic justice, and human rights on both sides of the U.S.–Mexico border).[133] With over 80 member organizations from the local to the national levels, MSN has a professional staff of six in several U.S. cities.

Solidarity activism at the regional and local levels overseas comprises another, looser layer of support.[134] Some of these groups are branches of national-level organizations, such as the Service Employees International Union, having a wide variety of other issues with which they are involved. Others focus on the Zapatistas but typically have only a handful of members and volunteer staffs. Most learn about events in Chiapas through information originally delivered through Internet listservs or Web sites run by national-level organizations. Some members of these groups have made regular trips to Chiapas, whereas others have confined their involvement to actions in their home countries. European solidarity activism follows this loose-knit pattern as well. Although some left-wing political parties, particularly in Italy, have expressed solidarity with the Zapatistas, most activists belong to ad hoc local groups, some of which have adopted the Zapatista ideal of mutual solidarity, pursuing their own local struggles most of the time while offering aid to the Zapatistas in times of crisis. In sum, the

---

[132] Global Exchange, "Global Exchange in Chiapas," http://www.globalexchange.org/countries/mexico/chiapas/program.html (accessed July 20, 2004).

[133] México Solidarity Network (MSN), "About MSN: Mission, Organization, History," http://www.mexicosolidarity.org/index.html (accessed July 20, 2004).

[134] For an extensive discussion, see Olesen, *International Zapatismo*, on which this paragraph is partially based.

solidarity network (like the advocacy and development networks) encompasses several distinct layers, from local Mexican organizations with deep ties to the Zapatistas, to transnational aid organizations with a relatively continuous presence in or contacts with Chiapas, to individual activists with sporadic involvement.

Conclusion

As the Zapatistas rightly state, they have not sold out to the Mexican government despite attractive offers of accommodation. Since 1996, they have maintained their demand for indigenous autonomy nationwide and have implemented it in their own communities. For years before their 2001 march on Mexico City, they rejected new talks with the government until army troops stationed near their communities were withdrawn. And throughout the conflict, they have literally stuck to their guns, although using them primarily for symbolic purposes. To survive for so many years, the Zapatistas relied not only on the loyalty of their base communities but also on the aid of third parties in their vibrant transnational network. To attract these outsiders, however, the Zapatistas had to market themselves. Before the rebellion, NGOs had neglected the plight of Mexico's poor and indigenous. Only the spectacular seizure of San Cristóbal attracted the media and opened the world's eyes, allowing the Zapatistas to bootstrap their way to real influence. Their initial accomplishments and extensive domestic support fostered a powerful mystique, convincing overseas audiences that the group had real promise. Since then, the Zapatistas have issued innumerable words, orchestrated large transnational talkfests, and exploited the Internet (though usually vicariously) – all with the aim of maintaining visibility.

In addition, the Zapatistas have accommodated themselves to the predilections of key supporters. In moving from military attacks to armed nonviolence, from socialist-inspired demands to indigenous rights, the Zapatistas have displayed great strategic flexibility. In some cases, these shifts were deliberate and proactive. Others corrected earlier missteps or responded to shifting opportunities in the political environment. Because the Zapatistas had not publicly staked out positions before they burst on the scene, they were not held to them, and because Zapatista grievances were so expansive at the start of the uprising, the group could easily shift into new avenues that looked promising. But matching also hinged on the movement's ability to convince supporters, particularly in the solidarity sector, to reconfigure their own priorities, tactics, and even identities. Zapatista marketing is thus not a case of cynical shifts meant to manipulate third parties. Rather, the changes the group has made are subtle and at times ambiguous, rooted in real aspects of the Zapatistas' identity but also in opportunism spurred by their need for assistance. And because of their high value to key international supporters, the Zapatistas have had the power to change their patrons also.

For the theory proposed here, the Zapatistas present a hard but fertile case. This tiny group literally came out of nowhere to galvanize a vibrant transnational network, illustrating a diversity of marketing strategies. The Zapatistas are also an unlikely group to have adopted such strategies since their ideology decries a global marketplace that robs the world of diversity. If even they have had to market themselves rather than relying on the automatic workings of a beneficent support "boomerang," it is all the more likely that others with fewer ideological qualms will do so. To their credit, the Zapatistas have not been crass or craven. They have refused offers of assistance they perceive as violating their dignity and have used frank language to puncture illusions about transnational networking (even while promoting others). Yet the overall trend is clear: Gaining major support requires techniques that effectively project and frame a movement for international audiences. The forces often extolled as weaving the contemporary world together – new technologies, a global consciousness – cannot by themselves explain how local movements attract backing. Nor can a "meritocracy of suffering" explain the contrast between successful and failed movements since there are few differences in relative need between the populations on whose behalf the EZLN and EPR rebelled. Rather, the key factors are resolutely political: organizational and material resources, knowledge of distant audiences' preferences, media savvy, and strategic skills. Only these allow groups like the Zapatistas to exploit opportunities available in the global support market.

But to what end? The Zapatistas certainly raised overseas awareness of Mexico's neglected and abused indigenous population. They galvanized advocacy and solidarity activism, both of which have endured over many years. And, on the international stage, they helped forge, energize, and symbolize today's often quixotic but nonetheless important global justice movement. Within Mexico, the Zapatistas have also had a significant impact, forcing the country to devote more resources to Chiapas and acknowledge Indian demands, rights, and identity. Although it is more difficult to show direct influence, the Zapatistas undoubtedly contributed to Mexico's democratization during the 1990s. On the other hand, neither the Zapatistas nor their domestic and international backers have succeeded in realizing the full promise of the San Andrés Accords. The vast bulk of Mexico's indigenous population remains poor and marginalized. And most of the ambitious goals with which the Zapatistas began their uprising have gone unmet. The entrenched power structures and deep divides of Mexican society go far in explaining these failings. The Zapatistas threatened key pillars of Mexico's decades-old political and economic system, making complete success for any challenger, let alone one composed of just a few thousand poor peasants, highly unlikely. Even Mexican President Vicente Fox found much of his reform program stymied in the Mexican legislature.

What of the effects of overseas aid on the Zapatistas themselves? The movement, its constituents, and neighboring communities have gained security and material boosts from foreign NGOs and activists. Just as important are the psychological consequences, the improvements in morale that have encouraged the Zapatistas to persist. There may also be a more subtle effect: The Zapatistas' access to the world has empowered more cosmopolitan and tolerant currents within the movement, thereby preventing other segments from shifting it toward ethnic exclusivity. Nonetheless, the quest for transnational backing has also exacted costs. Only by changing to please overseas audiences were the Zapatistas able to gain support. In the case of Zapatista tactics, the move to armed nonviolence rather than continued military force undoubtedly saved lives; the EPR experience suggests that guerrilla warfare in Mexico makes little sense. With regard to Zapatista goals, the costs of conforming to international concerns may be higher. As its earliest documents attest, the EZLN initially portrayed itself as a voice for all Mexico's poor and unrepresented. Yet the needs of the merely impoverished had little resonance domestically or internationally. Far more attractive was a framing of the revolt as indigenous, and the Zapatistas steadily moved in that direction. Indeed they have gone further, adopting a form of identity politics that champions "difference" in an age of globalized homogeneity. Although popular in many circles on the Left and an effective tool of mobilization, the sometimes mystical elevation of identity may obscure pressing issues of poverty and inequality around the globe.

5

Transnational Marketing and World Politics

The picture of transnational society presented here challenges both radical and liberal visions of globalization. Critics decry globalization's pernicious effects on the weak. In this view, overbearing states wield powerful new technologies to control their citizens. Rapacious corporations roam the world for the least regulated production sites, exploiting workers and despoiling environments. International financial institutions impose ruinous structural adjustment programs and heartless market policies. And a homogeneous global culture drains the globe of diversity. In all of this, the world's most vulnerable populations are relentlessly ground down.

Yet globalization has also opened the field of combat on which local movements resist these forces. Most obviously, it has widened conflict geographically. With the Internet, CNN, and the wide-bodied jet, talented marketers make their causes known overseas more easily and quickly than ever before. More subtly, globalization has expanded the ideological terrain on which small-scale disputes play themselves out. Christianity and Islam long served this purpose. For centuries, their global aspirations drew outsiders to distant corners of the globe. Since the nineteenth century, democracy, capitalism, Marxism, and nationalism have played similar roles. Insurgents, cognizant of these ideologies, have tapped them to draw intervention. Today, supplementing and in some cases supplanting them are other world-encompassing doctrines: environmentalism, human rights, and perhaps "global justice." All provide toeholds for astute challengers seeking to internationalize their causes: new sets of grievances, different names for old injuries, and a ready vocabulary for alerting distant audiences to local issues. Together, these developments create a climate primed for activism.

But those who see an emerging "global civil society" as an open and democratic forum for repressed groups are also off the mark. For many optimists, NGOs have come to embody a growing global consciousness and conscience. Their proliferation, along with advances in media and technology, has fired visions of a new force in world politics to counterbalance the power-hungry amorality of states and the grasping self-interest of corporations. In this view, principled activists reach across borders to rescue faraway people threatened by governments, multinational companies, and international institutions. Bound together by common humanity, rather than kinship, citizenship, or interest, they form transnational networks around pressing issues. In turn, these networks fundamentally restructure world politics, bringing new issues to the fore, new voices to the bargaining table, and, most importantly, a new morality to the global scene.

Despite the hype and the hope, however, for most movements the reality remains bleak. The cases examined here demonstrate the usefulness of viewing transnational support in market terms. On one side stand a host of challengers seeking aid, on the other NGOs who have resources, access, and clout. Sympathy and principle provide an important context for this market. Yet the magnitude of demand and the scarcity of supply mean that pragmatic considerations constantly vie with moral values. The transnational successes of the Zapatistas and Ogoni were therefore complex, eminently political processes marked by strategic maneuvers and resonant framing on the part of insurgents and by careful assessment of mutual interests and concerns on the part of NGOs. The growth of assistance involved two simultaneous but discrete steps, raising international awareness and matching key characteristics of potential supporters. With respect to the first, the two movements, both of which started in obscurity, exemplify contrasting strategies to achieve the same end. For the Ogoni, the primary mechanism was personal lobbying of key NGO staff in their home countries. In this way, MOSOP inched its way to international consciousness nonviolently and with limited though important aid from the press. By contrast, the Zapatistas initially used a much more transgressive and less controlled "spectacle" aimed at attracting the media, which in turn let the whole world know of the rebellion within hours of their attacks. These distinct tacks stemmed from varying characteristics of the two movements. The personal histories of their chief leaders and their dominant ideological influences played a role. In addition, Ken Saro-Wiwa's resources allowed him and other MOSOP leaders to engage in intensive overseas activity, while his preexisting contacts and standing afforded the Ogoni entrée to environmental and human rights gatekeepers. The Zapatistas had none of these advantages. But through the strategic use of surprise, drama, and force, they immediately shot to prominence. Once the two movements had obtained recognition, however, their means of holding international interest diversified and overlapped. The Zapatistas dropped the use of arms, although not of spectacle, and came into direct contact with advocacy and solidarity NGOs in Chiapas. Receptive audiences also had access to rebel writings in books, newspapers, and Web sites. For the Ogoni, as repression deepened, media reporting joined NGO lobbying in keeping the conflict in the spotlight. Nonetheless, for analytic purposes it is worth differentiating the two means of heightening awareness.

The differing mechanisms also had long-term consequences. For one thing, the Zapatistas had greater power than the Ogoni relative to prospective backers. This was because the Zapatistas sought aid *after* they had won attention and been certified not only by the media but also by key gatekeepers. In this case, the benefits of backing the Zapatistas loomed large and the costs small. Although the Zapatistas clearly needed assistance, their value to potential backers was initially higher than the Ogoni's. Many supporters flocked to Chiapas in the first days of the revolt, and others continued to stream in as the Zapatista phenomenon took off. By contrast, because the Ogoni were virtually unknown when Saro-Wiwa began lobbying, NGO staff worried about the risks of providing assistance, demanded proof of MOSOP's claims, and initially rejected his personal appeals.

Beyond raising awareness, both movements altered themselves to match supporters' key characteristics. Encompassing tactical, cultural, ethical, and organizational features, these changes affected NGO receptivity to the movements. And, as comparisons with the EPR and other Niger Delta movements indicated, the closer the match, the greater the likelihood of support. Most notably, the Shell and NAFTA connections helped make otherwise obscure conflicts in the developing world relevant to distant audiences. Environmental NGOs were explicit about the usefulness of the Ogoni case as a symbol of corporate malfeasance that might leverage change in a wide array of environmental conflicts around the world. And they saw the case, at least in part, as a way of "having a go" at an old enemy. Similarly, in their overseas presentations, the Zapatistas converted themselves into avatars of popular resistance against the juggernaut of "neo-liberalism." These framings were not cynical inventions by power-hungry movements; instead, they corresponded to real though secondary elements of the underlying conflicts. For overseas audiences, however, these became the primary aspects, evoking feelings of familiarity, sympathy, and responsibility.

Successful framing does not hinge only on adaptation. A movement's initial features also matter greatly. Local groups with vague and expansive goals, a wide variety of tactics, and flexible cultures will hold an advantage since their scope for repositioning will be larger than that for groups having more limited goals or rigid practices. The Zapatistas are a case in point. Yet a challenger's goals and tactics are not a simple matter of free choice. As a conflict deepens and becomes better-known abroad, choices narrow. Similarly, the reactions of opponents can force changes in direction. State repression injects a human rights dimension into diverse conflicts, and the involvement of multinational corporations or international financial institutions adds an obvious international hook. Movements that transform these threats into opportunities prosper overseas.

Both cases indicate that appropriate NGO targets may not be obvious, even to adept marketers. At first, the Ogoni won help only from the minority rights group UNPO, finding little sympathy or even understanding among the environmental and human rights groups they contacted. Moreover, identifying marketable frames may result as much from experiment as from calculation. The Zapatistas took a blunderbuss approach, testing a host of diverse issues early on, quickly dropping trial balloons such as socialism, and then emphasizing goals and tactics that soared internationally. In the Ogoni case, Saro-Wiwa learned of promising new emphases and directions through direct interactions with, and early rejections from, NGOs. He also received training from UNPO on how to market the movement more effectively in various venues. In the Zapatista case, learning initially occurred secondhand, through media reports of third parties demanding a halt to violence. In sum, knowledge of target audiences is crucial (although it will invariably be imperfect), as is continuous monitoring of the support market.

The Ambiguous Effects of Transnational Support

Although the Zapatistas and Ogonis beat the odds and won significant backing, the outcomes of their movements – Saro-Wiwa on the gallows, the Zapatistas still in conflict with the Mexican state – raise another question. What are the consequences of support? The empirical research and theoretical strands in this book, although not systematically aimed at answering this question, are nonetheless suggestive. Three effects should be considered: on conflict outcomes, on movements themselves, and on NGO supporters.

The questions are of obvious import, going ultimately to whether move-ments *should* seek aid and distant activists offer assistance.

There is much debate about the influence of NGO support on outcomes. The issue is difficult to settle for several reasons. First, the character and ambition of an insurgency's goals play a major role in determining its like-lihood of success. Given the complex conflicts in which many groups are involved, "outcomes" are seldom final, and tying a particular NGO's actions to a specific development in a conflict will always be controversial. Second, it is hard to separate the impacts of national and international factors. Is it pressure from the insurgency itself, from domestic allies, or from NGOs that leads to a policy change? Of course, movements and their backers have an interest in asserting the effectiveness of support, just as opponents have a strong reason to claim they have acted for other reasons. Analysts seeking an objective conclusion must rely primarily on evidence involving the tim-ing and circumstances of asserted causes and purported effects. Third, no matter what the level of outside interest, outcomes will vary depending on the opponent's identity and actions. How receptive is it to social movement pressure? How willing is it to accept intervention? States are often primary targets, and even when they are not – when a local powerholder, multi-national corporation, or international financial institution plays that role – government policy will be an important issue. Even within these categories, the upshot of support will vary depending on more specific features of the target. Among states, the character of political institutions, the security of a ruling regime, the openness of the political culture, and the concern about international reputation all play a role in determining receptivity.[1] Among corporations, an analogous set of issues affects vulnerability to pressure and likelihood of change.

Given these caveats and the different focus of this book, any conclusions about the impacts of support on targets must be tentative. Nonetheless, several possible effects may be identified as a basis for future research. For one thing, NGO intervention can raise a challenger's domestic standing, propelling new issues onto a target's agenda, as in the Zapatista and Ogoni cases. In itself, this is an achievement and can have positive (and nega-tive) consequences. Thus, to say that the Ogoni failed because MOSOP

---

[1] Susan Burgerman, *Moral Victories: How Activists Provoke Multilateral Action* (Ithaca, NY: Cornell University Press, 2001); Amy Gurowitz, "Mobilizing International Norms: Do-mestic Actors, Immigrants, and the Japanese State," *World Politics* 51, no. 3 (1999): 413–45; Thomas Risse-Kappen, ed., *Bringing Transnational Relations Back in: Non-State Actors, Domes-tic Structures and International Institutions* (Cambridge: Cambridge University Press, 1995).

was smashed misses the larger issues at stake – and the extent to which the movement raised the Niger Delta's international profile. Yet, as Saro-Wiwa recognized, "It is one thing being an issue, another achieving our aims."[2] And it is of course the latter, policy changes by the opponent, that are the most important. In both Nigeria and Mexico, there have been some improvements, and both movements deserve some of the credit for this. In addition, external involvement may encourage similarly situated communities to mobilize and pursue overseas aid. Certainly, in the Ogoni and Zapatista cases, there was an upsurge of mobilization nearby after the international spotlight shone on the regions. These broader consequences place additional pressure on states and may lead to changes in political agendas and policies. Research that seeks to probe the effects on targets should at a minimum consider these issues. But it should also be sensitive not only to positive but also negative repercussions: Did third-party action push issues off the agenda, harden existing policy positions, or drive opponents to adopt harsh policies? Under what circumstances will these results, rather than more positive ones, occur?

Although further research is needed to develop a clearer conclusion about the impacts of NGO support on outcomes, many movements *believe* it can help them. And, in one sense, it surely does – by giving them additional resources and greater leverage against their opponents, even if they do not "win" their conflicts. Foreign recognition can bolster a challenger's legitimacy and provide an important psychological boost to its members. In some cases, such as with the Ogoni, international certification may have a more fundamental effect, strengthening, and in some cases creating, ethnic or other identities. We should also consider several less visible consequences of the support market on movements. For one thing, the quest for backing, whether successful or not, can be costly. Overseas marketing is not free, and it necessarily diverts time, money, and staff from other ends. Even if such expenditures are relatively small in absolute terms, insurgents spend considerable amounts cultivating assistance, to the detriment of overall resources and goals. Indeed, within movements, there is frequent carping about jet-setting activists hopping from one international conference to another. Although outsiders should not second-guess a group's decision to "go global," the ways in which such decisions are made, whether by vote, consultation, or diktat, are worth investigating.

---

[2] Ken Saro-Wiwa, "Report to Ogoni Leaders Meeting at Bori, 3rd October, 1993," 2, Special Collections, Gumberg Library, Duquesne University.

More worrisome is that the quest for aid holds perils. Arousing international attention and altering one's image may require dangerous confrontations with opponents, as both the Zapatistas and Ogoni found. Intervention can generate a backlash against "traitorous" challengers, delaying or undermining the achievement of final ends. Of course, insurgents, or at least their leaders, weigh the dangers and take the initiative themselves. But the prospect of foreign help may also raise the possibility of moral hazard: Anticipating the availability and efficacy of transnational intervention, movements may take risky actions aimed at evoking it.[3] Yet, given the sway of sovereignty, NGOs may in fact be able to do little in repressive backwaters. Scholars have found that, in purely domestic contexts, third-party support fosters co-optation, demobilization, and decline, as movements bend to powerful patrons who encourage moderation.[4] Transnational intervention, however, presents the opposite problem. Distant activists, unfamiliar with local cultures or national politics, may encourage challengers in agendas that are inappropriate, unachievable, or dangerous. Yet the organizational imperatives driving NGOs sharply limit the time and resources they can commit to their clients, and few supporters can guarantee a movement's security, leaving vulnerable groups susceptible to attacks by angry foes. Some authorities, such as the Mexican government in early 1994, sometimes respond to pressure; others, such as the Nigerian military regime in 1995, will not. This is not an argument for nonintervention. Rather, NGOs must be realistic about the help they can offer and the threats their clients face. Promising too much and delivering too little may be worse than no action at all.

In the quest for support, pressures to conform to NGO concerns can contravene a movement's original goals and tactics. This can estrange leaders from their mass base or leave them less able to fulfill their domestic responsibilities. Backers also have incentives to use their clients as exemplars of larger problems or broader agendas. In turn, this may push insurgents

---

[3] Dane Rawlands and David Carment, "Moral Hazard and Conflict Intervention," in *The Political Economy of War and Peace*, Murray Wolfson, ed. (Boston: Kluwer Academic Publishers, 1998), 267–85; Alan J. Kuperman, "Humanitarian Hazard: Revisiting Doctrines of Intervention," *Harvard International Review* 26 (Spring 2004).

[4] Doug McAdam, *Political Process and the Development of Black Insurgency, 1930–1970*, 2nd ed. (Chicago: University of Chicago Press, 1999); J. Craig Jenkins and Craig M. Eckert, "Channeling Black Insurgency: Elite Patronage and Professional Social Movement Organizations in the Development of the Black Movement," *American Sociological Review* 51, no. 6 (1986): 812–29; Frances Fox Piven and Richard A. Cloward, *Poor People's Movements: Why They Succeed, How They Fail* (New York: Vintage Books, 1979).

to frame themselves further along internationally resonant lines. Thus, by the time the Ogoni had won worldwide exposure, some of their friends in the indigenous rights community were shaking their heads at how the movement's original demands for political autonomy had gone understated abroad compared with environmental and human rights issues. More dangerous still, NGO misunderstanding or even "hijacking" can alienate domestic constituencies and enrage opponents. In 2003, for instance, international supporters of a Nigerian woman condemned to death for adultery by a local shari'a court launched a blitz of e-mail messages incorrectly claiming that the country's Supreme Court had upheld the sentence. It is unclear whether this misinformation resulted from simple error or calculated overextension, but the campaign placed the woman at greater risk from radical Islamic elements, according to Nigerian women's rights organizations.[5] Although such mistakes are rare, the organizational imperatives and cultural chasms that facilitated it are common in the transnational market. In the case of diasporas, a parallel dynamic is well documented: Safe in their distant adopted societies, elements of the Tamil, Irish, and other diasporas have funneled cash and arms to radical coethnics while avoiding the consequences of the violence that followed.[6]

Once secured, NGO assistance also affects power dynamics within movements. When an insurgent marketer acts as an intermediary to overseas patrons, he or she obtains authority within a movement, often without distant supporters' awareness. Saro-Wiwa's stature within Ogoni society increased as he mobilized both distant NGOs and his domestic constituency. Rigoberta Menchú's international acclaim raised her from a foot soldier to a leader of the Guatemalan guerrilla movement.[7] More broadly, aid changes relationships in local communities, elevating particular organizations over others. In Mexico, for instance, the Zapatistas rapidly won greater leverage over the government than the country's many long-standing Indian and indigenous rights organizations.

---

[5] Somini Sengupta, "When Do-Gooders Don't Know What They're Doing," *New York Times*, May 11, 2003, Section 4, page 3. The errant messages were dispatched under the name of Amnesty International–Spain, which, however, denied having sent them.

[6] Stacy Sullivan, *Be Not Afraid, for You Have Sons in America: How a Brooklyn Roofer Helped Lure the U.S. into the Kosovo War* (New York: St. Martin's Press, 2004); Paul Hockenos, *Homeland Calling: Exile Patriotism and the Balkan Wars* (Ithaca, NY: Cornell University Press, 2003).

[7] David Stoll, *Rigoberta Menchú and the Story of All Poor Guatemalans* (Boulder, CO: Westview Press, 1999).

Both of these results occur because the quest for transnational support resembles a winner-take-all market, which often appears irrational in its exuberance for some causes and its apathy toward others.[8] In fact, as explained in this book, there is a logic to this market but not one that necessarily corresponds to the real needs of local populations. NGOs cannot, of course, assist every aspiring movement, and many are acutely aware of their own selectivity, justifying it with claims that their clients' fame will open opportunities for other challengers. The Ogoni and Zapatista cases confirm this view. The international profile of both southeastern Nigeria and Chiapas rose after the two movements gained support. But we need more research to determine the frequency of such "spillovers" and how much in fact trickles down to other groups. Moreover, when patrons seek clients, they do not necessarily look for the neediest cases. For one thing, they may have little time or ability to determine this. In any case, NGOs, caught in stiff competitions of their own for members and funding, often choose less desperate groups who appear more capable of using aid effectively. And when bandwagons develop, aid efforts duplicate one another, as NGOs pour into the latest media-saturated disaster zone.[9] As a result, outside help, even supposedly ameliorative capacity-building programs, can reinforce existing inequalities. By some lights, this is not a problem. After all, those who engender a network have proven themselves "fittest" in a rigorous global contest. Yet it is worth remembering that this competition is only for international support. It does not indicate which movements are most capable of achieving goals at home. Tibet's prolonged failure to achieve real autonomy, let alone independence, is a case in point.

The support market also has important consequences for NGOs. As we have seen, they spend much time and effort screening movements and then in a few cases aid them. Is this worthwhile? Asking this question, as all suppliers of aid do explicitly or implicitly, assumes that there are organizational as well as moral motives behind assistance. To answer it requires analysis of how involvement in a conflict will affect the patron's own resources, reputation, and in some cases membership. In the Ogoni and Zapatista cases, the results were generally positive, with the development

---

[8] Robert H. Frank and Philip J. Cook, *The Winner-Take-All Society: Why the Few at the Top Get so Much More than the Rest of Us* (New York: Free Press, 1995; New York: Penguin Books, 1996).

[9] Fiona Terry, *Condemned to Repeat?: The Paradox of Humanitarian Action* (Ithaca, NY: Cornell University Press, 2002); Michael Maren, *The Road to Hell: The Ravaging Effects of Foreign Aid and International Charity* (New York: Free Press, 1997).

of new programs, initiatives, and perspectives among external audiences. Although strategic considerations sometimes pulled NGOs in these new directions, the changes also had a realistic basis stemming from an enlarged understanding of the issues that the Ogoni and Zapatista movements helped create.

Taming the Market

Although the overall effects of support are uncertain, numerous movements will undoubtedly continue to pursue it. How then might some of the problems marring the transnational support market be alleviated? For insurgents, the first issue is the prudence of seeking aid. Leaders should consider the difficulties of finding and keeping patrons. What resources can they devote to pursuing overseas assistance and therefore forego for use at home? Do they have contacts that can ease their entrée to gatekeepers? What forms of support would be most helpful? Which organizations are most likely to provide such assistance? Related questions concern the non-monetary costs of a relationship with a patron. What motivates potential backers, and what effect will those motivations have? Will the movement be able to stay true to indigenous goals and tactics, or will the NGO make aid contingent on conformity to its own predilections and standards? Most importantly, leaders must consider the likely reactions of their opponents to foreign entry into a conflict. Will these reactions be violent, nonviolent, or indifferent? Will they help or hurt the challenger in achieving its goals? Of course, all of these assessments, if done carefully, will take considerable time and effort. Often, they will require a forthright comparison of the movement's situation and prospects with that of other similar groups that have sought support in the recent past. And they will require a level of sophistication unavailable to some local groups. In the heat of conflict, these evaluations are in any case difficult to undertake. Nonetheless, they are a useful set of considerations before any group opts to internationalize its struggle.

For their part, transnational supporters should ask a converse set of questions. NGOs already screen supplicants formally or informally for matching goals, tactics, culture, and ethics. To improve these assessments, they should rely as much as possible on unbiased sources of information and spend more time seeking to predict the likely effects of their intercession in a particular domestic context. The reactions of opponents should always be an area of concern. Experienced staff have considerable "folk knowledge" of such questions, although generalization, self-reflection, and frank organizational self-assessments are rare in the frenzied day-to-day life of today's activists. Sharing information within organizations is an easy and obvious fix. Pooling knowledge with other organizations, even rivals, would also be sensible and occasionally occurs today. Without second-guessing local leaders, prospective patrons could thereby reckon their support's likely impact on communities. With further investigation, NGOs might also determine who among a movement's constituency was consulted about a transnational campaign. Finally, outsiders should avoid hubris about their impacts. These will often be limited or perhaps deleterious, particularly when a client group seeks fundamental change against a recalcitrant foe. In any case, NGOs should refrain from action that encourages revolt where there is little likelihood of sufficient support.

Once NGOs decide to become involved in a conflict, how might they alleviate some of the inefficiencies endemic to the market? Bandwagons might be relieved through greater coordination from the earliest days rather than after duplication becomes visible. In the hectic initial days of an international campaign, planning is difficult. But given the benefits of more efficient operations, such efforts are worth pursuing. Making longer-term commitments, while tying them explicitly to reachable milestones, might also slow bandwagons and provide challengers with greater certainty. Solving the problems of "orphan" movements and the endemic inequalities of the transnational market is more difficult. An obvious but difficult option would be increasing the availability of support. Despite the deep concern of many, not least NGO staff, lack of resources in the face of overwhelming need underpins the market dynamic. Yet it is hard to imagine a boost in supply large enough to offset demand by myriad causes. This is not to say that few such resources are available – the world could do much more – only that competing demands and relative indifference make major expansion unlikely. Even without growth in resources, NGOs could make greater efforts to aid underserved populations by establishing programs that identify and target causes, groups, and regions with large populations suffering grave injuries or threats. Of course, defining these terms can be problematic, but that does not mean that nothing should be done. Researchers might, for instance, seek to develop head-to-head comparisons of various types and categories of at-risk populations and locales. New moves by human rights organizations to expand their mandates beyond the traditional core of civil and political rights to economic, social, and cultural rights set good examples. More generally, it would be sensible to pay greater attention to poverty and underdevelopment as important contributors to numerous grievances.[10] One model may be private sector initiatives such as the for-profit Geneva Global Inc., which researches, monitors, and certifies local projects among the world's neediest populations, then recommends them to individual, foundation, and religious donors seeking assurances that their philanthropic dollar is well spent.[11]

In a related vein, NGOs should be open to helping the less polished supplicants that knock on their doors. Typically, the causes that gain the most support are those spearheaded by more privileged local groups, who bring themselves to NGO attention first or most frequently. Instead, NGOs might establish programs that spread resources among diverse groups in a single needy region or those suffering a similar plight elsewhere. Alternatively, support programs might be made contingent on a client's helping other groups in the region. Of course, such programs might alienate the pioneering insurgency that took the initial risks and paid the largest costs, but it makes good sense from the perspective of patrons with broader agendas and concerns. And any charges of unfairness could be compensated by providing the client more than the other groups who benefited from the former's initiative. Similarly, NGOs should expand their relationships with movement personnel and constituencies. Often they have contact with only one or a few leaders since this is easiest and least costly. But this can reinforce or distort preexisting power structures within movements. At a minimum, NGOs need to be aware of how they affect their clients' internal dynamics.

As another step, NGOs could reorient capacity-building programs that seek to bolster a movement's international profile. Where there are few domestic channels for registering discontent, this focus may be beneficial. More sensibly, however, patrons should first assess whether their clients need that kind of training. The purpose of capacity building should be to help local groups meet their long-term goals. This might mean fewer

---

[10] Amnesty International, "Building an International Human Rights Agenda: Promoting Economic, Social and Cultural Rights," *Amnesty International Report 2004*, http://web.amnesty.org/report2004/hragenda-6-eng (accessed June 1, 2004); Paul Collier, V. L. Elliott, Havard Hegre, Anke Hoeffler, Marta Reynal-Querol, and Nicholas Sambanis, *Breaking the Conflict Trap: Civil War and Development Policy*, World Bank Policy Research Report (Washington, DC: World Bank; New York: Oxford University Press, 2003); Michael Klare, *Resource Wars: The New Landscape of Global Conflict* (New York: Henry Holt, Metropolitan/Owl Books, 2001).

[11] Geneva Global Inc., "The Geneva Way," http://www.genevaglobal.com/genevaway.shtml (accessed June 20, 2004).

programs on international law and fewer workshops on influencing the foreign media. In turn, this might require NGOs not to run such programs themselves but to fund locally based trainers adept at using domestic levers to influence national politics.

Although such programming shifts may be difficult, smaller changes would also be helpful. For one thing, NGO principals must constantly bear in mind the power dimension of their relationship with potential clients and the incentive this gives local groups to mold themselves accordingly. On the one hand, this underlines the need for careful investigation of insurgents seeking aid. Adopting a movement without thoroughly investigating its goals, leaders, tactics, and reputation is risky. NGOs must also understand that assistance frees resources for actions that they may disapprove.[12] Those concerned about "diversion" should consider limiting the types of support offered, earmarking funds, and closely monitoring usage. On the other hand, as the more powerful actors in most such relationships, NGOs should develop greater openness to varied tactics and cultural practices and should think carefully about imposing their own worldviews. In some cases, such impositions are appropriate, but not always. In either case, NGOs should act with awareness about the consequences of their own procedures and rules, in appropriate cases cultivating greater respect for differences rather than seeking to transform or "modernize" local groups. Although one cannot expect NGOs to aid challengers whose goals or tactics contradict their own, NGOs should consider giving a greater voice to alternative perspectives rather than encouraging movements to feign loyalty to alien ways.

Since redirecting operations in these ways would strongly affect NGOs, it would need to be done transparently. Informing donors and members of the difficulties they face in picking clients, of the criteria they use in doing so, and of the whipsaw they confront in balancing organizational needs and moral goals can only improve NGOs' standing in the long run. Similarly, they should stress that the groups they choose as clients are not necessarily the worst off, no matter how bad their situation. Finally, although it runs counter to the organizational dynamics at play among challengers and NGOs, the latter ought to avoid heroizing movements and their leaders. Although often courageous, these people are also engaged in a high-stakes competition for support. A candid description of these

---

[12] Alexander Cooley and James Ron, "The NGO Scramble: Organizational Insecurity and the Political Economy of Transnational Action," *International Security* 27, no. 1 (2002): 5–39.

considerations would rid the transnational market of some of its games-manship while also quieting those who criticize NGOs as being opaque and undemocratic.

Insurgent Marketing and World Politics

Much of today's research on transnational relations has sought to demonstrate the growing significance of NGOs, advocacy networks, and moral norms in international politics. Scholars in the "constructivist" school contend that these factors strongly influence global public opinion, international organizations, and states. These arguments buck dominant realist and liberal analyses that place states, power, and national interest at the heart of international politics. To make their heretical points, constructivists have focused on the most successful networks, the Northern NGOs that stud them, and their interactions with target states. This work has shown that in some important cases, such as the fall of apartheid in South Africa and the decline of communism in Eastern Europe, norms and non-state actors did play a role in "reconstituting" states, changing policies and even regimes.[13] Among activists and journalists there has also been considerable enthusiasm over the expansion of NGOs and new communications technologies.

The approach developed in this book supplements but sobers these views. Thematically, I highlight how disparate groups from around the world aggregate and ally rather than focusing on external campaigns by existing networks. Methodologically, I cover a wider sweep of cases. As Chapters 3 and 4 showed, the Zapatistas and Ogoni were not unique to their countries. Only their successes on the international stage were unusual. In countless geographic settings and for numerous issues, similar comparisons could be drawn. Analytically, I build on this enlarged perspective and find that although Keck and Sikkink's "boomerang model" is useful as a metaphor, transnational networking is more fully illuminated by thinking of it in terms of supply and demand. The comparative studies in this book have illustrated the usefulness of this perspective in diverse contexts: for movements having disparate goals, protest strategies, and domestic support; using both

---

[13] Audie Klotz, *Norms in International Relations: The Struggle against Apartheid* (Ithaca, NY: Cornell University Press, 1996); Daniel C. Thomas, *The Helsinki Effect: International Norms, Human Rights, and the Demise of Communism* (Princeton, NJ: Princeton University Press, 2001).

targeted lobbying and diffuse consciousness-raising; and attracting support from different sectors of the NGO "spectrum."

Invariably there will be multiple reasons that a particular insurgency gains major support; in the jargon of social science, such a complex outcome will always be "overdetermined," even where analysts control for numerous variables. Those seeking a deterministic theory of transnational support therefore face frustration. But this fact does not mean that analysts can say nothing – or that insurgents are powerless to influence events. The internationally successful and failed cases in this book teach much. At the most abstract level, they indicate both the market processes at work and the typical structure of that market, with many desperate groups demanding scarce support from a relatively small number of NGO suppliers. This is not a market based only on a cold calculation of interests; sympathy and altruism influence many of the exchanges that occur. But neither is this a realm in which transnational appeals will easily or invariably yield assistance. The relative power of the parties – their need for and value to one another – plays a key role. At a lower level of abstraction, the cases show that in this market the growth of support hinges both on a movement's gaining international visibility and on its demonstrating overlap with key NGO attributes. Although there is some tension between these two requirements, it is generally the case that the more visible a movement and the greater its fit with potential backers, the greater its likelihood of gaining support. Moving to a more concrete level, the cases demonstrated several strategies by which movements raise international consciousness and frame themselves around key NGO attributes. Both targeted lobbying of NGOs and more diffuse awareness-building through the media, exemplified by the Ogoni and Zapatista cases, respectively, are available – and have different repercussions for movements. With respect to matching, movements frame around five different attributes, and the degree to which they do so will depend on their relative power vis-à-vis potential supporters. Finally, these strategies are not equally available to all insurgents. Two broad sets of "structural" factors are critical to a movement's ability to use these strategies: its internal organizational features and its opponent's characteristics. Overall, the marketing perspective offers a comprehensive analytic framework for understanding the growth of NGO support for local movements. Other researchers might usefully extend this framework by seeking to rank strategic and structural factors in particular contexts.

Given the market processes I explored, the structure of contemporary transnational politics requires reconsideration. For one thing, the term "*global* civil society" implies a realm in which all have an equal chance of participating. The picture presented here is less comforting. There are huge rents in this society, with whole regions and vast populations absent or underrepresented. Even in regions where transnational interactions are thick, pockets remain outside the charmed circle. Needy groups unlucky enough to be located there have far less hope of making their causes known to audiences abroad than those from other places. Certain issues also stay persistently off the international radar screen. What plays best overseas seldom corresponds to what matters most domestically, as the Ogoni found when their initial ethnic appeals fell flat. Unfashionable, complex, or intractable conflicts fester in isolation, whereas those that match (or thanks to savvy marketing appear to match) international issues of the moment attract disproportionate interest. Thus, continuing ethnic and political turmoil in the Niger Delta remains far less notorious than the operations of multinational oil companies there.

At the domestic level, distressed populations also vary in their capacities to make their causes known to distant audiences. Material resources, technological know-how, preexisting contacts, and organizational expertise make a major difference. Because a central requirement is access to potential backers, movement opponents also exercise significant impact. This of course means that not all insurgents are created equal in the competition. Some, like the Ogoni and Zapatistas, are blessed with resources and special knowledge of the international scene. Adept leadership plays a major role, too. This goes beyond the truism that audiences latch onto a personal story better than a group's plight. In both the Zapatista and Ogoni cases, leaders not only symbolized the movements but in key ways *were* the movements, translating and linking the provincial and the global – even if they were also in some ways "made" by the support they excited.

Where networks do form, their structure differs from that which many optimists expect. For one thing, they are shot through with power differences and accompanying tensions. Mutual but unequal value and need underlie network operation, with desperate groups typically accommodating their powerful patrons by reframing their interests, culture, tactics, and ethics. Although some NGOs also change their perspectives and expand their missions in these interactions, movements bear the brunt of such "reconstitution." Moreover, although today's dominant international norms, such as respect for individual human rights, have the potential to strengthen dissident claims, they are themselves manifestations of power. Many are controversial and political, such as those surrounding environmental issues and even some human rights norms. Others are limited or one-sided, neglecting key issues affecting large populations. In their role as gatekeepers, major NGOs may act as brakes on more radical and exceptional ideas emanating from the developing world, and for that reason some important challengers eschew foreign ties.[14] Ultimately, the need for local groups to click with trendy issues fosters a homogeneity of humanitarianism. This is not an argument for cultural relativism – for aiding all groups equally regardless of their claims or tactics. Rather, the point is that even seemingly benign and democratic norms have unequal impacts.

Another aspect of network structure also demands review. Much of the academic literature suggests that relations among supporters are smooth and nonhierarchical, with networks composed of a large number of equally important entities. In fact, one or a few key NGOs or media typically act as "gatekeepers" to broader help from "followers," with "matchmakers" and "vouchers" playing lesser but important roles. Moreover, despite the image of a centerless network, follower NGOs often deal not with a distant movement but with a gatekeeper far from the target state, an organization they know and trust that acts as a clearinghouse for information about the challenger even if it has no formal authority in the network.

All of this suggests that the character of transnational advocacy merits rethinking. The term "global *civil* society" is often used to counterpose a realm of principle and morality against one marked by self-seeking, profit, and power. Yet this view, reflecting one aspect of transnational relations, obscures as much as it illuminates. For academics, it furnishes few analytic tools for explaining why some challengers excite major support while others, equally if not more worthy, remain orphans. More broadly, it misrepresents the underlying realities. The organizations and individuals composing networks are certainly motivated, in part, by high principles. But questions of organizational maintenance and survival also permeate NGO decision making. Viewing NGO motivations as fundamentally different from those of other international actors is therefore problematic.[15] Worthy movements that desire outside help must compete with one another and conform themselves to the predilections and demands of these patrons.

---

[14] Balakrishnan Rajagopal, *International Law from Below: Development, Social Movements, and Third World Resistance* (Cambridge: Cambridge University Press, 2003).

[15] Susan K. Sell and Aseem Prakash, "Using Ideas Strategically: The Contest between Business and NGO Networks in Intellectual Property Rights," *International Studies Quarterly* 48, no. 1 (2004): 143–75.

Many go unsupported or draw far less backing than their more fortunate cousins – for reasons that have little to do with their righteousness.

The marketing perspective therefore paints a stark picture of contemporary "global civil society." Without challenging the increasing role of advocacy networks and NGOs in world politics, the marketing approach places it in a different light. "Global civil society" is an arena of sharp competition where myriad weak groups fight for recognition and aid. It is a sphere in which hard-nosed calculation of costs and benefits constantly competes with sympathy and emotion. And it is a place where the real needs of local people are one factor, not necessarily the most important, in sparking international activism.

Appendix 1

NGO Standards for Supporting Local Movements

NGO decisions to support or reject local movements are based on criteria deriving from the NGOs' substantive, cultural, ethical, tactical, and organizational features. Often these factors remain unwritten and informal, known by key staff members and enforced by NGO managers. Some NGOs, particularly those hearing frequent appeals, formalize their criteria. In a few cases, NGOs have shared these documents with the public. The first sample below is from an Annual Report by the New York–based Human Rights Watch (HRW), one of the world's largest human rights organizations, which was founded in 1978 and is dedicated to "protecting the human rights of people around the world." Because of the report's public nature, the criteria discussed in it are rather vague.

The second document, from the San Francisco–based Sierra Club, is an internal memorandum obtained in 2001 from a high-level staff member and described as an "informal . . . starting point [including] some of the factors we weigh" in deciding which local causes to support.[1]

The third document is an excerpt from the Investigative Protocols of the Factory Assessment Program administered by the Workers Rights Consortium (WRC). WRC seeks to enforce codes of conduct covering labor practices for the manufacture of goods carrying collegiate logos and has more than one hundred affiliated colleges and universities. This section of the Protocols discusses the criteria that WRC weighs when deciding whether to conduct investigations of possible code violations.

---

[1] Interviewee 28 (Sierra Club manager), telephone interview by author, April 27, 2001.

Excerpt from Human Rights Watch's World Report 2001

The failure to include a particular country or issue often reflects no more than staffing limitations and should not be taken as commentary on the significance of the problem. There are many serious human rights violations that Human Rights Watch simply lacks the capacity to address. Other factors affecting the focus of our work...include the severity of abuses, access to the country and the availability of information about it, the susceptibility of abusive forces to outside influence, the importance of addressing certain thematic concerns, and the need to maintain a balance in the work of Human Rights Watch across various political divides. (Human Rights Watch, "Introduction," *Human Rights Watch World Report 2001*, http://www.hrw.org/wr2kl/intro/index.html (accessed May 18, 2004))

"General Sierra Club Criteria for Involvement in Human Rights Cases"

The Sierra Club's Human Rights and the Environment Campaign is particularly interested in protecting the fundamental civil liberties of individuals worldwide who wish to advocate nonviolently for environmental protection. Such liberties are more closely related to our mandate as a grassroots environmental organization. The kinds of rights that are most involved with providing these critical assurances are those: guaranteeing rights of political participation; guaranteeing personal security; and guaranteeing personal autonomy (e.g., freedom to speak, organize, etc.)

The Sierra Club prefers to confine its involvement in the human rights area to pursuing civil and political rights of this sort for all people in all places who are advocates for environmental protection. We would pursue these as rights to be recognized and guaranteed under international law.

As a corollary, we would not involve ourselves in promoting – as rights under international law – "social, economic or cultural rights." While these deal with important human concerns, they lack the same character as pre-conditions for our work.

General Human Rights and the Environment Campaign Support Questions

1. Is there a local grassroots organization that we can work with? (As a primarily domestically focused, US-based organization, the Sierra Club prefers to support indigenous environmentalists rather than to organize a country-specific campaign from abroad.)
2. Does this individual or community group wish our assistance?
3. Would the Sierra Club's involvement help or harm this individual/community? Will our involvement make a positive difference?
4. Is the environmental cause in keeping with Sierra Club policy on that issue? If the above are answered affirmatively, then...

5. Do we expect this to be a long or short term campaign? How winnable is it?
6. Will Sierra Club members be sympathetic to this issue/country/community?
7. Is there a U.S. government or corporate hook? (Sierra Club, "General Sierra Club Criteria for Involvement in Human Rights Cases," memorandum, n.d.)

Excerpt from Workers Rights Consortium Factory Assessment Program, "Investigative Protocols"

Substantive Criteria for the Decision to Proceed with an Investigation . . .

A. Mandatory Threshold Criteria. No Investigation shall proceed unless it meets each of the following two criteria:
   1. There is reasonable cause to believe that a party has engaged in actions constituting a non-trivial violation of University Codes of Conduct . . . or there is good cause, based on the WRC's objectives and principles, to Investigate whether there is such reasonable cause in a particular facility or category of facilities.
   2. There is substantial cause to believe that the workers who are or may be affected by an Investigation desire that the WRC initiate an Investigation.
      a. In the case of a Complaint-triggered Investigation, a Complaint submitted by affected or potentially affected workers shall suffice to establish such substantial cause.
      b. In the case of an Investigation initiated by a Complaint submitted by a party other than the affected or potentially affected workers, . . . the Executive Director shall rely on information provided by all parties, including local groups, organizations, and advocates, in determining whether there is such substantial cause. The expressed views of the affected or potentially affected workers and their communities shall presumptively establish whether there is substantial cause to believe that the affected or potentially affected workers desire that the WRC initiate an Investigation.
B. Other Criteria that Shall be Weighed. If the potential Investigation meets each of the two threshold criteria . . . , then the following criteria shall be considered in deciding which Investigations should proceed, that is, in deciding how WRC resources and time should be allocated among potential Investigations:
   1. The relative importance of the substantive rights or standards which allegedly have been violated. In making this judgment about the prioritization of matters that are the subject of potential Investigations, primary consideration shall be given to the views of affected or potentially affected workers.
   2. The relative severity of the alleged violation – that is, the degree of harm caused by the alleged violation of the rights or standards at issue. In making this judgment, primary consideration shall be given to the views of affected

or potentially affected workers about the relative severity of the alleged violation.

3. The relative pervasiveness of the violation, that is, the relative number of workers, communities, factories, or regions allegedly harmed by the violation.

4. The relative probability that the potential WRC Investigation, if conducted, will result in actual remediation, or progress toward remediation, of any violations that may be found in the Investigation.

5. The degree to which, and the probability that, the potential Investigation, in addition to promising remediation of any violation, will concurrently empower and strengthen the capacity of local groups, organizations, and advocates, especially the affected workers and their communities, to participate in future WRC Investigations or to undertake future investigations and remediation conducted by the local parties themselves without WRC assistance.

6. The probability that the potential Investigation, in addition to promising remediation of violations and empowerment of local groups, will yield information, education, and constructive innovation serving the general purposes and activities of the WRC, including data-collection, extension and improvement of the WRC's networking activities, the WRC's constructive interaction with interested parties (including licensees and contractors), public disclosure and education about compliance with labor rights and standards, and improvement of other policies and practices of the WRC, including improvement of these Protocols. (Workers Rights Consortium Factory Assessment Program, "Investigative Protocols," http://www.workersrights.org/wrc_protocols.asp (accessed August 10, 2003))

Appendix 2

Interviews

For the empirical portions of this book, particularly Chapter 3, I spoke with more than 60 people in North America and Europe, in some cases multiple times, primarily during 1996–98 but also in later years. For the Nigerian case study, my primary target was the MOSOP leadership, who I identified through a review of American, European, and Nigerian periodicals as well as other published materials, including most importantly Ken Saro-Wiwa's illuminating *A Month and a Day: A Detention Diary*. After contacting this group of leaders by telephone or letter, I used a "snowball" technique to expand my list, identifying other subjects through an initial interview round, a review of newly collected primary documents, or by chance presence at an interview location. (However, I conducted all interviews with individual subjects.) In several instances, I met with newly identified subjects when I attended MOSOP strategy meetings, public discussions, or other events in the United States and Europe. When I conducted the bulk of my interviews, during 1996–98, the height of the brutal dictatorship of Sani Abacha, most of the still-living MOSOP leadership were exiled in Europe or North America, where I met with them. I interviewed primarily men but also several women prominent in the movement. The interviews are of elites involved in MOSOP's international strategizing rather than the Ogoni masses, and they include highly educated MOSOP leaders, some of them relatives of Ken Saro-Wiwa. Because my focus was on understanding MOSOP's success on the international stage, I did not interview Ogoni who opposed the movement. For information on other Niger Delta ethnic groups that have failed to gain international support, my interviewing was more limited, but I used similar techniques to identify key subjects.

In my interviews with NGOs from the Ogoni support network, I sought information not only about why the Ogoni gained major support beginning in 1993 but also why they failed to do so earlier and why other Niger Delta minorities remained isolated. I first sought to find the most prominent organizations involved in the Ogoni network during the mid-1990s using the sources indicated. I then contacted these organizations and pinpointed principals involved in key decisions to support the Ogoni. I again conducted a first round of interviews, primarily in the NGOs' offices in North America and Europe, identifying further subjects through snowballing and serendipity. (My lengthy interview with a top leader of Papua New Guinea's Bougainville Interim Government, exiled to the Netherlands from the Solomon Islands only days before I met him, is an example of the latter "method.") To the extent possible, I sought to interview both NGO staff members and managers – and found interesting tensions between them. I interviewed approximately equal numbers of men and women, most of them deeply involved in Ogoni support activities. In several instances, I also interviewed journalists who reported on the Ogoni conflict. Although I sought an "on the record" interview with Shell, this was refused, and I was able to secure only an extended background talk with a member of the company's public affairs department in the Netherlands in July 1996.

For my study of the Mexican cases, I interviewed some NGO principals on my own but relied primarily on contemporaneous interviews of Zapatista leaders, especially Subcomandante Marcos, conducted by journalists, activists, and other academics. Although there is a heavy focus on Marcos's views in Chapter 4, this is justified because of his central role in the movement's strategizing and because, as discussed, his persona itself has been central to the Zapatistas' international successes. The Zapatistas' fame has resulted in a wealth of interviews as well as primary documents issued by the movement and by NGO supporters which I used in writing the chapter. In writing about the EPR, I relied primarily on journalistic interviews, the group's own primary documents, and secondary sources.

My interviews – conducted in person, by telephone, or both – generally lasted from one to two hours. Although I began each interview with a set of written questions developed earlier, I used a dialogical technique – and frequently uncovered new information and insights that I followed up. (For shorter and less formal interchanges, I use the term "discussion.") In most of my personal and telephone interviews, informants agreed to my use of a tape recorder. Where this was not the case, I transcribed interviewees' responses. Because the Ogoni and Zapatista conflicts continue today in both domestic and international arenas and because some of the information I collected is sensitive, I offered anonymity to my subjects. In a few cases (marked with asterisks), I conducted interviews with subjects who had read and were reacting to my *Foreign Policy* article in which I made some of the arguments discussed in this book. The list that follows, arranged by Interviewee Number, gives a brief description of my primary informants' affiliations or activities at the time of the events they discuss. I have deposited copies of my audiotapes, notes, or transcripts in Special Collections, Gumberg Library, Duquesne University, Pittsburgh, PA. Included below is information about the most important of my interviews. Copies of notes from briefer exchanges, my attendance at public events and private strategy sessions, and numerous primary documents are also archived in Gumberg Library.

1. Greenpeace International communications officer, telephone interview, July 24, 1996, transcript.
2. Friends of the Earth-Netherlands staffperson, personal interview, Amsterdam, the Netherlands, July 17, 1996, audiotape.
3. Unrepresented Nations and Peoples Organization (UNPO) staffperson, personal interview, Littlehampton, England, July 18, 1996, audiotape.
4. Rainforest Action Group activist, personal interview, Oxford, England, July 19, 1996, audiotape.
5. Filmmaker and Greenpeace International consultant, telephone interview, June 25, 1996, transcript.
6. Greenpeace International staffperson, telephone interview, July 16, 1996, transcript.
7. Environmental activist, personal discussion, London, England, July 23, 1996, notes.
8. Greenpeace International manager, telephone interview, July 29, 1996, transcript.
9. Greenpeace International staffperson, personal interview, Amsterdam, the Netherlands, July 14, 1996, audiotape.
10. Survival International staffperson, telephone interview, June 18, 1996, transcript; personal interview, London, England, July 22, 1996, audiotape.
11. Movement for the Survival of the Ogoni People–United Kingdom (MOSOP-UK) leader, personal interview, London, England, July 23, 1996, audiotape.
12. Movement for the Survival of the Ogoni People (MOSOP) leader, personal interview, London, England, July 23, 1996, audiotape.

13. UNPO manager, personal interview, The Hague, the Netherlands, July 11, 1996, audiotape.
14. Greenpeace International consultant, telephone interviews, June 26, 1996 and July 24, 1996, transcripts.
15. UNPO staffperson, personal interview, The Hague, the Netherlands, July 12, 1996, audiotape.
16. MOSOP activist, personal discussion, London, England, July 21, 1996, audiotape.
17. MOSOP-UK leader, personal interview, London, England, July 21, 1996, audiotape.
18. MOSOP leader, personal interview, London, England, July 21, 1996, audiotape; personal discussion, St. Louis, MO, March 14, 1998, notes.
19. Ijaw activist, personal interview, London, England, July 23, 1996, audiotape.
20. Amnesty International staffperson, personal interview, Amsterdam, the Netherlands, July 17, 1996, audiotape.
21. UNPO staffperson, personal interview, The Hague, the Netherlands, July 11, 1996, audiotape.
22. Greenpeace–United States manager, telephone interview, June 21, 1996, transcript.
23. MOSOP-USA leader, personal discussion and public talk, St. Louis, MO, March 14, 1998, notes.
24. MOSOP activist, personal discussion and public talk, St. Louis, MO, March 14, 1998, notes.
25. MOSOP activist, personal discussion, St. Louis, MO, March 14, 1998, notes.
26. Human Rights Watch staffperson, telephone interview, May 2, 2001, transcript.
27. Human Rights Watch manager, personal interview, New York, NY, March 14, 2001, audiotape.
28. Sierra Club manager, telephone interview, April 27, 2001, audiotape.
29. Ijaw Youth Council leader, telephone interview, June 27, 2001, audiotape; personal interview, Pittsburgh, PA, April 24, 2002, audiotape.
30. Bougainville Interim Government official, personal interview, The Hague, the Netherlands, July 13, 1996, audiotape.
31. Human Rights Watch staffperson, telephone interviews, April 10, 2001 and April 20, 2001, audiotapes.

32. Free Nigeria Movement leader, personal discussion, St. Louis, MO, March 14, 1998, notes.
33. The Body Shop social issues manager, personal interview, Littlehampton, England, July 18, 1996.
34. *Guardian* (London) reporter, telephone interview, July 24, 1996, transcript.
35. British Broadcasting Company reporter, telephone interview, July 25, 1996, transcript.
36. MOSOP activist, personal interview, London, England, July 21, 1996, audiotape.
37. Stakeholder Democracy Network activist, telephone interview, May 10, 2002, audiotape.*
38. Robert F. Kennedy Memorial manager, telephone interview, May 2, 2001, audiotape.
39. Ford Foundation program officer, telephone interview, May 16, 2001, audiotape.
40. Students for a Free Tibet manager, telephone interview, June 6, 2002, audiotape.*
41. Human Rights Watch communications officer, New York, NY, personal interview, March 14, 2001, transcript.
42. Ambedkar Center for Justice and Peace leader, telephone interview, April 26, 2001, audiotape.
43. Unitarian Universalist Holdeen India Program manager, telephone interview, May 1, 2001, audiotape.
44. Unitarian Universalist Service Committee staffperson, personal interview, Cambridge, MA, April 13, 1996, transcript.
45. International Foundation for Election Systems manager, telephone interview, June 10, 2002, transcript.*

Bibliography

Note: This bibliography includes unpublished or rare primary documents that I collected during my research. I have archived them, as well as other unpublished sources not cited in this book and copies of newspaper articles from Nigerian and Mexican sources, in the Special Collections section of Duquesne University's Gumberg Library, Pittsburgh, PA. Entries that include the term "Gumberg Library" are available to the public there.

Ackerman, Peter, and Christopher Kruegler. *Strategic Nonviolent Conflict: The Dynamics of People Power in the Twentieth Century*. Westport, CT: Praeger, 1994.

Adamson, Fiona. "The Diffusion of Competing Norms in Central Asia: Transnational Democracy Assistance Networks vs. Transnational Islamism." Paper presented at the 2003 Annual Meeting of the American Political Science Association, Philadelphia, PA, August 27–31, 2003.

Addendum to the Ogoni Bill of Rights. August 26, 1991. In Ken Saro–Wiwa, *A Month and a Day: A Detention Diary*. New York: Penguin Books, 1995, 89–92.

Aguilera, Eugenio, Ana Laura Hernández, Gustavo Rodríguez, and Pablo Salazar Devereaux. Interview with Subcomandante Marcos, May 11, 1994. In EZLN, *¡Zapatistas! Documents of the New Mexican Revolution* (December 31, 1993–June 12, 1994), Autonomedia, ed. and trans. New York: Autonomedia, 1994, 289–309.

Al-Sayyid, Mustapha Kamel. "A Clash of Values: U.S. Civil Society Aid and Islam in Egypt." In *Funding Virtue: Civil Society Aid and Democracy Promotion*, Marina Ottaway and Thomas Carothers, eds. Washington, DC: Carnegie Endowment for International Peace, 2000, 48–73.

Americas Watch. *Unceasing Abuses: Human Rights in Mexico One Year After the Introduction of Reform*. New York: Human Rights Watch, 1991.

Amnesty International. "Building an International Human Rights Agenda: Promoting Economic, Social and Cultural Rights." *Amnesty International Report 2004*. http://web.amnesty.org/report2004/hragenda-6-eng.

Amnesty International USA. "Just Earth!" http://www.amnestyusa.org/justearth/index.do (accessed June 28, 2004).

Applied Anthropology Computer Network, Chiapas News Archive. Rochester, MI: Oakland University. ftp://vela.acs.oakland.edu/pub/anthap/ Chiapas_News_Archive/ (accessed January 26, 1997; site now discontinued).

Arquilla, John, and David Ronfeldt. *Networks and Netwars*. Santa Monica, CA: RAND, 2001.

Bailey, F. G. *Humbuggery and Manipulation: The Art of Leadership*. Ithaca, NY: Cornell University Press, 1988.

Bardach, Ann Louise. "Mexico's Poet Rebel." Includes an interview with Subcomandante Marcos, March 25, 1994. *Vanity Fair*, July 1994, 68.

Barnes, Robert H., Andrew Gray, and Benedict Kingsbury, eds. *Indigenous Peoples of Asia*. Ann Arbor, MI: Association for Asian Studies, 1995.

Barreiro, Jose. "Native Response to Chiapas." *Akwe:kon: A Journal of Indigenous Issues* 11, no. 2 (1994): 78–80.

Bassey, Nnimmo, and Oronto Douglas. "Prize Ceremony – Speech by the Prize Winner, 1998 – Environmental Rights Action, Nigeria," June 15, 1998. http://www.sophieprize.org/ (accessed June 28, 2004).

Bates, Crispin. "'Lost Innocents and the Loss of Innocence': Interpreting Adivasi Movements in South Asia." In *Indigenous Peoples of Asia*, Robert H. Barnes, Andrew Gray, and Benedict Kingsbury, eds. Ann Arbor, MI: Association for Asian Studies, 1995, 103–19.

Baumgartner, Frank, and Bryan Jones. "Agenda Dynamics and Policy Subsystems." *Journal of Politics* 53, no. 4 (1991): 1044–74.

Beltrán del Río, Pascal. "Hay que eliminar a los Zapatistas: Recomendación del Chase Manhattan Bank al Gobierno Mexicano, *Proceso*, February 13, 1995, n.p.

Benjamin, Medea. "Interview: Subcomandante Marcos," n.d. [March 25, 1994?]. In *First World, Ha Ha Ha! The Zapatista Challenge*, Elaine Katzenberger, ed. San Francisco: City Lights Books, 1995, 57–70.

Bjornlund, Eric. "Democracy Inc." *Wilson Quarterly*, Summer 2001, 18–24.

Blau, Peter M. *Exchange and Power in Social Life*. New Brunswick, NJ: Transaction Books, 1964.

Bob, Clifford. "Beyond Transparency: Visibility and Fit in the Internationalization of Internal Conflict." In *Power and Conflict in the Age of Transparency*, Bernard I. Finel and Kristin M. Lord, eds. New York: Palgrave/St. Martin's Press, 2000, 287–314.

Bob, Clifford. "Globalization and the Social Construction of Human Rights Campaigns." In *Globalization and Human Rights*, Alison Brysk, ed. Berkeley: University of California Press, 2002, 133–47.

Bob, Clifford. "Marketing Rebellion: Insurgent Groups, International Media, and NGO Support." *International Politics* 38, no. 3 (2001): 311–34.

Bob, Clifford. "Merchants of Morality," *Foreign Policy*, March/April 2002: 36–45.

Bob, Clifford. "Overcoming Indifference: Internationalizing Human Rights Violations in Rural Mexico." *Journal of Human Rights* 1, no. 2 (2002): 247–61.

Bob, Clifford. "Political Process Theory and Transnational Movements: Dialectics of Protest among Nigeria's Ogoni Minority." *Social Problems* 49, no. 3 (2002): 395–415.

Boli, John, and George M. Thomas, eds. *Constructing World Culture: International Nongovernmental Organizations since 1875*. Stanford, CA: Stanford University Press, 1999.

Bottelier, Pieter. "Was World Bank Support for the Qinghai Anti-Poverty Project in China Ill-Considered?" *Harvard Asia Quarterly* 5, no. 1 (2001). http://www.fas.harvard.edu/~asiactr/haq/200101/0101a007.htm (accessed August 3, 2004).

Brouwer, Imco. "Weak Democracy and Civil Society Promotion: The Cases of Egypt and Palestine." In *Funding Virtue: Civil Society Aid and Democracy Promotion*, Marina Ottaway and Thomas Carothers, eds. Washington, DC: Carnegie Endowment for International Peace, 2000, 21–48.

Bruhn, Kathleen. "Antonio Gramsci and the *Palabra Verdadera*: The Political Discourse of Mexico's Guerrilla Forces." *Journal of Interamerican Studies and World Affairs* 41, no. 2 (1999): 29–55.

Brysk, Alison. "From Above and Below: Social Movements, the International System, and Human Rights in Argentina." *Comparative Political Studies* 26, no. 3 (1993): 259–85.

Brysk, Alison. "Turning Weakness into Strength: The Internationalization of Indian Rights." *Latin American Perspectives* 23, no. 2 (1996): 38–57.

Brysk, Alison. *From Tribal Village to Global Village: Indian Rights and International Relations in Latin America*. Stanford, CA: Stanford University Press, 2000.

Burgerman, Susan. *Moral Victories: How Activists Provoke Multilateral Action*. Ithaca, NY: Cornell University Press, 2001.

Burguete Cal y Mayor, Araceli. "The de Facto Autonomous Process: New Jurisdictions and Parallel Governments in Rebellion." In *Mayan Lives, Mayan Utopias: The Indigenous Peoples of Chiapas and the Zapatista Rebellion*, Carlos Pérez, trans., Jan Rus, Rosalva Aída Hernández Castillo, and Shannan L. Mattiace, eds. Lanham, MD: Rowman & Littlefield, 2003, 191–218.

Castillo, Carmen, and Tessa Brisac. "Apéndice: Historia de Marcos y de los hombres de la noche," interview with Subcomandante Marcos, October 24, 1994. In Adolfo Gilly, Subcomandante Marcos, and Carlo Ginzburg, *Discusión sobre la historia*. Mexico City: Taurus, 1995, 129–42.

Ceceña, Ana Esther. "Zapata in Europe." In *Auroras of the Zapatistas: Local and Global Struggles of the Fourth World War*, Midnight Notes Collective, eds. Brooklyn, NY: Autonomedia, 2001, 79–103.

Chomsky, Noam. "Time Bombs." In *First World, Ha Ha Ha! The Zapatista Challenge*, Elaine Katzenberger, ed. San Francisco: City Lights Books, 1995, 175–82.

Christian Aid. "Behind the Mask: The Real Face of Corporate Social Responsibility." London: Christian Aid, 2004. http://www.christian-aid.org.uk/indepth/0401csr/index.htm (accessed June 30, 2004).

Christian Aid. *Shell in Nigeria: Oil and Gas Reserves and Political Risks: Shared Concerns for Investors and Producer-Communities*. Lewes, United Kingdom: Christian Aid, 2004.

Churchill, Ward. "A North American Indigenist View." In *First World, Ha Ha Ha! The Zapatista Challenge*, Elaine Katzenberger, ed. San Francisco: City Lights Books, 1995, 141–56.

Civil Liberties Organisation. *Ogoni: Trials and Travails* (Lagos, Nigeria: Civil Liberties Organisation, 1996).

Clark, Ann Marie, Elisabeth Friedman, and Kathryn Hochstetler. "The Sovereign Limits of Global Civil Society: A Comparison of NGO Participation in UN World Conferences on the Environment, Human Rights, and Women." *World Politics* 51, no. 1 (1998): 1–35.

Cleaver, Harry. "Background on Chiapas95." http://www.eco.utexas.edu/faculty/Cleaver/bkgdch95.html (accessed July 15, 2004).

Cleaver, Harry. "Zapatistas in Cyberspace: A Guide to Analysis and Resources." http://www.eco.utexas.edu/faculty/Cleaver/zapsincyber.html (accessed July 15, 2004).

Colburn, Forrest D. *The Vogue of Revolution in Poor Countries*. Princeton, NJ: Princeton University Press, 1994.

Collier, George A. "Roots of the Rebellion in Chiapas." *Cultural Survival Quarterly* 18, no. 1 (1994): 14–18.

Collier, Paul, V. L. Elliott, Havard Hegre, Anke Hoeffler, Marta Reynal-Querol, and Nicholas Sambanis. *Breaking the Conflict Trap: Civil War and Development Policy*. World Bank Policy Research Report. Washington, DC: World Bank; New York: Oxford University Press, 2003.

Colonial Office. *Nigeria: Report of the Commission Appointed to Enquire into the Fears of Minorities and the Means of Allaying Them (Willink Commission Report)*. London: Her Majesty's Stationery Office, 1958. Reprint, Port Harcourt, Nigeria: Southern Minorities Movement, 1996.

Cooley, Alexander, and James Ron. "The NGO Scramble: Organizational Insecurity and the Political Economy of Transnational Action." *International Security* 27, no. 1 (2002): 5–39.

Corro, Salvador. "En una sangrienta noche de terror, las fuerzas del EPR destruyerion el mito de la pantomima." *Proceso*, September 1, 1996, 13–17.

Coy, Patrick. "Cooperative Accompaniment and Peace Brigades International in Sri Lanka." In *Transnational Social Movements and Global Politics: Solidarity beyond the State*, Jackie Smith, Charles Chatfield, and Ron Pagnucco, eds. Syracuse, NY: Syracuse University Press, 1997, 81–100.

Davis, Morris. *Interpreters for Nigeria: The Third World and International Public Relations*. Urbana: University of Illinois Press, 1977.

Debray, Régis. "Si Desaparemos, sólo quedará la violencia, una Yugoslavia en el sureste Mexicano." Includes an interview with Subcomandante Marcos, April 1996. In *EZLN: La utopía armada: Una visión plural del movimiento Zapatista*, Marcelo Quezada and Maya Lorena Pérez-Ruiz, eds. La Paz, Bolivia: Plural Editores/CID, 1998, 291–99.

Downs, Anthony. "Up and Down with Ecology: The 'Issue-Attention Cycle.'" *Public Interest* 28 (Summer 1972): 38–50.

Bibliography

Economist. "Mexico's Second Class Citizens Say Enough Is Enough." January 8, 1994, 41–42.

Economist. "The Shock Waves Spread." January 15, 1994, 39.

Eguruze, Stanley E. "The Federation of Ijaw Communities (FEDICOM): The Marketing of a Non-Governmental Organisation (NGO) in Nigeria." M.A. dissertation, School of Marketing, University of Greenwich, July 1996. Gumberg Library.

Ekeocha, Okey. "A Cry for Justice – Or Drum Beats of Treason?" *African Guardian,* May 17, 1993, 21.

Enlace Civil. "Enlace Civil." http://www.enlacecivil.org.mx/lm_enlace.html (accessed July 19, 2004).

Ejército Popular Revolucionario (EPR). "Manifiesto de Aguas Blancas," June 28, 1996. http://www.pengo.it/PDPR-EPR/doctos_basicos/manifiest_aguas.htm (accessed July 20, 2004).

Ejército Zapatista de Liberación Nacional (EZLN). "Cuarta Declaración de la Selva Lacandona," January 1, 1996. *¡Ya Basta!* http://www.ezln.org/documentos/1996/19960101.es.htm (accessed August 1, 2004).

EZLN. "Declaración de la Selva Lacandona: Hoy decimos ¡basta!" December 31, 1993. In EZLN, *Documentos y comunicados,* vol. 1. Mexico City: Ediciones Era, 1994, 33–35.

EZLN. *Documentos y comunicados,* vol. 1. Mexico City: Ediciones Era, 1994.

EZLN. *EZLN: La utopía armada: Una visión plural del movimiento Zapatista.* Marcelo Quezada and Mya Lorena Pérez-Ruiz, eds. La Paz, Bolivia: Plural Editores/CID, 1998.

EZLN. *Los hombres sin rostro: Dossier sobre Chiapas,* vol. 1. Mexico City: CEE–SIPRO, 1994.

EZLN. "Pliego de demandas," March 1, 1994. In *Documentos y comunicados,* vol. 1. Mexico City: Ediciones Era, 1994, 178–85.

EZLN. "Segunda Declaración de la Selva Lacandona," June 10, 1994. *¡Ya Basta!* http://www.ezln.org/documentos/1994/19940610.es.htm (accessed July 15, 2004).

EZLN. *Shadows of Tender Fury: The Letters and Communiqués of Subcomandante Marcos and the Zapatista Army of National Liberation,* Frank Bardacke, Leslie López, and the Watsonville, California Human Rights Committee, trans. New York: Monthly Review Press, 1995.

EZLN. "Tercera Declaración de la Selva Lacandona," January 1, 1995. *¡Ya Basta!* http://www.ezln.org/documentos/1995/199501xx.es.htm (accessed July 15, 2004).

EZLN. *Voice of Fire: Communiqués and Interviews from the Zapatista National Liberation Army,* Ben Clarke and Clifton Ross, eds.; Clifton Ross, et al., trans. Berkeley, CA: New Earth Publications, 1994.

EZLN. *¡Ya Basta!* http://www.ezln.org (accessed July 15, 2004).

EZLN. *¡Zapatistas! Documents of the New Mexican Revolution (December 31, 1993–June 12, 1994),* Autonomedia, ed. and trans. New York: Autonomedia, 1994.

Falk, Richard A. *On Humane Governance: Toward a New Global Politics – The World Order Models Project Report of the Global Civilization Initiative*. University Park: Pennsylvania State University Press, 1995.

Fisher, William F. "Development and Resistance in the Narmada Valley." In *Toward Sustainable Development?: Struggling Over India's Narmada River*, William F. Fisher, ed. Armonk, NY: M. E. Sharpe, 1995, 3–46.

Fisher, William F., and Thomas Ponniah, eds. *Another World Is Possible: Popular Alternatives to Globalization at the World Social Forum*. New York: Palgrave MacMillan, 2003.

Flood, Andrew. "The Story of How We Learnt to Dream at Reality: A Report on the First Intercontinental Gathering for Humanity and against Neoliberalism," n.d. [1997?]. http://flag.blackened.net/revolt/andrew/encounter1_report.html (accessed August 4, 2004).

Florini, Ann M., ed. *The Third Force: The Rise of Transnational Civil Society*. Tokyo: Japan Center for International Exchange; Washington: Carnegie Endowment for International Peace, 2000.

Fourth World Bulletin, "Self-Determination and Maya Rebellion in Chiapas: Commentary." *Fourth World Bulletin* 3, no. 2 (1994): 1–6.

Frank, Robert H., and Philip J. Cook. *The Winner-Take-All Society: Why the Few at the Top Get So Much More than the Rest of Us*. New York: Free Press, 1995; New York: Penguin Books, 1996.

Free West Papua Movement, OPM (Organisesi Papua Merdeka). http://www.converge.org.nz/wpapua/opm.html (accessed June 1, 2004).

Frontline. "The Gate of Heavenly Peace." Show no. 1418. Boston: WGBH Educational Foundation, 1996.

Frynas, Jedrzej Georg. *Oil in Nigeria: Conflict and Litigation between Oil Companies and Village Communities*. Munster: Lit Verlag, 2000.

Gamson, William A. *The Strategy of Social Protest*, 2nd ed. Belmont, CA: Wadsworth Publishing, 1990.

Gandhi, Mahatma. *The Collected Works of Mahatma Gandhi*, vol. XXVI. Delhi: Publications Division, Ministry of Information and Broadcasting, 1958.

Garfinkel, Simson. "The Free Software Imperative." *Technology Review*, February 2003, 30.

Garrow, David J. *Protest at Selma*. New Haven, CT: Yale University Press, 1978.

Gatsiopoulos, Georgina. "The EPR: Mexico's 'Other' Guerrillas." *NACLA Report on the Americas* 30, no. 4 (1997): 33.

Geneva Global Inc. "The Geneva Way." http://www.genevaglobal.com/genevaway.shtml (accessed June 20, 2004).

Gilly, Adolfo. *Chiapas: La Razon Ardiente: Ensayo sobre la rebelión del mundo encantado*. Mexico City: Ediciones Era, 1997.

Global Exchange. "Current Campaigns: Guerrero." http://www.globalexchange.org/countries/mexico/campaigns.html (accessed July 20, 2004).

Global Exchange. "Foreigners of Conscience: The Mexican Government's Campaign against International Human Rights Observers in Chiapas." http://www.globalexchange.org/countries/mexico/observers/report/ (accessed July 20, 2004).

Bibliography

Global Exchange. "Global Exchange in Chiapas." http://www.globalexchange.org/countries/mexico/chiapas/program.html (accessed July 20, 2004).

Gray, Andrew. "The Indigenous Movement in Asia." In *Indigenous Peoples of Asia*, Robert H. Barnes, Andrew Gray, and Benedict Kingsbury, eds. Ann Arbor, MI: Association for Asian Studies, 1995, 35–58.

Gray, Virginia, and David Lowery. *The Population Ecology of Interest Representation: Lobbying Communities in the American States*. Ann Arbor: University of Michigan Press, 2000.

Greenpeace International. *Shell-Shocked: The Environmental and Social Costs of Living with Shell in Nigeria*. London: Greenpeace International, 1994.

Greenpeace Netherlands. "Ogoni Blood on Shell's Hands." Press release, October 31, 1995. Gumberg Library.

Gurowitz, Amy. "Mobilizing International Norms: Domestic Actors, Immigrants, and the Japanese State." *World Politics* 51, no. 3 (1999): 413–45.

Gutiérrez, Maribel. *Violencia en Guerrero*. Mexico City: La Jornada Ediciones, 1998.

Halleck, Deedee. "Zapatistas On-Line." *NACLA Report on the Americas* 28, no. 2 (1994): 30–32.

Hammer, Joshua. "The Making of a Legend." *Newsweek*, December 18, 1995, 47.

Hammond, Allen L. "Digitally Empowered Development." *Foreign Affairs*, March/April 2001, 96–106.

Harper's Magazine. "The Glorious Struggle for Market Share," April 1996, 30.

Harvey, Neil. *The Chiapas Rebellion: The Struggle for Land and Democracy*. Durham, NC: Duke University Press, 1998.

Harvey, Neil. "Playing with Fire: The Implications of *Ejido* Reform." *Akwe:kon: A Journal of Indigenous Issues* 11, no. 2 (1994): 20–27.

Hayden, Tom. "In Chiapas." In *The Zapatista Reader*, Tom Hayden, ed. New York: Thunder's Mouth Press/Nation Books, 2002, 76–97.

Hayden, Tom, ed. *The Zapatista Reader*. New York: Thunder's Mouth Press/Nation Books, 2002.

Hernández Navarro, Luís. "The Chiapas Uprising." *Transformation of Rural Mexico*, no. 5. La Jolla: Center for U.S.–Mexican Studies, University of California, San Diego, 1994, 51–64.

Hinojosa, Oscar. "Por el TLC, Salinas Omitió a la Guerrilla: Marcos." *El Financiero*, February 21, 1994. Quoted in Dolia Estévez, "Chiapas: An Intelligence Fiasco or Coverup?" *CovertAction*, Spring 1994, 44–48.

Hockenos, Paul. *Homeland Calling: Exile Patriotism and the Balkan Wars*. Ithaca, NY: Cornell University Press, 2003.

Holloway, John. *Change the World without Taking Power: The Meaning of Revolution Today*. London: Pluto Press, 2002.

Homelands. "Autonomy, Secession, Independence and Nationalist Movements." http://www.visi.com/~homelands (accessed May 15, 2004).

Hull, Jennifer Bingham. "Cecilia Rodriguez: Zapatista, Feminista." *Ms.*, November/December 1996, 28–31.

Human Rights Watch. *Human Rights Watch World Report: Events of 1992*. New York: Human Rights Watch, 1993.

Human Rights Watch. "Introduction." In *Human Rights Watch World Report 2001*. http://www.hrw.org/wr2k1/intro/index.html (accessed May 18, 2004).

Human Rights Watch. "Opportunism in the Face of Tragedy: Repression in the Name of Anti-Terrorism." http://www.hrw.org/campaigns/september11/opportunismwatch.htm (accessed August 3, 2004).

Human Rights Watch. *The Price of Oil: Corporate Responsibility and Human Rights Violations in Nigeria's Oil Producing Communities*. New York: Human Rights Watch, 1999.

Human Rights Watch/Africa. "Nigeria: The Ogoni Crisis: A Case-Study of Military Repression in Southeastern Nigeria." *Human Rights Watch/Africa Report* 7, no. 5 (1995).

Human Rights Watch/Americas. "Mexico: The New Year's Rebellion: Violations of Human Rights and Humanitarian Law During the Armed Revolt in Chiapas, Mexico." *Human Rights Watch/Americas Report* 6, no. 3 (1994).

Huntington, Samuel. "Transnational Organizations in World Politics." *World Politics* 25 (April 1973): 333–68.

Ikelegbe, Augustine. "Civil Society, Oil and Conflict in the Niger Delta Region of Nigeria: Ramifications of Civil Society for a Regional Resource Struggle." *Journal of Modern African Studies* 39, no. 3 (2001): 437–69.

International Foundation for Election Systems. "Mission and Goals." http://www.ifes.org/mission.htm (accessed July 15, 2004).

International Human Rights Law Group. "Advocacy Bridge Project." http://www.hrlawgroup.org/site/programs/Adbridge.htm (accessed July 17, 2004).

International Rivers Network. "About International Rivers Network." http://www.irn.org/index.asp?id=/basics/about.html (accessed July 17, 2004).

Jenkins, J. Craig, and Craig M. Eckert. "Channeling Black Insurgency: Elite Patronage and Professional Social Movement Organizations in the Development of the Black Movement." *American Sociological Review* 51, no. 6 (1986): 812–29.

Jenkins, J. Craig, and Charles Perrow. "Insurgency of the Powerless: Farm Worker Movements (1946–1972)." *American Sociological Review* 42, no. 2 (1977): 249–68.

John D. and Catherine T. MacArthur Foundation. "Program on Global Security and Sustainability." http://www.macfound.org/programs/gss/nigeria.htm (accessed June 30, 2004).

Jordan, Lisa, and Peter van Tuijl. "Political Responsibility in Transnational NGO Advocacy." *World Development* 28, no. 12 (2000): 2051–65.

Kampwirth, Karen. *Women and Guerrilla Movements: Nicaragua, El Salvador, Chiapas, Cuba*. University Park: Pennsylvania State University Press, 2002.

Kane, Joe. *Savages*. New York: Vintage Books, 1996.

Katzenberger, Elaine, ed. *First World, Ha Ha Ha! The Zapatista Challenge*. San Francisco: City Lights Books, 1995.

Keck, Margaret E., and Kathryn Sikkink. *Activists beyond Borders: Advocacy Networks in International Politics*. Ithaca, NY: Cornell University Press, 1998.

Keohane, Robert O., and Joseph S. Nye, Jr., eds. *Transnational Relations and World Politics*. Cambridge, MA: Harvard University Press, 1971.

Khagram, Sanjeev, James V. Riker, and Kathryn Sikkink, eds. *Restructuring World Politics: Transnational Social Movements, Networks, and Norms*. Minneapolis: University of Minnesota Press, 2002.

Kingdon, John W. *Agendas, Alternatives, and Public Policies*. New York: Harper Collins, 1984.

Klare, Michael. *Resource Wars: The New Landscape of Global Conflict*. New York: Henry Holt, Metropolitan/Owl Books, 2001.

Klotz, Audie. *Norms in International Relations: The Struggle against Apartheid*. Ithaca, NY: Cornell University Press, 1996.

Kratochwil, Friedrich. *Rules, Norms, and Decisions: On the Conditions of Practical and Legal Reasoning in International Relations and Domestic Affairs*. Cambridge: Cambridge University Press, 1989.

Kretzmann, Steve. "Realidad Check." *In These Times*, April 17, 1995, 31.

Kudirat Initiative for Development. "KIND's Vision: Our Work." http://www.kind.org/work.php3 (accessed September 15, 2004).

Kuperman, Alan J. "Humanitarian Hazard: Revisiting Doctrines of Intervention." *Harvard International Review* 26 (Spring 2004): 64–68.

Lapidus, Gail. "Contested Sovereignty: The Tragedy of Chechnya." *International Security* 23, no. 1 (1998): 5–49.

Lawyers Committee on Human Rights. *Critique: Review of the Department of State's Country Reports on Human Rights Practices for 1992*. New York: Lawyers Committee on Human Rights, 1993.

Le Bot, Yvon, with the collaboration of Maurice Najman. *El sueño Zapatista*. Interviews with Subcomandante Marcos, Major Moíses, and Comandante Tacho, August 1996. Barcelona: Editorial Anagrama, 1997.

Leñero, Vincente. "El Subcomandante se abre." Interview with Subcomandante Marcos, February 17, 1994. *Proceso*, February 21, 1994, 15.

Leton, Garrick B., Edward N. Kobani, Ken B. Saro-Wiwa, and Albert T. Badey. "The Ogoni Case." Memorandum, n.d. [1990?]. Gumberg Library.

Lichbach, Mark I. *The Rebel's Dilemma*. Ann Arbor: University of Michigan Press, 1998.

Lipschutz, Ronnie D. "Reconstructing World Politics: The Emergence of a Global Civil Society." *Millennium: Journal of International Studies* 21, no. 3 (1992): 389–420.

Lipsky, Michael. "Protest as a Political Resource." *American Political Science Review* 62, no. 4 (1968): 1144–58.

Livingston, Steven. "Suffering in Silence: Media Coverage of War and Famine in Sudan." In *From Massacres to Genocide: The Media, Public Policy, and Humanitarian Crises*, Robert I. Rotberg and Thomas G. Weiss, eds. Cambridge, MA: World Peace Foundation, 1996.

Lopez, Donald S., Jr., *Prisoners of Shangri-La: Tibetan Buddhism and the West*. Chicago: University of Chicago Press, 1998.

Madsen, Douglas, and Peter G. Snow. *The Charismatic Bond: Political Behavior in Time of Crisis*. Cambridge, MA: Harvard University Press, 1991.

Madsen, Richard. "Understanding Falun Gong." *Current History*, September 2000, 243–47.

Mancillas, Jorge. "The Twilight of the Revolutionaries." In *The Zapatista Reader*, Tom Hayden, ed. New York: Thunder's Mouth Press/Nation Books, 2002, 153–65.

Manheim, Jarol B. *Strategic Public Diplomacy and American Foreign Policy: The Evolution of Influence*. New York: Oxford University Press, 1994.

Mansbach, Richard W., Yale H. Ferguson, and Donald E. Lampert. *The Web of World Politics: Non-State Actors in the Global System*. Englewood Cliffs, NJ: Prentice-Hall, 1976.

Marcos, Subcomandante. "Chiapas: la guerra," November 20, 1999. *¡Ya Basta!* http://www.ezln.org/documentos/1999/19991120a.es.htm (accessed July 18, 2004).

Marcos, Subcomandante. "Chiapas, 13th Stele: Part 2, a Death." Irlandesa, trans., August 1, 2003. http://www.sf.indymedia.org/news/2003/08/1631948.php (accessed July 18, 2004).

Marcos, Subcomandante. *Our Word Is Our Weapon: Selected Writings*, Juana Ponce de León, ed. New York: Seven Stories Press, 2001.

Maren, Michael. *The Road to Hell: The Ravaging Effects of Foreign Aid and International Charity*. New York: Free Press, 1997.

Martínez Carvajal, Alejandro. *Ejército Popular Revolucionario (Guerrero)*. Acapulco: Editorial Sagitario, 1998.

McAdam, Doug. *Political Process and the Development of Black Insurgency, 1930–1970*, 2nd ed. Chicago: University of Chicago Press, 1999.

McAdam, Doug, Sidney Tarrow, and Charles Tilly. *Dynamics of Contention*. Cambridge: Cambridge University Press, 2001.

McAdam, Doug, Sidney Tarrow, and Charles Tilly. "To Map Contentious Politics." *Mobilization: An International Journal* 1, no. 1 (1996): 17–34.

McCarthy, John D., and Mayer N. Zald. "Resource Mobilization and Social Movements: A Partial Theory." *American Journal of Sociology* 82, no. 6 (1977): 1212–41.

McGreal, Chris. "The Plight of the Ogoni." *Newsweek*, September 20, 1993, 43.

Melucci, Alberto. "Getting Involved: Identity and Mobilization in Social Movements." In *From Structure to Action: Comparing Social Movement Research across Cultures*, Bert Klandermans, Hanspeter Kriesi, and Sidney Tarrow, eds. Greenwich, CT: JAI Press, 1988, 329–48.

México Solidarity Network (MSN). "About MSN: Mission, Organization, History." http://www.mexicosolidarity.org/index.html (accessed July 20, 2004).

Meyer, Carrie A. "Opportunism and NGOs: Entrepreneurship and Green North–South Transfers." *World Development* 23, no. 8 (1995): 1277–89.

Meyer, David S., and Suzanne Staggenborg. "Movements, Countermovements, and the Structure of Political Opportunity." *American Journal of Sociology* 101, no. 6 (1996): 1628–60.

Midnight Notes Collective, eds. *Auroras of the Zapatistas: Local and Global Struggles of the Fourth World War*. Brooklyn, NY: Autonomedia, 2001.

Minkoff, Debra C. "Macro-Organizational Analysis." In *Methods of Social Movement Research*, Bert Klandermans and Suzanne Staggenborg, eds. Minneapolis: University of Minnesota Press, 2002, 260–85.

Minnesota Advocates for Human Rights. *Civilians at Risk: Military and Police Abuses in the Mexican Countryside*. New York: North America Project, World Policy Institute, August 1993.

Minnesota Advocates for Human Rights. *Conquest Continued: Disregard for Human and Indigenous Rights in the Mexican State of Chiapas*. New York: North America Project, World Policy Institute, October 1992.

Moffat, David, and Olof Lindén. "Perception and Reality: Assessing Priorities for Sustainable Development in the Niger River Delta." *Ambio* 24 (1995): 527–38.

Moseley, Christopher, and R. E. Asher. *Atlas of the World's Languages*. London: Routledge, 1994.

Movement for the Survival of the Ogoni People (MOSOP). *Constitution of the Movement for the Survival of the Ogoni People (MOSOP)*. Pamphlet, 1993. Gumberg Library.

Movement for the Survival of the Ogoni People (MOSOP). "Shell's Genocide against Ogoni People." Briefing note, August 1993. Gumberg Library.

Naanen, Ben. "Effective Nonviolent Struggle in the Niger Delta." http://www.iisg.nl/~sephis/ogonipeople.pdf (accessed July 30, 2004).

Nadelmann, Ethan. "Global Prohibition Regimes: The Evolution of Norms in International Society." *International Organization* 44, no. 4 (1990): 479–526.

Nash, June. "The Reassertion of Indigenous Identity: Mayan Responses to State Intervention in Chiapas." *Latin American Research Review* 30, no. 3 (1995): 7–41.

Nash, June C. *Mayan Visions: The Quest for Autonomy in an Age of Globalization*. New York: Routledge, 2001.

National Commission for Democracy in Mexico. *Against Neoliberalism and for Humanity*. Compilation of articles and communiqués, n.d. [1996?]. Gumberg Library.

National Commission for Democracy in Mexico. "Contribute $10 Towards National Press Campaign! Help Break the Media Blockade on the Low-Intensity War in Chiapas." Fund-raising flyer, n.d. [1996?]. Gumberg Library.

Nations, James D. "The Ecology of the Zapatista Revolt." *Cultural Survival Quarterly*, Spring 1994, 31–33.

NativeWeb. "Resources for Indigenous Cultures around the World." http://www.nativeweb.org/hosted/ (accessed May 15, 2004).

Nelson, Joyce. "The Zapatistas versus the Spin-Doctors." *Canadian Forum*, March 1994, 18–25.

Nembe Creek Oil Field Community. *An Open Letter to the Head of State and Commander in Chief of the Armed Forces of Nigeria*. Letter, December 22, 1993. Gumberg Library.

Nigeria, Rivers State. "Judicial Commission of Inquiry into Umuechem Disturbances under the Chairmanship of Hon. Justice Opubo Inko-Tariah (Rtd.)." Report, January 1991. Gumberg Library.

Nigh, Ronald. "Zapata Rose in 1994: The Indian Rebellion in Chiapas." *Cultural Survival Quarterly* 18, no. 1 (1994): 9–11.

Nsirimovu, Anyakwee. *The Massacre of an Oil Producing Community: The Umuechem Tragedy Revisited*. Port Harcourt, Nigeria: Institute of Human Rights and Humanitarian Law, 1994.

O'Beirne, Kate. "A Faraway Country... about Which We Know a Lot." *National Review*, March 5, 2001, 30.

Ogoni Bill of Rights. August 26, 1990. In Ken Saro-Wiwa, *A Month and a Day: A Detention Diary*. New York: Penguin Books, 1995, 67–70.

Olagbaju, Folabi K., and Stephen Mills. "Defending Environmental Defenders." *Human Rights Dialogue* 2, no. 11 (2005): 32.

Olesen, Thomas. *International Zapatismo: The Construction of Solidarity in the Age of Globalization*. London: Zed Books, 2005.

Olson, Mancur. *The Logic of Collective Action: Public Goods and the Theory of Groups*. Cambridge, MA: Harvard University Press, 1965.

Onishi, Norimitsu. "Deep in the Republic of Chevron." *New York Times Magazine*, July 4, 1999, 26.

Osaghae, Eghosa E. "The Ogoni Uprising: Oil Politics, Minority Agitation and the Future of the Nigerian State." *African Affairs* 94 (1995): 325–44.

Ottaway, Marina. "Reluctant Missionaries." *Foreign Policy*, July/August 2001, 44–54.

Ottaway, Marina, and Thomas Carothers, eds. *Funding Virtue: Civil Society Aid and Democracy Promotion*. Washington, DC: Carnegie Endowment for International Peace, 2000.

Partido Democrático Popular Revolucionario/Ejército Popular Revolucionario (PDPR/EPR). "Mexico: Partido Democrático Popular Revolucionario/Ejército Popular Revolucionario." http://www.pengo.it/PDPR-EPR/ (accessed July 15, 2004).

PDPR/EPR. "La lucha de clases en el campo" [Class Struggle in the countryside], *El Insurgente*, February 2003, http://www.pengo.it/PDPR-EPR/El_insurgente/el_insurgente51/texto/insurgente51.htm (accessed July 28, 2004).

Paz, Octavio. "The Media Spectacle Comes to Mexico." *New Perspectives Quarterly*, Spring 1994, 59–60.

Peltier, Leonard. "Statement of Support." In *First World, Ha Ha Ha! The Zapatista Challenge*, Elaine Katzenberger, ed. San Francisco: City Lights Books, 1995, 139–40.

Peterson, M. J. "Transnational Activity, International Society and World Politics." *Millennium: Journal of International Studies* 21, no. 3 (1992): 271–88.

Petras, James, and Steve Vieux. "Myths and Realities of the Chiapas Uprising." *Economic and Political Weekly*, November 23, 1996, 3054–56.

Petrich, Blanche. "Voices from the Masks." In *First World, Ha Ha Ha! The Zapatista Challenge*, Elaine Katzenberger, ed. San Francisco: City Lights Books, 1995, 41–54.

Petrich, Blanche, and Elio Henríquez. Interviews with Subcomandante Marcos, February 4–7, 1994. In EZLN, *Los hombres sin rostro: Dossier sobre Chiapas*, vol. 1. Mexico City: CEE-SIPRO, 1994, 145–64.

Physicians for Human Rights and Human Rights Watch/Americas. *Mexico: Waiting for Justice in Chiapas*. Boston: Physicians for Human Rights, 1994.

Piven, Frances Fox, and Richard A. Cloward. *Poor People's Movements: Why They Succeed, How They Fail*. New York: Vintage Books, 1979.

Pochon, Thomas R. *Mobilizing for Peace: The Antinuclear Movements in Western Europe*. Princeton, NJ: Princeton University Press, 1988.

Power, Samantha. "To Suffer by Comparison?" *Daedalus: Proceedings of the American Academy of Arts and Sciences* 128, no. 2 (1999): 31–67.

Preston, Julia, and Samuel Dillon. *Opening Mexico: The Making of a Democracy*. New York: Farrar, Straus and Giroux, 2004.

Princen, Thomas, and Matthias Finger. *Environmental NGOs in World Politics: Linking the Local and the Global*. London: Routledge, 1994.

Rajagopal, Balakrishnan. *International Law from Below: Development, Social Movements, and Third World Resistance*. Cambridge: Cambridge University Press, 2003.

Rawlands, Dane, and David Carment. "Moral Hazard and Conflict Intervention." In *The Political Economy of War and Peace*, Murray Wolfson, ed. Boston: Kluwer Academic Publishers, 1998, 267–85.

Risse, Thomas, Stephen C. Ropp, and Kathryn Sikkink, eds. *The Power of Human Rights: International Norms and Domestic Change*. Cambridge: Cambridge University Press, 1999.

Risse-Kappen, Thomas. "Bringing Transnational Relations Back in: Introduction." In *Bringing Transnational Relations Back in: Non-State Actors, Domestic Structures, and International Institutions*, Thomas Risse-Kappen, ed. Cambridge: Cambridge University Press, 1995.

Rivers Chiefs. "The Endangered Environment of the Niger Delta: An NGO Memorandum of the Rivers Chiefs and Peoples Conference, Port Harcourt, Nigeria for the World Conference of Indigenous Peoples on Environment and Development and UNCED, Rio de Janeiro, Brazil, 1992." Memorandum. Gumberg Library.

Ron, James. "Ideology in Context: Explaining Sendero Luminoso's Tactical Escalation." *Journal of Peace Research* 38, no. 5 (2001): 569–92.

Ronfeldt, David, John Arquilla, Graham E. Fuller, and Melissa Fuller. *The Zapatista Social Netwar in Mexico*. Santa Monica, CA: RAND, 1998.

Rosenau, James N. *Along the Domestic–Foreign Frontier: Exploring Governance in a Turbulent World*. Cambridge: Cambridge University Press, 1997.

Ross, John. *Rebellion from the Roots: Indian Uprising in Chiapas*. Monroe, ME: Common Courage Press, 1995.

Ross, John. "Unintended Enemies: Save a Rainforest, Start a Revolution." *Sierra*, July/August 1994, 45–47.

Rotberg, Robert I., and Thomas G. Weiss, eds. *From Massacres to Genocide: The Media, Public Policy, and Humanitarian Crises*. Cambridge, MA: World Peace Foundation, 1996.

Rowell, Andy. "Outrage in Nigeria: Did Shell Oil Help Execute Ken Saro-Wiwa?" *Village Voice*, November 21, 1995, 21.

Rus, Jan, Shannan L. Mattiace, and Rosalva Aída Hernández Castillo. "Introduction." In *Mayan Lives, Mayan Utopias: The Indigenous Peoples of Chiapas and the Zapatista Rebellion*, Jan Rus, Shannan L. Mattiace, and Rosalva Aída Hernández Castillo, eds. Lanham, MD: Rowman & Littlefield, 2003, 1–26.

Rus, Jan, Shannan L. Mattiace, and Rosalva Aída Hernández Castillo, eds. *Mayan Lives, Mayan Utopias: The Indigenous Peoples of Chiapas and the Zapatista Rebellion*. Lanham, MD: Rowman & Littlefield, 2003.

Sachs, Aaron. *Eco-Justice: Linking Human Rights and the Environment*. Worldwatch Paper no. 127. Washington, DC: Worldwatch Institute, 1995.

Saideman, Stephen M. "Discrimination in International Relations: Analyzing External Support for Ethnic Groups." *Journal of Peace Research* 39 (2002): 27–50.

Saro-Wiwa, Ken. "Before the Curtain Falls." Speech, October 10, 1991. In Ken Saro-Wiwa, *A Month and a Day: A Detention Diary*. New York: Penguin Books, 1995, 82–7.

Saro-Wiwa, Ken. *First Letter to Ogoni Youth*. Port Harcourt, Nigeria: Saros International, 1983.

Saro-Wiwa, Ken. Foreword to *Ogoni Bill of Rights Presented to the Government and People of Nigeria October 1990 with an Appeal to the International Community*. Port Harcourt, Nigeria: Saros International, 1992; *Fourth World Bulletin* 5, nos. 1–2 (1996): 17–18.

Saro-Wiwa, Ken. "Ethnic Energies Are Needed to Unscramble Africa: Guest Column." *Africa Analysis*, August 21, 1992, 15.

Saro-Wiwa, Ken. *Genocide in Nigeria: The Ogoni Tragedy*. Port Harcourt, Nigeria: Saros International, 1992.

Saro-Wiwa, Ken. *A Month and a Day: A Detention Diary*. New York: Penguin Books, 1995.

Saro-Wiwa, Ken. *The Ogoni Nation Today and Tomorrow*. Original 1968. Reprint, 2nd ed. Port Harcourt, Nigeria: Saros International, 1993.

Saro-Wiwa, Ken. "Report to Ogoni Leaders Meeting at Bori, 3rd October, 1993." Speech. Gumberg Library.

Saro-Wiwa, Ken. Speech before Kagote Club, December 26, 1990. In Ken Saro-Wiwa, *A Month and a Day: A Detention Diary*. New York: Penguin Books, 1995, 71–77.

Saro-Wiwa, Ken. "Statement of the Ogoni People to the Tenth Session of the Working Group on Indigenous Populations, Palais des Nations, Geneva, July 1992." Written statement, July 28, 1992. Gumberg Library.

Schattschneider, E. E. *The Semisovereign People: A Realist's View of Democracy in America*. Hinsdale, IL: Dryden Press, 1960.

Bibliography

Scherer García, Julio. "La entrevista insólita." Interview with Subcomandante Marcos, March 10, 2001. *Proceso*, March 11, 2001. http://www.ezln.org/entrevistas/20010309.es.htm.

Schulz, William F. *In Our Own Best Interest: How Defending Human Rights Benefits Us All.* Boston: Beacon Press, 2001.

Scobie, Richard S. "Report from Mexico." Pamphlet, December 1995. Cambridge, MA: Unitarian Universalist Service Committee. Gumberg Library.

Sell, Susan K., and Aseem Prakash. "Using Ideas Strategically: The Contest between Business and NGO Networks in Intellectual Property Rights." *International Studies Quarterly* 48, no. 1 (2004): 143–75.

Selznick, Philip. *TVA and the Grassroots: A Study of Politics and Organization.* Berkeley: University of California Press, 1984.

Serra, Sonia. "Multinationals of Solidarity: International Civil Society and the Killing of Street Children in Brazil." In *Globalization, Communication and Transnational Civil Society*, Sandra Braman and Annabelle Sreberny-Mohammadi, eds. Cresskill, NJ: Hampton Press, 1996, 219–41.

Sharp, Gene. *The Politics of Nonviolent Action.* Boston: Porter Sargent Publishers, 1973.

Shattuck, John. Assistant Secretary of State for Human Rights and Humanitarian Affairs. Testimony and statement, February 2, 1994. U.S. House of Representatives, Committee on Foreign Affairs, Subcommittee on the Western Hemisphere. *Mexico: The Uprising in Chiapas and Democratization in Mexico.* 103rd Congress, 2nd session, February 2, 1994, 16–35, 71–76.

Shaw, Martin. "Civil Society and Global Politics: Beyond a Social Movements Approach." *Millennium: Journal of International Studies* 23, no. 3 (1994): 647–67.

Shaw, Martin. *Civil Society and Media in Global Crises: Representing Distant Violence.* London: Pinter, 1996.

Shell International Petroleum Company, Group Public Affairs. "'The Heat of the Moment.'" Information Brief. London: Shell International Petroleum Company, October 1992. Gumberg Library.

Shell International Petroleum Company, Group Public Affairs. "Operations in Nigeria." Shell Briefing Note. London: Shell International Petroleum Company, May 1994. Gumberg Library.

Shell International Petroleum Company, Group Public Affairs. "Shell in Nigeria." Shell Briefing Note. London: Shell International Petroleum Company, December 1995. Gumberg Library.

Shell International Petroleum Company, Group Public Affairs. "Tensions in Nigeria." Information sheet, n.d. [May 1993?], photocopy. Gumberg Library.

Sierra Club. "International Campaigns: Mexico." http://www.sierra-club.org/human-rights/Mexico/ (accessed July 20, 2004).

Sikkink, Kathryn. "Human Rights, Principled Issue-Networks, and Sovereignty in Latin America." *International Organization* 47, no. 3 (1993): 411–41.

Sikkink, Kathryn. "Social Equity and Environmental Politics in Brazil: Lessons from the Rubber Tappers of Acre." *Comparative Politics* 27, no. 4 (1995): 409–24.

Sikkink, Kathryn. "Restructuring World Politics: The Limits and Asymmetries of Soft Power." In *Restructuring World Politics: Transnational Social Movements, Networks, and Norms*, Sanjeev Khagram, James V. Riker, and Kathryn Sikkink, eds. Minneapolis: University of Minnesota Press, 2002, 301–18.

Sikkink, Kathryn, and Jackie Smith. "Infrastructures for Change: Transnational Organizations, 1953–93." In *Restructuring World Politics: Transnational Social Movements, Networks, and Norms*, Sanjeev Khagram, James V. Riker, and Kathryn Sikkink, eds. Minneapolis: University of Minnesota Press, 2002, 24–44.

Silverstein, Ken, and Alexander Cockburn. "Chase Memo Tumult: Come Blow Our Horn." *Counterpunch*, February 15, 1995, 3.

SIPAZ. "What is SIPAZ?" http://www.sipaz.org/fini_eng.htm (accessed July 19, 2004).

Smith, Brian H. *More Than Altruism: The Politics of Private Foreign Aid*. Princeton, NJ: Princeton University Press, 1990.

Smith, Jackie. "Characteristics of the Modern Transnational Social Movement Sector." In Jackie Smith, Charles Chatfield, and Ron Pagnucco, *Transnational Social Movements and Global Politics: Solidarity beyond the State*. Syracuse: Syracuse University Press, 1997, 42–58.

Smith, Jackie, Charles Chatfield, and Ron Pagnucco. *Transnational Social Movements and Global Politics: Solidarity beyond the State*. Syracuse: Syracuse University Press, 1997.

Smithey, Lee, and Lester R. Kurtz. "We Have Bare Hands: Nonviolent Social Movements in the Soviet Bloc." In *Nonviolent Social Movements: A Geographical Perspective*, Stephen Zunes, Lester R. Kurtz, and Sarah Beth Asher, eds. New York: Blackwell Publishers, 1999, 96–124.

Snow, David A., and Robert D. Benford. "Master Frames and Cycles of Protest." In *Frontiers in Social Movement Theory*, Aldon D. Morris and Carol McClurg Mueller, eds. New Haven, CT: Yale University Press, 1992, 133–55.

Snow, David A., E. Burke Rochford, Jr., Steven K. Worden, and Robert D. Benford. "Frame Alignment Processes, Micromobilization, and Movement Participation." *American Sociological Review* 51, no. 4 (1986): 464–81.

Sophie Foundation. "About the Sophie Prize." http://www.sophieprize.org/ (accessed June 28, 2004).

Soyinka, Wole. *The Open Sore of a Continent*. Oxford: Oxford University Press, 1997.

Stephen, Lynn. "In the Wake of the Zapatistas: U.S. Solidarity Work on Chiapas." In *Cross Border Dialogues: U.S.–Mexico Social Movement Networking*, David Brooks and Jonathan Fox, eds. La Jolla: Center for U.S.–Mexican Studies, University of California, San Diego, 2002, 303–28.

Stephen, Lynn. *¡Zapata Lives! Histories and Cultural Politics in Southern Mexico*. Berkeley: University of California Press, 2002.

Stoll, David. *Rigoberta Menchú and the Story of All Poor Guatemalans*. Boulder, CO: Westview Press, 1999.

Stone, Deborah. "Causal Stories and the Formation of Policy Agendas." *Political Science Quarterly* 104, no. 2 (1989): 281–300.

Bibliography

Suberu, Rotimi T. *Federalism and Ethnic Conflict in Nigeria*. Washington, DC: United States Institute of Peace Press, 2001.

Sullivan, Stacy. *Be Not Afraid, for You Have Sons in America: How a Brooklyn Roofer Helped Lure the U.S. into the Kosovo War*. New York: St. Martin's Press, 2004.

Survival International. "Niger Delta: Shell Destroys Land and Lives." Press release, May 16, 1995. Gumberg Library.

Survival International. "Nigeria: Government Repression of the Peoples of the Oil Producing Areas, Rivers and Delta States." Press release, November 1, 1995. Gumberg Library.

Tacho, Comandante. Interview by Yvon Le Bot, August 1996. In Yvon Le Bot, with the collaboration of Maurice Najman, *El sueño Zapatista*. Barcelona: Editorial Anagrama, 1997, 200–207.

Tamir, Yael. "Hands off Clitoridectomy: What Our Revulsion Reveals about Ourselves." *Boston Review*, Summer 1996. http://bostonreview.net/BR21.3/Tamir.html (accessed July 17, 2004).

Tarrow, Sidney. "Fishnets, Internets and Catnets: Globalization and Transnational Collective Action." Working Paper no. 1996/78. Madrid: Center for Advanced Study in the Social Sciences, Instituto Juan March de Estudios e Investigaciones.

Tarrow, Sidney. *Power in Movement: Social Movements and Contentious Politics*, 2nd ed. Cambridge: Cambridge University Press, 1998.

Tennant, Chris. "Indigenous Peoples, International Institutions, and the International Legal Literature from 1945–1993." *Human Rights Quarterly* 16, no. 1 (1994): 1–57.

Terry, Fiona. *Condemned to Repeat? The Paradox of Humanitarian Action*. Ithaca, NY: Cornell University Press, 2002.

Thomas, Daniel C. *The Helsinki Effect: International Norms, Human Rights, and the Demise of Communism*. Princeton, NJ: Princeton University Press, 2001.

Trejo Delabre, Raúl. *Chiapas: la comunicación enmascarada; los medios y el pasamontañas*. Mexico City: Diana, 1994.

L'Unitá (Rome). "El Comandante Marcos, al Periodico L'Unitá: 'Mejor morir combatiendo que morir de disenteria.'" Interview with Subcomandante Marcos, January 1, 1994. *Proceso* (Mexico City), January 10, 1994, 8.

United States House of Representatives, Committee on Foreign Affairs, Subcommittee on the Western Hemisphere. *Mexico: The Uprising in Chiapas and Democratization in Mexico*. 103rd Congress, 2nd session 1994.

United States Information Agency, International Visitor Program. "Mr. Ken Saro-Wiwa: National Itinerary." Itinerary of U.S. visit, n.d.[1990]. Gumberg Library.

Unrepresented Nations and Peoples Organization. "About UNPO." http://www.unpo.org/news_detail.php?arg=01&par=153 (accessed August 3, 2004).

Unrepresented Nations and Peoples Organization. "The First Three Years." n.d. [1994?]. Gumberg Library.

Unrepresented Nations and Peoples Organization. "General Assembly IV: Summary Report and Documentation, UNPO's 4th General Assembly, January 20–26, 1995, The Hague, The Netherlands." Report, March 15, 1995. Gumberg Library.

Unrepresented Nations and Peoples Organization. "Members of the UNPO." http://www.unpo.org/members_list.php (accessed July 15, 2004).

Uyghur Information Agency. "Media Advisory." http://www.uyghurinfo.com (accessed July 17, 2004).

Van Cott, Donna Lee. *Defiant Again: Indigenous Peoples and Latin American Security*. Washington, DC: Institute for National Strategic Studies, National Defense University, 1996.

Velin, Jo-Anne, Human Rights Internet, and International Centre for Humanitarian Reporting. *Reporting Human Rights and Humanitarian Stories: A Journalist's Handbook* (1997). http://www.hri.ca/doccentre/docs/handbook97/ (accessed July 17, 2004).

Vickers, Miranda. *Between Serb and Albanian: A History of Kosovo*. New York: Columbia University Press, 1998.

WAC Global Services. "Peace and Security in the Niger Delta: Conflict Expert Group Baseline Report." Working Paper for Shell Petroleum Development Corporation, December 2003. Gumberg Library.

Waldman, Sidney R. *Foundations of Political Action: An Exchange Theory of Politics*. Boston: Little, Brown, 1972.

Walker, R. B. J. *One World, Many Worlds: Struggles for a Just World Peace*. Boulder, CO: Lynne Rienner Publications; London: Zed Books, 1988.

Walker, R. B. J. "Social Movements/World Politics." *Millennium: Journal of International Studies* 23, no. 3 (1994): 669–700.

Wapner, Paul. *Environmental Activism and World Civic Politics*. Albany: State University of New York Press, 1996.

Welch, Claude E., Jr. "The Ogoni and Self-Determination: Increasing Violence in Nigeria." *Journal of Modern African Studies* 33, no. 4 (1995): 635–50.

Welch, Claude E., Jr. *Protecting Human Rights in Africa: Strategies and Roles of Non-Governmental Organizations*. Philadelphia: University of Pennsylvania Press, 1995.

Welch, Claude E., Jr., and Marc Sills. "The Martyrdom of Ken Saro-Wiwa and the Future of Ogoni Self-Determination." *Fourth World Bulletin* 5, nos. 1–2 (1996): 5–16.

Wente-Lukas, Renate. *Handbook of Ethnic Units in Nigeria*. Stuttgart: F. Steiner Verlag Wiesbaden, 1985.

Willetts, Peter, ed. *Pressure Groups in the Global System: The Transnational Relations of Issue-Oriented Non-Governmental Organizations*. New York: St. Martin's Press, 1982.

Wiwa, Ken. *In the Shadow of a Saint*. Toronto: Alfred A. Knopf Canada, 2000.

Wolfsfeld, Gadi. *Media and Political Conflict: News from the Middle East*. Cambridge: Cambridge University Press, 1997.

Womack, John. *Rebellion in Chiapas: An Historical Reader*. New York: New Press, 1999.

Workers Rights Consortium Factory Assessment Program. "Investigative Protocols." http://www.workersrights.org/wrc_protocols.asp (accessed August 10, 2003).

Bibliography

World Bank, Industry and Energy Operations Division, West Central Africa Department, Africa Region. *Defining an Environmental Development Strategy for the Niger Delta*. Washington, DC: World Bank, 1995.

World Bank Group. *World Development Report 2000/2001: Attacking Poverty*. Washington, DC: World Bank, 2000.

Zunes, Stephen, Lester R. Kurtz, and Sarah Beth Asher, eds. *Nonviolent Social Movements: A Geographic Perspective*. New York: Blackwell Publishers, 1999.

Newspapers and News Services

Bloomberg.com

Daily Sunray (Port Harcourt, Nigeria)

El País (Madrid)

Guardian (Lagos)

Guardian (London)

Guardian on Sunday (Lagos)

Houston Chronicle

Independent (London)

Inter Press Service

La Jornada (Mexico City)

Los Angeles Times

National Concord (Lagos)

New York Times

Newswatch (Lagos)

Observer (London)

Reuter Library Report

Reuters

Sunday Sketch (Ibadan, Nigeria)

Tell (Lagos)

Vanguard (Ilorin, Nigeria)

Wall Street Journal

Index

Index

EPR, views of, 167, 171
frames: indigenous, 153, 154–55,
  156, 159; NAFTA, 157–60, 180;
  neoliberal, 157–60, 180
identity, 127, 129, 152, 153, 154–55,
  156, 177
ideology, 124, 152
and indigenous movements:
  compared to EZLN, 130, 185;
  international, 155–56, 169;
  Mexican, 119, 154, 156, 173,
  185
international campaign, 141;
  awareness-raising, 127–39, 175;
  effects, 118–19, 144, 177, 186–87;
  structure (of NGO network),
  171–75
and Internet, 117, 118, 132–33,
  137–38, 144
and marketing theory, 176;
  exchange, with NGOs, 164–70,
  171; power, relative to NGOs,
  120, 180
matching, 139–58, 171, 180–81;
  cultural, 161–64; ethical, 139–50;
  organizational, 164–71;
  substantive, 150–61
and media, 120, 128–30, 133, 145,
  154, 165–66; strategy, 136–37
and Mexican government:
  negotiations, 125, 141, 154, 156,
  158; repression, 146–47
MOSOP, compared to, 12, 120, 139,
  179–81
New Year's Day attacks, 119, 127–30,
  140
and NGOs, 118, 142;
  environmental, 160–61; human
  rights, 165–66, 171–72; social
  justice, 172–73; solidarity, 133–34,
  144, 147–48, 169–70, 173–75
polls, 143–44
Revolutionary Laws, 141, 150–51,
  153, 157, 163
romanticism, 147–48, 155, 163

and socialism, 150–51, 153, 181
and Switzerland, 160
and United States, 160, 174
violence, 139–41, 144–48
vouchers, 120, 154, 166
women, 163–64
see also Marcos, Subcomandante;
  Mexico; National Committee for
  Democracy in Mexico

Fair Trade campaign (NGO), 158
Falk, Richard, 3
Falun Gong, 41
female genital mutilation, 29
First Intercontinental Encounter for
  Humanity and against
  Neoliberalism, 135, 143, 158,
  170
FLN (Fuerzas de Liberación
  Nacional), 123–24, 163
Flood, Andrew, 170
follower, NGO, 19, 40, 194
Forces of National Liberation, *see*
  FLN
Fox, Vicente, 127
framing, 4, 27–28, 30–33, 180–81
  branding, 28, 47, 170–71
  information and, 28, 181
  limitations, 27, 52, 181
  master frames, 28
  process, 28
  vagueness, 27, 152, 175, 181
  see also marketing theory; matching
Fray Bartolomé Human Rights Center,
  136, 171
  see also Ruiz, Samuel
Free West Papua Movement, 3, 48
Friends of the Earth
  and Environmental Rights Action
    (ERA), 109–10
  as gatekeeper, 98
  and MOSOP, 71, 74, 80, 86, 95
FZLN (Frente Zapatista de Liberación
  Nacional), 144
  see also EZLN

229

Index

Index

National Indigenous Congress, 156
National Youth Council of Ogoni
    People (NYCOP), 63, 66
    see also MOSOP
NCDM (National Committee for
    Democracy in Mexico), 133, 135,
    147, 164
"netwar," 138
    see also Internet, and EZLN
networks, *see* transnational networks
New York Times, 145, 166
NGO Coordination for Peace
    (CONPAZ), 149, 169, 172
NGOs (nongovernmental
    organizations)
  bandwagoning, 40–41, 94–95, 99,
    188
  competition among, 18, 28–29, 95
  definition, 2, 8, 14; advocacy, 8–9,
    37–38; solidarity, 8–9, 37–38
  hierarchies among, 21–22
  organizational needs, 26–27, 37–41
  power, relative to movements,
    20–22, 75–76, 77, 120, 190
  as principled actors, 3, 9, 14, 22–23,
    37, 42; limitation as analytic
    concept, 5, 7, 14–15, 42
  proliferation, 17
  resources, 17–18, 186
  roles, in transnational networks,
    18–20; follower, 19, 40, 194;
    gatekeeper, 18–19, 40, 194;
    matchmaker, 19, 173, 194;
    voucher, 40, 194
  as strategic actors, 5, 14–15, 21–22,
    184, 186
    see also global civil society; NGO
    support; transnational networks;
    specific NGO names
NGO support, for social movements
  advantages to movement, 4, 8
  benefits to NGO, 14–15, 41
  costs to NGO, 37–41
  defined, 8
  disadvantages to movement, 6,
    184–86, 193–94

effects of, 181–86, 187, 189
exchange aspects, 5, 14–15, 20–22
maintaining, 41–42
measuring, 10
reforms to, 187–88
selection process, 21–22, 76, 187–88,
    197
  see also global civil society; NGOs;
  transnational networks
Niger Delta Development
    Commission (NDDC), 115
Niger Delta minorities (non-Ogoni),
    55, 56–58, 78–79
  grievances, 58–60, 61, 62
  international campaigns, 68, 104–10
  and MOSOP, 66, 70, 78–79, 104,
    112; compared to, 68–71, 104–10
  national convention, demand for, 78,
    102
  protests, 62, 78–79, 104–10
  violence, 107
    see also Etche minority; Ijaw
    minority; Itsekiri minority; Ogoni
    minority
Niger Delta Republic, 58
Nigeria
  Biafran Civil War, 25–26, 58
  colonial period, 56–58
  democracy movement, 100–1
  election (1993), 78, 92
  Mobile Police Force, 70
  National Constitutional Conference
    (1994–95), 114
  national convention, demand for, 78,
    102
  oil production, 59–60, 61; revenue
    distribution, 59–61, 102, 114–15
  repression, of MOSOP, 79, 92–93
  sanctions against, 99
  shari'a law, death sentence case, 185
  state creation, 58–59, 66, 114
  Treason and Treasonable Offenses
    Decree (1993), 79, 115
  Umuechem massacre, 70, 81, 89
    see also Niger Delta minorities; *names
    of country's leaders*

Index

Index